STUDIES IN IMPERIALISM

general editor John M. MacKenzie

When the 'Studies in Imperialism' series was founded more than twenty-five years ago, emphasis was laid upon the conviction that 'imperialism as a cultural phenomenon had as significant an effect on the dominant as on the subordinate societies'. With more than ninety books published, this remains the prime concern of the series. Cross-disciplinary work has indeed appeared covering the full spectrum of cultural phenomena, as well as examining aspects of gender and sex, frontiers and law, science and the environment, language and literature, migration and patriotic societies, and much else. Moreover, the series has always wished to present comparative work on European and American imperialism, and particularly welcomes the submission of books in these areas. The fascination with imperialism, in all its aspects, shows no sign of abating, and this series will continue to lead the way in encouraging the widest possible range of studies in the field. 'Studies in Imperialism' is fully organic in its development, always seeking to be at the cutting edge, responding to the latest interests of scholars and the needs of this ever-expanding area of scholarship.

Wales and the British overseas empire

I0809469

MANCHESTER 1824

Manchester University Press

SELECTED TITLES AVAILABLE IN THE SERIES

FROM JACK TAR TO UNION JACK
Representing naval manhood in the British empire, 1870–1918
Mary A. Conley

EUROPEAN EMPIRES AND THE PEOPLE
Popular responses to imperialism in France, Britain, the Netherlands, Belgium, Germany and Italy
Edited by John MacKenzie

THE SCOTS IN SOUTH AFRICA
Ethnicity, identity, gender and race, 1772–1914
John MacKenzie with Nigel R. Dalziel

IRELAND, INDIA AND EMPIRE
Indo-Irish radical connections, 1919–64
Kate O'Malley

ENDING BRITISH RULE IN AFRICA
Writers in a common cause
Carol Polsgrove

Wales and the British overseas empire

Interactions and influences, 1650–1830

Edited by H. V. Bowen

MANCHESTER
UNIVERSITY PRESS

Published by Manchester University Press
Altrincham Street, Manchester M1 7JA, UK
www.manchesteruniversitypress.co.uk

British Library Cataloguing-in-Publication Data is available

Library of Congress Cataloging-in-Publication Data is available

ISBN 978 1 7849 9352 8 *paperback*

First published by Manchester University Press in hardback 2011

This edition first published 2016

Printed by Lightning Source

CONTENTS

LIST OF TABLES

NOTES ON CONTRIBUTORS

H. V. Bowen is Professor of Modern History at Swansea University. He has published many books, articles and essays on British economic, imperial and political history during the eighteenth century. His most recent book is *The Business of Empire: The East India Company and Imperial Britain, 1756–1833* (Cambridge, 2006).

Trevor Burnard is Professor and Head of School, School of Historical and Philosophical Studies, University of Melbourne, having previously taught at universities in Britain, New Zealand and Jamaica. He is the author of *Mastery, Tyranny, and Desire: Thomas Thistlewood and His Slaves in the Anglo-Jamaican World* (Chapel Hill, 2004).

Chris Evans is Professor of History at the University of Glamorgan. His most recent books are *Slave Wales: The Welsh and Atlantic Slavery, 1660–1850* (Cardiff, 2010) and (co-authored with Göran Rydén) *Baltic Iron in the Atlantic World in the Eighteenth Century* (Leiden, 2007).

Neil Evans is an Honorary Research Fellow in the School of History and Archaeology, Cardiff University. He was joint editor of *Llafur: The Journal of Welsh People's History*, 1995–2010. He has published extensively on Welsh historiography and is currently writing an essay which offers a general interpretation of the British Empire in the nineteenth century for a volume on European empires edited by Stefan Berger and Alexei Miller.

David Ceri Jones is a Lecturer in History at Aberystwyth University. He is the editor of the *Proceedings of the Wesley Historical Society* and the author of *'A Glorious Work in the World': Welsh Methodism and the International Evangelical Revival, 1735–1750* (Cardiff, 2004) and one of the co-authors of *The Elect Methodists: Calvinistic Methodism in England and Wales, 1735–1811* (forthcoming). He is currently writing a popular history of the evangelical movement, *The Fire Divine: Introducing Evangelicalism* (forthcoming).

Andrew Mackillop is a Lecturer in the Department of History, University of Aberdeen. His research focuses upon Scottish, Irish and Welsh involvement in the eighteenth-century English East India Company. His recent publications include: 'A union for empire? Scotland, the English East India Company and the British union', *Scottish Historical Review*, 87 (2008), and 'Dundee, London and the empire in Asia', in

Charles McKean, Bob Harris and Christopher A. Whatley (eds), *Dundee: Renaissance to Enlightenment* (Dundee, 2009).

Martyn J. Powell is Senior Lecturer in Modern British History at Aberystwyth University. A specialist in eighteenth-century Irish political and social history, his publications include *Britain and Ireland in the Eighteenth-Century Crisis of Empire* (Basingstoke, 2003), *The Politics of Consumption in Eighteenth-Century Ireland* (Basingstoke, 2005), *Piss-Pots, Printers and Public Opinion in Eighteenth-Century Dublin* (Dublin, 2009), and many articles and essays.

GENERAL EDITOR'S FOREWORD

In 1821, Sir William Lloyd of the East India Company visited Simla. The celebrated hill station (now Shimla), which was to become the summer capital of India, barely existed at this point, but Lloyd felt an immediate attraction to the area. He found the mountain air immensely invigorating and discovered that the landscape made him think of his native Wales:

> This day's journey I shall always remember, for it reminded me of home, the days of my boyhood, my mother, and the happiest of varied recollections. It was not, however, the effect of the prospects, for they were unlike those among the Welsh hills, but it was because I recognised a great number of trees and flowers common there; such as the fir, the oak, the apricot, the pear, the cherry, together with wild roses, raspberries, thistles, dandelion, nettles, daisies, and many others. There was, too, an indescribable something in the breeze which brought back a comparative similarity of feeling. I shall never forget this day.[1]

Those who have worked on the subject of the Scots overseas will find this reaction familiar. Scots around the world frequently found landscapes or flora that reminded them of their native heath. This invocation of Welsh memories is rarer, but it reflects the extent to which Welsh people, like others from different parts of the United Kingdom, found solace in aspects of environmental familiarity. It also explains why so many of them were keen to retire to Wales and reinvest their incomes from imperial activity in houses, land or further economic opportunity at home.

The notion of a 'four-nation' (Welsh, English, Scottish and Irish) approach to British imperial history is of relatively recent origin, but it is rapidly growing in popularity.[2] It is clear that the notion that migrants or sojourners could be Welsh (or whatever) at home, but 'British' in the empire does not really fit the case. Like Lloyd, many seem to have retained aspects of their specific ethnicity overseas, perhaps within a layering of multiple identities. Indeed, as I have argued in the past, it may well be that the British Empire ironically served to maintain such identities rather than obscure them. Thus, it is essential to avoid a purely Anglocentric (or even Londinocentric) history of empire if its cultural, religious, educational, environmental and economic forms are to be fully understood. Moreover, it is increasingly important to examine the manner in which each of these identities interacted within Britain itself, interactions which often had a significant imperial dimension to them.

As the editor of this volume points out, studies of the Irish and the Scots overseas have almost become commonplace, but in the case of the Welsh (and, to a certain extent, this must also be said of the English) much less so. When I conducted research in South Africa to consider the role of Scots in that region, I examined the censuses for places of birth and encountered the category 'England and Wales'. I remember reflecting on how lucky I was that the Scots had a separate column, unlike the Welsh.

This phenomenon is alluded to several times in this book, but the contributions here reflect the manner in which this collapsing of two ethnicities can be overcome. Moreover, the relative absence of Wales in the historiography is particularly true of the period covered by the chapters in this volume, spanning as they do the years 1650–1830. Thus this book is genuinely pioneering, both in terms of the recognition that there is indeed a significant story of imperial Wales to be told and in respect of its chronological focus.

The innovative studies here cover a historiographical survey of the writing of empire into Welsh history (or not, as the case might be) in the nineteenth and twentieth centuries (Neil Evans); a striking examination of a region bounded by the Irish Sea and the Severn estuary, South Wales, south-west England and the Irish province of Munster (Chris Evans); and the rivalries and interactions between Ireland, Scotland and Wales in Britain, within a significant imperial framework (Martyn Powell). Most would accept that one of the prime formers of Welsh identity lies in religion. Wales has been generally constructed from the seventeenth century as a quintessentially Protestant country, one where revivalism and so-called Nonconformity were always prominent. This receives appropriate attention from David Ceri Jones (and indeed some of the most illuminating recent studies of the Welsh in the empire relate to missionary activity). There is also an intriguing study (by Trevor Burnard) of the notable reinvestment of a West Indian fortune, derived from slave plantations, in industrial developments in North Wales. While not unique, this case is striking for the very considerable sums involved. Andrew Mackillop brings his extensive knowledge of the personnel of the East India Company to bear upon the Welsh contribution, showing that, while Wales was indeed represented in the EIC (as in the case of Lloyd at the beginning of this introduction), it was probably in a proportion somewhat below what should have been the case given the comparative scale of the Welsh population within Britain. Finally, the editor, Huw Bowen, ranges widely over connections among India, the East India Company and the Welsh economy. All of this adds up to a realisation that there were indeed significant connections between Wales and empire which need to be explored.

One of the purposes of this book is to stimulate further research. It will certainly do that. Moreover, this volume cries out to be succeeded by one considering Wales and the British Empire in the nineteenth and twentieth centuries. Work on this is already proceeding and will surely be published in the not-too-distant future.

John M. MacKenzie

Notes

1 Sir William Lloyd and Captain Alexander Gerard, *Narrative of a Journey from Caunpoor to the Boorendo Pass* (London, 1840), quoted in Raja Bhasin, *Simla, the Summer Capital of British India* (New Delhi, 1992), pp. 24–5.

2 For preliminary statements, see John M. MacKenzie, 'Irish, Scottish, Welsh and English worlds? A four-nation approach to the history of the British Empire', *History Compass*, 6 (2008), 1244–63, and also 'Irish, Scottish, Welsh and English worlds? The historiography of a four nations approach to the history of the British Empire', in Catherine Hall and Keith McClelland (eds), *Race, Nation and Empire: Making Histories, 1750 to the Present* (Manchester, 2010), pp. 133–53.

ACKNOWLEDGEMENTS

The essays in this volume are based upon papers that were first presented at a research workshop held at Aberystwyth University in September 2007. The workshop was part of a programme of work on Wales and the British overseas empire funded by a British Academy small research grant (SG-44820), and I would like to acknowledge the Academy's generous support for that project. While the essays in this volume focus on the years between 1650 and 1830, the papers presented at the workshop covered a longer period of time, which extended the analysis of the relationship between Wales and the empire up to 1960. This meant that, in addition to those who have written the essays that follow, the authors of post-1830 papers also played a full part in the proceedings, as well as in the discussions that contributed to the eventual making of this book. Consequently, I am indebted to the following for their stimulating contributions to the workshop: Jane Aaron, Gwyn Campbell, Bill Jones, Paul O'Leary, Chris Williams and Gareth Williams. Others in attendance at the workshop also made very helpful comments, for which I am grateful, but special thanks go to Geraint H. Jenkins who offered a general critique of the papers. As with so many historians of the British Empire, I owe a great debt to John MacKenzie who, as general editor of the 'Studies in Imperialism' series, has provided unwavering support for this exploratory venture into uncharted historical waters. Professor MacKenzie has long been concerned that, by comparison with Ireland and Scotland, Wales is underrepresented in historical writing on the empire, and the patient encouragement he has offered to me during the preparation of the volume has helped to ensure that the balance can now be redressed at least to some small degree.

LIST OF ABBREVIATIONS

BL	British Library, London
IOR	India Office records
NLW	National Library of Wales, Aberystwyth
TNA	The National Archives, London
WHR	*Welsh History Review*

Map: Welsh counties and towns in 1800

Introduction

H. V. Bowen

Without much fear of contradiction it can be stated that Wales and the Welsh have always been located at the very outer margins of British imperial historiography; and similarly it can be said that the British Empire has never loomed very large in writing on the domestic history of Wales. Several landmark publications on the broad sweep of British imperial history published in the last decade or so barely mention Welsh involvement in the overseas empire,[1] and recent examinations of the impact of empire on Britain have next to nothing to say about Wales.[2] On the other side of the coin, few general historical studies of Wales have ever devoted much space to the imperial or international dimensions of the Welsh historical experience, and readers will usually search Welsh history book indexes in vain for the words 'empire' or 'British Empire', which is somewhat ironic in view of the fact that it was a London Welshman, the polymath John Dee, who was the first to use the term 'British Empire' in 1577.[3]

There is in fact nothing at all novel about these opening observations, however, because many such remarks have been made, often by those who have contrasted the lack of work on Wales and the empire with the continuing flow of studies of British imperialism framed with reference to Ireland and Scotland. But, although the situation is slowly changing, there is still no comprehensive account of Welsh engagement with the empire and, as Neil Evans explains in the opening essay in this volume, students seeking to make sense of Welsh imperial relationships still need to piece together some very scattered 'fragments' of writing on the subject. This impoverished state of our knowledge about the Welsh contribution to the British Empire means that any claim about a 'Welsh empire' coexisting with the recently invoked 'empires' of Ireland or Scotland would be absurd;[4] and it currently seems far beyond the realms of possibility that a volume devoted to Wales will ever stand alongside those on Ireland and Scotland that provide 'companions' to *The Oxford History of the British Empire*.[5] In short, scant attention has ever been paid to historical connections between Wales and British overseas expansion, and considerable *lacunae* exist in our understanding of the histories of both British imperialism and Wales itself.

What is to be made of the fact that so little has ever been written about Wales and the empire? Are we to conclude that the empire was never of any great significance to Wales and the Welsh, or is it simply the case that the subject is yet to attract sustained attention from historians? Neil Evans explores these issues in detail but in general terms logic dictates that two possible explanations can be offered in response to such questions. The first is that the Welsh were not ever engaged to any great degree with the processes of British overseas expansion and hence, despite their best research efforts, historians have been unable to unearth archival evidence that points to much by way of interest, activity or involvement. If this is indeed so then such a conclusion is itself of some considerable importance because it points to relationships between Wales and the empire that were markedly weaker than those that linked Ireland and Scotland to the wider *imperium*. It could then be inferred that Welsh attitudes towards the empire were quite different from those of the Irish and Scots who have been identified as prominent agents of expansion in all spheres of British overseas activity. The Welsh, it might be concluded, were not an imperial people. A second possible explanation is that historians have not actually attempted to explore links between Wales and the empire, and as result judgement has to be suspended on a whole range of important issues which have been analysed thoroughly in relation to the other constituent parts of the British Isles: the nature and distribution of the overseas presence, participation rates, the establishment of imperial networks, the economic impact of expansion, attitudes towards the wider world and indigenous peoples, the place of empire in identity construction and so on. In other words, it could be argued that the empire has yet to capture the attention of scholars interested in the history of Wales.

There is in fact little to indicate that it is a scarcity of primary sources that lies behind the failure of historians to consider more thoroughly the relationships that might have existed between Wales and the overseas empire, and indeed the essays in this volume attest to the fact that there is an abundance of archival material on the subject to be found in Wales and elsewhere. The National Library of Wales is a rich mine of empire-related records, yet it is only in recent years that researchers have been opening up its 'imperial' seams, and many previously hidden gems are now also being unearthed in local record offices.[6] It thus becomes necessary to consider why historians have devoted so little attention to Wales and the empire.

There is perhaps no great mystery with regard to historians of the overseas empire, because their limited discussion of the Welsh simply reflects the fact that those from Wales have often failed to catch the eye. As far as the identification of individuals is concerned, for example, it is sometimes easy for researchers to overlook Welsh people whose surnames were also commonplace in England. The bureaucratic legacy of the early political and administrative assimilation of Wales into England also led to Welsh people sometimes being described as 'English', and Wales was routinely included under the heading of 'England and Wales' in collections of statistics or schemes of classification.[7] These practical research problems have often made it difficult for historians to spot the Welsh in the historical record or disaggregate their numbers from larger totals. Yet, even so, there is no escaping the hard fact that in comparison with others from Britain there were never many Welsh men or women in the wider world, and it has been well documented that across time and space their overseas presence usually paled into insignificance alongside the English, Irish and Scots. The numbers of the Welsh were seldom sufficient for them to establish and sustain the types of groups, networks, institutions and traditions that were characteristic of the Irish and Scots and thereby gave them the very visible presence in the wider world that has attracted so much attention from scholars. The thin scattering of those from Wales across the empire has prevented them making a similar collective impression on the consciousness of imperial historians and this has led to claims that because the Welsh were 'rarities everywhere' their impact on the colonies was very much a 'story of individuals'.[8] In fact, detailed research on post-1850 Welsh migrations serves to qualify this notion, but such assessments are unsurprising when offered by historians presenting an overview of movements of Britons into the overseas empire.

Historians with a more specific interest in Wales are presented with the same problems of identifying and quantifying the Welsh overseas presence, and they acknowledge that this makes it difficult for them to be precise about movements of people from Wales into the wider world.[9] But other reasons also help to explain why only limited examinations have ever been made of the part played by the Welsh in the creation and extension of the British overseas empire, and why there has not yet been any systematic examination of the effects that expansion had upon the economy, society and culture of Wales. It is of course worth remembering that compared with the size of academic communities in Ireland and Scotland the number of professional historians of Wales is actually quite small, which necessarily means that some important subject areas have been neglected as scholarly fashions have waxed and waned. The history of Wales and the empire is by no means unique in this sense, and thus, to take just two other examples, very little recent research has been conducted on Welsh economic history or early mediaeval Welsh history.

Yet the fact that only a relatively small number of historians engage in the study of Wales does not by itself explain why the empire has been neglected. An important part of the explanation lies in the fact that since the Second World War the very subject matter of Welsh history has been quite narrowly circumscribed, and it is now commonly observed that a disproportionate amount of attention has been focused on the social, labour and political aspects of working-class life during the nineteenth and twentieth centuries.[10] At the same time, those inclined to view Wales as colony of England have been reluctant to concede that a colonised Welsh people could ever have become active and enthusiastic participants in British imperial enterprise.[11] Of course, much the same can be said of Ireland and the Irish, but whereas historians of Ireland have explored fully the complexities of the colonised/coloniser relationship few Welsh historians have taken up the challenge.[12] Instead, a blind eye, or at least a partially blind eye, has been turned to Welsh involvement in the empire, with the result that is not possible for a clear sight to be gained of how, and to what extent, Wales was shaped by the process of imperial expansion. This cutting adrift of a significant part of the nation's past was noted by Gwyn Alf Williams who sketched out a late nineteenth-century 'imperial South Wales', 'the sense and feel and smell of which, no doubt because of the formative experience of Depression, Socialism and Welsh Nationalism, Welsh historiography seems largely to have lost'.[13]

The steering of Welsh historical writing in particular directions has meant that important groups of people are conspicuous by their absence from mainstream studies of Wales, as has been pointed out by Russell Davies in a trenchant overview of modern Welsh history.[14] Until quite recently women were almost entirely ignored, as were the urban middle classes,[15] and certain categories of men have been similarly marginalised or excluded altogether. Hence, little attention has ever been paid to businessmen, industrialists and entrepreneurs by Welsh historians, and scant notice has been granted to those individuals from the middle and upper classes who made their way in the world as adventurers, plantation owners, merchants, sea captains, army and navy officers, doctors or colonial administrators. And next to nothing is known about the Welsh mercenaries, freebooting sailors and foot-soldiers of empire who served and frequently died far from their homeland. This has helped to ensure that Welsh history sometimes has a self-contained and inward-looking feel to it, as befits a subject organised, conceptualised and explained without much reference to external influences emanating from British overseas expansion. In other words, the very way in which Welsh historians have collectively defined their subject has served to ensure that the empire has not yet been fully integrated into the history of Wales.

Of course, it would be quite wrong to suggest that the history of Wales has been entirely sealed off from the empire. Migrants and missionaries have always received their fair share of attention, although a focus on their activity has perhaps served to deflect attention away from Welsh engagement with the harder edges of imperialism which found expression in acts of violence, coercion, exploitation and plunder that often characterised British actions in the wider world. And historians have occasionally placed Wales and the Welsh people within terms of analytical reference defined by engagement with the empire. As already noted, Gwyn Alf Williams marked out the existence of a nineteenth-century 'imperial South Wales', arguing that 'industrial Wales – and the Welsh working class within it – were products of an imperial formation located in buoyant export enterprise which gave south Wales a world empire'.[16] More recently, Aled Jones and Bill Jones have explored the relationship between the 'Welsh world' and the British Empire, and although they point to a diversity of experience they suggest that 'similar motivational, linguistic, cultural, and religious impulses were shared by a significant proportion of the actors involved'.[17]

These two much-quoted studies focus on the years after 1850 and it is striking that the literature that does exist on Wales and the empire is weighted very heavily in favour of the late nineteenth and early twentieth centuries. The dangers inherent in this situation are obvious, especially if historians invoke examples of Welsh interactions with the empire drawn from the years after 1850 and use them as proxies to generalise about imperial relationships in earlier times. This can lead to the creation of a static and one-dimensional picture of Welsh engagement with the empire, which does little justice to change over time. In order to address this problem, relationships between Wales and the empire need to be set in a much longer-term perspective than has hitherto been the case, for only then can conclusions be drawn about the extent to which the contributions that the Welsh made to the empire in, say, 1750 differed from those that existed a hundred years later. As things stand, very little of substance is known about Wales and the empire before 1850, and those modern studies that do exist are very few in number.

In fact, the period covered by this volume, from 1650 to 1830, offers plenty of scope for the detailed exploration of different relationships between Wales and British overseas expansion, and there is much to suggest that the empire bore rather more heavily upon Wales than one might assume from the paucity of literature on the subject. Indeed, it is surprising that little sustained attention has been paid to Wales and the empire before 1830, not least perhaps because Wales and its emblems were often inscribed into the overseas empire through the names that were given to colonies, settlements and ships. Most notably, what was originally called 'New Wales' became the New South Wales of Australia, and if things had worked out only a little differently Nova Scotia might today be known as Nova Cambrensis. The 'Welsh Tract' of Pennsylvania contained a substantial community of Welsh-speakers in the American colonies; a number of estates or slave plantations in the Caribbean adopted Welsh place names such as Swansea and Denbigh; and the East India Company settlement at Cuddalore on the Coromandel Coast of India was protected by nearby Fort St David. At sea, East Indiamen named *Anglesey*, *Cardigan*, *Carmarthen* and *Monmouth* plied the routes between Britain and Asia, and during the early nineteenth century privately owned trading vessels called *Owen Glendower* and *Upton Castle* operated out of Madras.

The names given to places and ships help to establish the geographical range of the Welsh overseas presence during the eighteenth century, and this has encouraged historians to look at the underlying colonial communities that had their origins in Wales. Over the years, the place of Welsh religious groups in North America has been noted in general studies of early modern migration and colonial identities, and attention has been paid to settlement, especially where it was most concentrated in Pennsylvania.[18] In addition, some detailed works have concentrated on the founding of specific Welsh communities, such as Cardigan established by West Walian migrants in New Brunswick in 1819.[19] Historians have also often noted in passing that Welshmen, or at least men connected with Wales, were capable of making their way in the wider world, some of them with a considerable degree of success. There are the usual suspects such as Henry Morgan, Elihu Yale, David Samwell, Sir Thomas Picton, and the great oriental scholar Sir William Jones, a London Welshman who was from an Anglesey family. And there are prominent figures who are not often thought of as having been Welsh, such as the writer on imperial politics Josiah Tucker and the great Surveyor-General of India, Sir George Everest. But there were also plenty of other lesser-known individuals of the second or third rank who used the opportunities provided by imperial expansion to advance their careers, interests and fortunes. Historians have located them across the empire, ranging from Nova Scotia, which had Richard Philipps as its first long-serving although often absent Governor between 1717 and 1749, to Madras where Sir Henry

Gwillim, the 'Welshman and a fiery Briton in all senses', served as a controversial judge in the Supreme Court during the early years of the nineteenth century.[20] Many other such figures feature in the essays that follow.

It is also the case that historians have occasionally identified signs that some contemporaries believed that, for good or ill, the empire had the capacity to exert influence on the society and economy of Wales during the eighteenth century. It has been noted, for example, that some critics feared that the empire was proving to be too much of an attraction for Welshmen, so that not enough attention was being paid to domestic economic improvement. As early as 1748 Lewis Morris of Anglesey condemned in typically robust fashion those Welsh landlords who went fortune-seeking overseas, thus preferring to 'rummage the East and West Indies for money rather than to go fifty or a hundred yards underground in our own island'.[21] Evidence such as this offers tantalising glimpses of interactions between Wales and the empire, but studies of groups and individuals remain unconnected, making it difficult to discern any meaningful patterns or trends, and as yet no attempt has been made to draw together different strands of enquiry into one consolidated study of the Welsh dimensions of British imperialism.

In responding to the challenge of filling a considerable gap that exists in Welsh historiography, this collection of essays does not aspire to offer a comprehensive history of Wales and the British Empire between 1650 and 1830. Too many aspects of the subject remain under-researched for such a project to be feasible. Instead, the volume represents a somewhat tentative first step in the exploration of various interactions that occurred between Wales and the many processes of British overseas expansion. And even this step has required some very basic groundwork to be undertaken by the contributors whose essays are founded upon extensive archival research. In some cases, it has been necessary to map out and establish more fully the extent of Welsh participation in imperial activity even though, as noted earlier, this is by no means a straightforward task. Of course, simple head counts and cataloguing of individual achievement can take us only far, as has recently been pointed out.[22] And, as Neil Evans notes below, when taken to extremes, the claiming of important imperial figures for Wales can be a rather pointless exercise, which then becomes a very misleading one if it is implied that such men brought something distinctively 'Welsh' to the process of expansion. To take an example already cited, Sir George Everest might (or perhaps might not) have been born near Crickhowell but, although this happy event is now useful for the local tourist board, there is nothing to suggest that Everest ever regarded himself as Welsh.[23] Indeed, many of the Welshmen at the forefront of British imperial endeavour in the period under review do not appear to have been self-consciously Welsh to any great degree, partly because a good proportion of them emerged from Anglicised minor gentry families and as a result were not much inclined to differentiate themselves from their English counterparts across the border. Nonetheless, identification and quantification are tasks of considerable importance because they underpin the reconstruction of linkages, networks and connections that facilitated two-way movements of people, goods, resources, ideas and knowledge between Wales and the wider world.

Mapping connections between Wales and the empire requires that some consideration be given to the nature of Wales itself as well as to how it fitted into wider political and economic frameworks. This is necessary not only because the structure of the Welsh economy and society bore heavily on how connections with the empire developed, but also more broadly because some historians have recently been advocating the adoption of a 'four-nation' approach to the history of the British Empire. Such an approach, as articulated by John MacKenzie, suggests: 'The four nations [of the British and Hibernian Isles] each had separate relationships with the empire and each identity was developed and enhanced rather than destroyed by the imperial experience.'[24] Rather than the expansion of the empire serving to dissolve differences by engaging the Irish, English, Scots and Welsh in a common external endeavour, the reality was altogether more complex because 'Members of each ethnicity interacted with empire, and its indigenous peoples, in different ways.'[25]

There is much to commend in such an approach, not least because it acknowledges the importance of the different ethnicities and identities that existed among 'Britons', but accommodating Wales and the Welsh for the long eighteenth century is difficult for several reasons, one of which has already been touched upon. Both Ireland and Scotland have mature and rich historical literatures which allow for meaningful comparisons and contrasts to be made with England and between each other; and substance can be given to claims about the existence of an 'Irish empire' or 'Scottish empire' which made unique and distinctive cultural, economic, military and social contributions to British overseas enterprise over a long period of time. But, as we have seen, those seeking insights into the relationship between Wales and the empire are forced to draw conclusions from only a very small handful of modern articles and chapters, all of which relate to the years after 1850, and this hinders very significantly the full implementation of any 'four-nation' approach to the study of the empire. At the same time, there is the problem of employing the 'nation' as an analytical term of reference or organisation across all the constituent parts of the British Isles because while Ireland and Scotland are sharply formed as distinct entities in the minds of historians, the same cannot be said of Wales. Defining Wales has always been problematic, because it is not entirely clear when in the past it has existed as a 'nation', and thus Welsh historians have always had to address some rather basic questions which do not occupy historians of other parts of the British Isles to anything like the same degree. Some have asked 'when was Wales?' and even 'did Wales exist?';[26] and so too it is quite legitimate to pose the questions 'what was Wales?' and indeed 'where was Wales?' This is not the place to offer elaborate answers to these broad questions, but it is necessary to sketch in outline terms the Wales that existed during the period under review because this will serve to contextualise the volume as a whole as well as some of the comparisons, contrasts and connections with other parts of the British and Irish Isles that are made in the essays of Chris Evans and Martyn Powell.

Here Wales is defined in geographical terms as the twelve historic shire counties that were subject to the jurisdiction of the Court of Great Sessions between 1542 and 1830, as well as Monmouthshire. Throughout the long eighteenth century covered by the book, it was a territory routinely described by visitors as a foreign country marked out by its remoteness, separateness and backwardness, and this often gave rise to stark comparisons with neighbouring England.[27] At the same time, English commentators and satirists were wont to suggest, often very unflatteringly, that the Welsh possessed unique characteristics that served to define them as a people. And, as Martyn Powell shows in his essay, Irish and Scottish writers also pointed out ways in which those in Wales were different from their supposedly fellow Celts. Yet in many ways these views from the outside served to impose a uniformity and cohesion upon Wales and the Welsh that simply did not exist in reality. Wales itself had no political unity, nor had it coalesced into a single integrated economic entity, and this served to retard its emergence as a nation in any modern sense of that term. Physical barriers prevented much by way of direct contact or interaction between North and South Wales, and lines of communication ran along west–east axes, which extended to key nodal points in England. This meant that, until the emergence of Swansea as a thriving industrial port town during the second half of the eighteenth century, Bristol served as the 'metropolis' of South Wales, and Hereford, Shrewsbury, Chester and Liverpool all exerted economic, social and cultural pulls of their own on people across many parts of mid- and North Wales.

Moreover, in the border counties centuries of local movement across Offa's Dyke had blurred lines of linguistic and cultural difference between England and Wales, especially as far as the gentry were concerned, and elsewhere in-migration had long served to ensure that parts of Glamorgan and Pembrokeshire contained significant pockets of English-speakers. By the same token, of course, there were still very large majorities of Welsh-speakers across much of West, mid- and North Wales, and the survival of the language in these areas encouraged those among the middling orders who were promoting a Welsh renaissance and attempting to revive notions of a nation defined by its own native culture and unique historical experience. But, crucially, any (re-)emerging sense of Welsh identity or nationality was not yet reinforced by the creation of national institutions or organisations, and this meant that cross-border administrative, political, legal and religious structures continued to bind Wales into greater English frameworks of organisation. The effect of all this was to ensure that imaginings of Wales as a nation were as yet only partially formed in the minds of many Welsh people, if they existed at all.[28]

Wales remained both tightly harnessed to England in a political and administrative sense during the period under review and increasingly integrated with its neighbour in economic terms, and this determined the nature of many of its interactions with the empire and the international economy. As is well documented, Wales was short of both investment capital and financial institutions and as a result was heavily dependent on injections of funds from resident or absentee English entrepreneurs, a process that can be identified as having been at work across a range of enterprises. Some Welsh businessmen, such as the Anglesey solicitor and 'copper king' Thomas Williams, were certainly capable of undertaking large-scale investment and outflanking English competitors,[29] but a general scarcity of savings in Wales meant that external injections of start-up finance and credit were often essential for the development of trade and industry. At a similarly basic level, before the late-eighteenth-century development of Swansea the lack of a major port precluded early Welsh involvement in the transoceanic bulk-carrying trades, and the absence of a long-distance merchant fleet dictated that the flow of people and goods from Wales into the wider world mostly had to be filtered through Bristol, Liverpool, Cork and London, as well as a number of minor English provincial ports. Consequently, although some emigrants departed for the New World from small ports such as Cardigan, Wales established few direct links of its own with the North American colonies, Africa and the Caribbean, and by comparison with Ireland and Scotland the movements of Welsh ships were very narrowly circumscribed. As Chris

Evans shows in his essay, this served in important ways to shape relations between Wales, southern Ireland and south-west England, which in their turn determined patterns of Welsh engagement with the wider Atlantic economy. And as far as connections with Asia are concerned, the existence of the monopolistic East India Company meant London was the only (legal) point of departure for shipping destined for the Orient, which again meant that the movement of Welsh people and commodities into the empire had to be channelled through England. These very same general economic circumstances also served to ensure that inward flows of people, goods and wealth from the empire into Wales were seldom direct, and those Welsh people who stayed at home usually found themselves at some distance removed from contact with the processes that underpinned overseas expansion.

The absence of a clearly defined Welsh nation or self-standing Welsh economy thus poses challenges to historians wishing to explore connections between Wales and the empire. But the adoption of what might be called an integrationist approach by collapsing Wales into England and using 'England and Wales' as a unit of analysis does not offer a way forward. Not only can this lead to a lazy, old-style 'for Wales, see England' type of attitude to the past, which portrays Wales as an undifferentiated junior partner of England, but it also proceeds on the assumption that a process of cultural, economic, political and social assimilation had been completed. This was in fact far from being the case because the relationships that existed between Wales and England were at no point cast in stone to the extent that the foregoing summary descriptions might suggest. Some further convergence between England and Wales was undoubtedly still taking place, but there are signs that towards the end of the eighteenth century elements of divergence were also beginning to occur, a process that would lead eventually to the 'rebirth' of a Welsh nation together with the creation of a mature export industrial economy that forged its own direct links with the wider world through the ports of Cardiff, Newport and Swansea. Here, the relationship between Wales and the empire cut both ways. On the one hand, overseas expansion promoted further integration between Wales and England because it helped incorporate Welsh people in a pan-British enterprise in ways that served to emphasise common purposes, interests and outlooks; while on the other hand the growth of the empire helped to stimulate the development of a Welsh industrial economy and society that was no longer wholly dependent on English resources, support and facilities. This is one of the central points that emerges from the essays: in some ways interactions with the empire during the long eighteenth century served further to blur distinctions between Wales and England while they also helped directly and indirectly to lay foundations for much of what was to become unique and distinctive about Wales in the nineteenth and twentieth centuries.

In the essays that follow, the authors have adopted, and sometimes combined, a number of different frameworks of analysis. Some such as Huw Bowen, Trevor Burnard and Andrew Mackillop have taken one particular connection – West Indian in the case of Burnard, East Indian in the case of Bowen and Mackillop – and then examined and quantified different interactions that occurred between Wales and the overseas empire. Both Bowen and Mackillop stress how expansion in Asia served to draw Wales and the Welsh into the domestic and overseas worlds of the London-based East India Company, while Bowen and Burnard explore aspects of the impact that expansion had upon the development of the Welsh economy. Others such as Chris Evans and David Ceri Jones have adopted an Atlantic perspective, which enables them to locate Wales in wider worlds. In Evans's case the focus is on Atlantic-facing parts of the Welsh economy, while Jones explores how British expansion in the Atlantic basin opened up opportunities for people from Wales to take a prominent place in international communities of religious thought and belief. As Jones shows, participation in an expanding spiritual empire brought like-minded individuals together in transoceanic networks and this engagement helped to shape the emergence of Welsh evangelical identities.

Chris Evans's essay is also explicitly comparative because it traces the different trajectories of economic development followed by three Atlantic provinces – Wales, Munster and the South West region of England – and this reveals much about why the Welsh economy developed along some lines and not others. Martyn Powell similarly utilises comparison as a tool of analysis as he explores how overseas expansion generated frictions between Ireland, Scotland and Wales, which in turn gave rise to articulations of difference and rivalry that bore on Celtic self-perceptions. This very usefully shifts attention away from England and serves as an antidote to the by now standard and rather tired Anglo–Celtic contrasts and comparisons that punctuate the large number of works that have been devoted to the formation of British identity and identities during the eighteenth century.

The volume opens with Neil Evans's scene-setting study of the place of the empire in Welsh historiography. The essays by Chris Evans and Martyn Powell then locate Wales within wider domestic frameworks of interpretation by exploring how different forms of imperial expansion and crisis bore upon relations with other parts of the British and Irish Isles. Thereafter, David Ceri Jones and Trevor Burnard examine ways in which British expansion in the Atlantic world influenced Wales in different ways before, finally, Andrew Mackillop and Huw Bowen turn eastwards to analyse Welsh interactions with the nascent British empire in India.

Notes

1 See, most significantly, Wm Roger Louis (editor-in-chief), *The Oxford History of the British Empire* (5 vols, Oxford, 1998).

2 For example, Wales is mentioned only twice in passing in Bernard Porter, *The Absent-Minded Imperialists: Empire, Society, and Culture in Britain* (Oxford, 2004); and the Welsh fare little better in Andrew Thompson, *The Empire Strikes Back? The Impact of Imperialism on Britain from the Mid-Nineteenth Century* (Harlow, 2005). Many of the so-called 'new imperial histories' are similarly Anglocentric, despite their supposedly 'British' perspectives on the empire. Hence in Kathleen Wilson, *A New Imperial History. Culture, Identity, and Modernity in Britain and the Empire, 1660–1840* (Cambridge, 2004), the only 'Wales' to make an appearance is William Wales, the astronomer who accompanied Captain Cook on his second voyage. A full listing of such examples would be very long indeed.

3 For notable exceptions to this general rule see Gwyn A. Williams, *When was Wales? A History of the Welsh* (Harmondsworth, 1985), and Russell Davies, *Hope and Heartbreak: A Social History of Wales and the Welsh, 1776–1871* (Cardiff, 2005). There is a single reference to 'British Empire (the term)' in the index to several editions of John Davies, *History of Wales,* although even this is absent from the most recent revised edition published in London in 2007.

4 Keith Jeffery (ed.), *An Irish Empire? Aspects of Ireland and the British Empire* (Manchester, 1996); Michael Fry, *The Scottish Empire* (East Linton and Edinburgh, 2001); T. M. Devine, *Scotland's Empire, 1600–1815* (London, 2003).

5 Kevin Kenny (ed.), *Ireland and the British Empire* (Oxford, 2004); John M. MacKenzie and T. M. Devine (eds), *Scotland and the British Empire* (Oxford, forthcoming).

6 See, for example, Douglas Fraser's richly detailed studies of the connections between Tenby and the tea and opium trades, as established by John Rees and other Pembrokeshire men who traded in eastern seas, to be found in *Pembrokeshire Life* (February 2007), 12–16, and (December 2009) 10–14.

7 On the problems of generating Welsh historical statistics because Wales did not often provide a basis for the collection of information see John Williams, 'Figures in Welsh history', in John Williams, *Was Wales Industrialised? Essays in Modern Welsh History* (Llandysul, 1995), pp. 79–96 (esp. pp. 82–6).

8 Ged Martin and Benjamin E. Kline, 'British emigration and new identities', in P. J. Marshall (ed.), *The Cambridge Illustrated History of the British Empire* (Cambridge, 1996), p. 265.

9 Aled Jones and Bill Jones, 'The Welsh world and the British Empire, c.1851–1939: an exploration', *Journal of Imperial and Commonwealth History,* 31 (2003), 58.

10 See for example, *ibid.,* 57–8, and Julie Light, 'The middle classes as urban elites in nineteenth-century South Wales', *WHR,* 24 (2009), 27–34. For an identification and analysis of the trends in the writing of Welsh history between 1945 and 1990 which caused this situation see Neil Evans, 'Writing the social history of modern Wales: approaches, achievements, and problems', *Social History,* 17 (1992), 479–92.

11 Jones and Jones, 'The Welsh world', 58.

12 For a robust discussion of why it is 'not meaningful to view contemporary Wales as "post-colonial"', see Chris Williams, 'Problematizing Wales: an exploration in historiography and postcoloniality', in Jane Aaron and Chris Williams (eds), *Postcolonial Wales* (Cardiff, 2005), pp. 3–22 (esp. 1–11; quotation on p. 11).

13 Gwyn A. Williams, *The Welsh in Their History* (London, 1982), pp. 184–5.

14 Davies, *Hope and Heartbreak,* pp. 1–28.

15 For an article that begins to redress the balance a little by focusing on the middle classes of nineteenth-century South Wales see Light, 'The middle classes'.
16 Williams, *The Welsh in Their History*, pp. 183–4.
17 Jones and Jones, 'The Welsh world', 61.
18 For a summary and references see H. V. Bowen, *Elites, Enterprise, and the Making of the British Overseas Empire, 1688–1775* (Basingstoke and London, 1996), pp. 158–9, 168–9. For a now dated but still useful identification and enumeration of Welsh settlements and prominent men of Welsh origin in the thirteen American colonies see Edward George Hartmann, *Americans from Wales* (Boston, 1967), pp. 39–60.
19 Peter Thomas, *Strangers From a Secret Land. The Voyages of the Brig 'Albion' and the Founding of the First Welsh Settlements in Canada* (Toronto, 1986).
20 Ralph A. Griffiths, 'Governor Richard Philipps and the province of Nova Scotia', *Transactions of the Honourable Society of Cymmrodorion*, Session 1968, Part II, 265–92. This description of the irascible libertarian Gwillim was made by Governor-General Lord Minto, as quoted in Stephen Taylor, *Storm and Conquest. The Battle for the Indian Ocean, 1809* (London, 2007), p. 42.
21 Quoted in Geraint H. Jenkins, *The Foundations of Modern Wales. Wales 1642–1780* (Oxford, 1993), p. 280.
22 Jones and Jones, 'The Welsh world', 59–60.
23 For a careful but ultimately inconclusive discussion of Everest's place of birth see J. R. Smith, *Everest: the Man and the Mountain* (Caithness, 1999), pp. 6–7. The Everest family undoubtedly had strong connections with the area and owned property there but George's actual place of birth remains obscure and he was baptised in Greenwich six months after he was born.
24 John M. MacKenzie, 'Irish, Scottish, Welsh and English worlds? A four-nation approach to the history of the British Empire', *History Compass*, 6 (2008), 1244–63 (quotation from abstract on 1244).
25 *Ibid.*
26 Williams, *When was Wales?*; Williams, 'Figures in Welsh history', p. 82. In answer to his own question about the existence of Wales for statistical purposes, John Williams writes that Wales 'forms as natural a geographical unit as England or Scotland' but notes that there are 'many other categories for which does not (or did not) form the obvious basis for the collection of statistics'.
27 For a good summary of English views of Wales and the Welsh before 1847 see Gwyneth Tyson Roberts, *The Language of the Blue Books: the Perfect Instrument of Empire* (Cardiff, 1998), pp. 9–24.
28 For the view that 'in the context of British politics, "Wales" itself only came into being during the mid-Victorian period', which meant that before then it was 'an unimagined nation', see Matthew Cragoe, *Culture, Politics, and National Identity in Wales, 1832–1886* (Oxford, 2004), p. 2.
29 For Williams see below, p. 185.

CHAPTER 1

Writing Wales into the empire: rhetoric, fragments – and beyond?[1]

Neil Evans

Empire has not figured prominently in Welsh historiography. A key problem is that empire does not fit with the self-images of many Welsh people. There is a preference for regarding the Welsh as a colonised people, rather than a colonising one. The literary and cultural critic Ned Thomas, writing in 1971, sets out the issue:

> It is better in the end to belong to an oppressed group than an oppressing one. The Welsh identity is dearer to me precisely because it lacks the strain of militarism and imperialism which there is in the British identity. I should make it clear that I am not exonerating Welshmen from having participated in British imperialism. It is merely that when they did they did so as Britishers, not as Welshmen. The Welsh language was not part of that imperialism, and as the Welsh speaker in his own country the Welshman was himself the victim of a kind of imperialism.[2]

This is not a unique experience, of course, and it can be found in many other parts of the empire. Canadian historians, for instance, have also faced the issue of whether their people were colonisers or colonised – and coming to terms with the fact that they have been both.[3] But in Wales the discussion has been remarkably one-sided: there has been little sustained interest in the place of Welsh people in the empire. Imperialism has entered Welsh discussion mainly as internal colonialism, in the now rather tired debates initiated by Michael Hechter. More usefully, it has been reprised, with cultural variations, in the recent volume on *Postcolonial Wales*.[4]

It is not intended to re-enter these domestic lists, but rather to address the issue of the historiography of Welsh people as imperialists and the impact of the empire upon Wales. There are two sides to this: what Welsh historians have written on the issue and the recognition of their role by British imperial historians. The Welsh in the empire have fallen down some black hole between these galaxies. They are conspicuous mainly by their absence. The historiography can be divided into three broad periods since the emergence of history as a professional subject in Wales – which means from the early twentieth century. This will be set against the broader trends in imperial historiography which emerged at the same time, to assess what chances there were of any meeting of minds in these three eras.

The first period runs from 1890 to 1950, and embraces the work of historians mainly born between 1850 and 1900. This was the era in which Welsh history was established as a grounded academic subject. But this was mainly the case for the medieval period and coverage of the early modern and modern periods was sketchy. Sir John Edward Lloyd (1861–1947) was the foremost historian of the period, but his scholarly and documented accounts of Welsh history concluded with the death of Owain Glyndwr around 1415. Much of what was written on these later periods was by amateurs and even when written by professionals it was usually not the product of thorough research.[5]

From this work we can find two sorts of writing. One was windy rhetoric with often fine and flowery flourishes; the other centred on detailed reports of events or issues but lacked any real context or overall perspective. They may remind some of the famous distinctions which C. Wright Mills made in the 1950s between 'grand theory' and 'abstracted empiricism' in sociology.[6] Rarely if ever did the two tendencies in Welsh writing meet and neither was very substantial.

The classic statement of the first kind was the flourish – the political *hwyl* perhaps? – with which Owen M. Edwards (1858–1920) closed his best-selling volume *Wales* of 1901, in the 'Stories of the Nations' series.[7] Here he simply claimed that there was an ever-closer integration of Wales and the empire but it was not a theme which arose in any prominent way in his text and indeed references to empire are few and far between: 'The development of Wales has been twofold – in national intensity and in the expansion of imperial sympathy.'[8] None of this has much support in the text. Of the potential heroes he mentions in elsewhere in this passage, Gam, Nott and Picton do not rate discussion in the text while Henry Morgan figures only as 'a warped continuation' of the 'energy of the Cavalier', which was not really a compliment from a historian whose chapter on the seventeenth century was entitled 'Blind loyalty'.[9] It was far from uncharacteristic of his work to be able to find little relationship between detailed evidence and general assertion.[10] Though Edwards had held a fellowship at Lincoln College, Oxford, and as such he was a scholar, he was hardly a professional historian by the emerging standards of the period and may be seen as a prime example of the kind of college tutor engaged in getting pupils through examinations and providing instruction in morals and nationalism rather than original research, which was more characteristic of the professors.[11]

The other tendency in Welsh writing on connections with the empire was for occasional detailed work, which was not made into any patterned argument and remained as isolated fragments. This remains largely the case – though the fragments get much bigger and better! Perhaps there was a problem of finding sufficient evidence to go with the rhetoric. Another writer revealed the difficulties. Howell T. Evans (1877–1950), the author of some of the most successful school textbooks in the period before the First World War, was much more ambivalent in his attitudes to the empire and we can find contrasting approaches in his work. He was a teacher and later a headmaster and his writing shows that there was some justice in claims in the Conservative *Western Mail* that he was a Liberal partisan in his work.[12] His first reference to anything more or less imperial is dismissive; on the Napoleonic Wars: 'The battlefields saw the heroism of the soldier prostituted for the military glory of the squire. There was greater heroism at home in the poor hillside cottage of Ap Vychan.'[13] Yet when he came to consider the educational reforms of the late nineteenth century he had a different attitude and saw positive contributions to Welsh identity. He did clearly think that schoolchildren needed imperial heroes as role models and offered the examples of Generals Nott and Picton.[14] But this co-existed with a fervent attitude to the land question and much implied praise for Henry Richard and his pacifism – perhaps not an approach which chimed with the imperial history of the day. Indeed the imperial heroes were always members of the gentry and Welsh Liberalism tended to regard them as so Anglicised as to be excluded from the nation.

Howell Evans also offered an encomium to Lloyd George which suggested that his pre-eminence in the politics of the empire was as significant as his ascendancy among Welsh members. But here 'the empire' means not specifically imperial aspects but the full range of British politics – and especially to his presidency of the Board of Trade.[15] Very much the same is true of Sir John Lloyd who wrote a general history of Wales in 1930: 'David Lloyd George . . . had ultimately on his shoulders the responsibility of piloting the Empire to a successful issue in the World War.'[16]

On the other hand, Llewelyn Williams (1867–1922), the Liberal MP and barrister, who was quite a prolific writer on more recent Welsh history, saw Wales as having a pivotal place in the history of the empire and offered perhaps the most coherent and reasoned overview: '[In the 1530s] the boon of a constitution was extended to Wales. . . . The grant of a free constitution was an instantaneous success. The same "wonderful issue" attended it in Wales as has since attended it in Canada, South Africa, and in every part of the British Dominions in which it has been tried.' He also saw the inclusion of a subject race in its own government as had happened in Wales as a precedent for the system of dyarchy in India. Yet this was not necessarily either the end of the story or completely beneficial. He also invoked the principle of self-determination, and in doing so stressed that the literature, piety and self-respect of the Welsh had almost been destroyed, though happily this had now been averted – though not thanks to the state or the wealthy, but by the native energy of the people who had 'renewed their youth like the eagle'.[17]

Williams, then, more successfully than Owen M. Edwards, integrated general claims and detailed study. One of his latter efforts was a study of the pirate Henry Morgan, in which he expressed a certain pride about his celebrity.[18] But this was a general British fame, he thought, which was not shared in Wales.[19] What he revealed was that there was little general consciousness of any part played by Welsh people in the history of the empire in the Wales of his day. None of this prevented popular historians of Wales from trying to point out the connections and make as much of them as possible. But there is a distinct sense that they were swimming against a tide of indifference and ignorance when compared with the relative success of promoting knowledge about the two great ages of Welsh history, the age of the princes in the middle ages and the age of the people marked by the expansion of Nonconformity, education and Liberal politics.[20]

The history of Wales written by W. Watkin Davies (1895–1973) for the Home University Library had the kind of integrationist view of Wales's place in the empire that we can find in most historical works in the period. His concluded that:

> Wales has come to be actively and amicably associated with England in her high destinies. Everywhere Welshmen are participating to the uttermost in the wider life of the Empire. The people have seen a fairer vision . . . of a Commonwealth living a life of ordered prosperity; upholding and illustrating the great principles of justice, equality and freedom, . . . a Commonwealth in which Wales, in virtue of its splendid tradition of passionate idealism and of tireless spiritual efforts, shall enjoy a foremost place.[21]

Davies saw Welsh people as colonisers taking with them their language, patriotic societies and chapels.[22] J. E. Lloyd's very short and popular general history of Wales elaborated this view of the Welsh as having 'an aptitude for colonisation' despite being 'not so widely dispersed as the Irish and the Scotch': Patagonia was the prime example of this.[23] Lloyd was almost confirming what another – now forgotten – historian had said a few years previously in going back to the earliest Welsh effort at colonisation. Edward Roland Williams rooted the Patagonian colony in a tradition stretching back to Cambiol in the early seventeenth century and even beyond into the ranks of Raleigh's settlers in Virginia.[24] He saw Welsh people as sharing fully in the lust for wealth in the period and this as underlying the buccaneering activities in which Welsh people took part.[25] Similar themes ran through the contemporaneous work of Frederick J. Harries who chronicled Welsh involvement against the Armada, their role in exploration and the importance of Roger Williams, the founder of the Rhode Island colony and a puritan, leading him to this conclusion: 'The records of this period show that they rendered conspicuous service in helping to lay the foundations of the British Empire. That is a circumstance of which modern Welshmen have every reason to feel proud.'[26] Llewelyn Williams had a rather similar perspective on this process, stressing the Welsh descent of many colonisers in New England and Virginia while not averse to yoking in Cromwell's Welsh ancestry to claim a Welsh role in the annexation of Jamaica, reminding his readers of the role of Henry Morgan there – the subject of his earlier specialised study.[27]

Owen Rhoscomyl (Arthur Owen Vaughan, 1863–1919) does not belong in the company of professional historians, but he was an important myth-maker in Edwardian Wales and his work carried the imprimatur of scholars like Sir John Rhŷs and Kuno Meyer.[28] He offered a view which was very similar, from the perspective of the reign of Henry VIII: 'The effect of [the Act of Union] was seen at once. Read all the splendid activity of the people, sailors, traders, and seekers after strange things, in the reigns of the next few monarchs. You will see that the Cymru jostled shoulder to shoulder to the front with the English, in all the glorious bustle of those brave days and we held in honour as brave men, and given due credit for all they did.'[29] In giving a bush to this heady wine, the eminent philologist and Celtic scholar Sir John Rhŷs (1840–1915) offered the view that the individual's sense of Welsh nationality was developing to the full and: 'That development could not help making him a better man and a better citizen of the mighty Anglo-Celtic Empire, in which the accidents of place and history have made him a piece of the mosaic'.[30] Such viewpoints were sustained in a limited number of more detailed pieces of research on Welsh emigration and the Welsh in America in particular.[31]

What this exemplifies is a Liberal consensus that Wales and England were now united harmoniously and that Welsh achievements could be seen everywhere, including in the empire. The fact that this was challenged by Vyrnwy Morgan (1861–1925) is the exception which proves the rule.[32] That contrarian of all that Liberal Wales held dear predictably registered his dissent. As against all those celebrations of great men in nineteenth-century Wales, the alpine peaks of *Cofiannau*,[33] Morgan asserted that Wales had fewer great men than any country in Europe and compared with Ireland little impact on the empire: 'Does Wales lead Ireland? . . . She does not lead in the number of great men she has given to the service of the Empire. Ireland has given some of her greatest sons, from a Napier and a Wellesley to a Dufferin and a Lord Roberts.'[34] Vyrnwy Morgan aside, there was a view of Welsh participation in the empire and it was a consistent one through most of the popular historiography of the period. Wales was seen as actively promoting the imperial enterprise, though there were some reservations about this. There was little overt anti-imperialism. Even right-wing Welsh writers generally shared such a view, making Vyrnwy Morgan even more of an exception. H. J. W. Edwards (1910–91) in his idiosyncratic history of the Rhondda managed to make out-migration a positive feature of the interwar period, and one which led to the creation of what he called 'Imperial Rhondda'. The boom years of coal were not its glory days even if 'There are still those who would call that progress but it is a kind of progress that has dirtied the Rhondda, given no direct spiritual help to the pilgrims and left them penniless.'[35] The depression was giving the Rhondda a chance to improve its image and to participate in a wider Welsh tradition of colonisation:

> . . . they are slowly building up a Rhondda Empire. There is a Rhondda man now running a chemist's shop in Honolulu, there are Rhondda folk in Australia and Canada . . . Stanley the explorer, commented on the Welsh genius for emigration when he told of his experience on reaching an African village where no white man to his knowledge had ever been, and of his surprise when a compatriot came up to his boat and sold him some bootlaces.[36]

But if empire was part of the myth of Welsh identity it was rarely one of the first thoughts that Welsh historians had when thinking about the history of their country. There was no sustained and developed work on this, or on modern history, in general. The angels of Welsh historiography of the time remained within the celestial sphere of medievalism; they feared to tread in the modern world.

This Welsh tradition of writing coincided with the first era of writing British imperial history which may be neatly marked off between the publication of Sir John Seeley's *The Expansion of England* in 1883 and its going out of print in 1956, the year of Suez. Seeley provided the foundations for a large body of writing which culminated in *The*

Cambridge History of the British Empire, published in eight volumes between 1929 and 1963. There was a variety of different approaches but they agreed on a basic need to rouse the nation to interest in empire (which meant syntheses rather than monographic research) and to create a distinct subject, rather than accepting a role as a sub-field of domestic history. Gradually the writing extended its range and coverage, until in the work of Keith Hancock in the 1930s – generally considered the finest historian of the empire in the first phase – it extended beyond the usual constitutional concerns to embrace the economy, religion and demography.[37]

This imperial historigraphy focused on a period later than that which was the concern of most Welsh historians and its contributors had almost no interest in Wales. There are a total of twelve references to Wales in *The Cambridge History* – and to arrive at this figure it is necessary to use the most generous criteria possible, including counting the *Prince* of Wales (see Table 1.1). Scotland and Ireland do rather better, though the Anglocentricity of the enterprise is apparent. Only two Welsh historians seem to have contributed: J. F. Rees and R. B. Pugh, neither of whom wrote on Wales.

Welsh history was becoming professionalised in the same period and from the early 1930s three chairs in the subject were created. William Rees (1887–1978) in Cardiff had made his reputation through a study of South Wales and the march between 1284 and 1415. His chronological range extended little beyond the incorporation of Wales into the English state in 1536. R. T. Jenkins (1881–1969) was a schoolteacher

Table 1.1 *References to Wales, Scotland and Ireland in* The Cambridge History of the British Empire

Volume	Wales	Indirect	Ireland	Scotland
I	0	6	23	20
II	1	0	37	4
III	0	0	14	2
IV	0	0	0	1
V	0	0	2	1
VI	1	1	18	9
VII[a]	0	1	8	10
VIII	0	2	0	1
Total	2	10	102	48

Note: [a] Includes both parts of volume. Throughout, the most generous criteria have been used. Occasionally there are references to Wales or Welsh people (for instance, Roger Williams), though not acknowledged as such.
Source: *The Cambridge History of the British Empire* (8 vols, Cambridge, 1929–63).

and popular writer who hold an independent lecturership at Bangor (subsequently elevated to a chair) but his concerns were mainly with literature and Welsh domestic politics in the eighteenth and early nineteenth centuries. E. A. Lewis (1880–1940) at Aberystwyth was essentially a medieval economic and institutional historian, though his work did take him to the edge of the Industrial Revolution and included editing port books. But none could really connect with the imperial subject which had been established in the dominant academic triangle of Oxford, Cambridge and London. It was here that there could be a tenuous connection. Caroline Skeel (1872–1951) was a historian of Welsh descent who was the first female professor of history in the University of London. Some of her later work in the economic and social history of the Welsh woollen industry was inspired by material which one of her students had found in the papers of the Royal African Company. This is probably the closest connection between Wales and the empire established by a professional historian in the period.[38]

Imperial history was, of course, essentially a story of diplomacy and administration, of the white settler colonies, with India as a major erratic that was too big to ignore but too different to fit in. Seeley had set his stall up in opposition to the stress on constitutional progress and liberty which he found to be the main concern of English historians and it was the lack of interest in the process of the growth of the empire to which he was referring in his famous – and often misunderstood – remark about the British Empire being created in a fit of absence of mind.[39] But if Welsh historians connected with any English history it was to this Whig story – with Nonconformity as the essence of liberty. Indeed there was a Liberal and Whiggish variant of imperial history which stressed constitutional development and the export of the Westminster model abroad. To the extent that Welsh writers acknowledged the empire they bought into this story and could even find Wales to be the pioneer and exemplar of the story. But there was no reciprocal interest in such a perspective from the imperial historians. Generally, imperial history remained apart from the story of English constitutional triumphs and the three chairs created in Oxford (1905), Cambridge (1919) and London (1919) were not followed by any others, despite the ambitions of the generation inspired by Seeley to establish them everywhere.[40] Welsh scholarship found a very different course. It was in the same era that the University College of Wales, Aberystwyth gained Britain's first chair of international politics – clearly meant to promote peace and international understanding rather than imperial expansion and fascination. This, perhaps, fitted in with the dominant Welsh political concerns much better than a chair of imperial history. London and Oxford followed Aberystwyth in establishing chairs of international relations; no Welsh University seems to have founded a chair of imperial history. But this is only half the story; while no chair of colonial history survived in Aberystwyth, one did exist between 1907 and 1934. In a fit of enthusiasm for tariff reform the Welsh coal-owner David Davies created an appointment and T. Stanley Roberts held it throughout its existence. In its later years the chair ran concurrently with the chair of international relations, which David Davies had also endowed after his experiences on the Western Front. But the colonial history chair never really become established; the incumbent was sometimes described as an assistant professor and certainly did assist the professor of history. When he retired the chair was converted into additional teaching appointments in history – but including a lectureship in imperial history.[41]

Other parts of the globe than the empire tended to claim the attention of Welsh historians. Welsh writers were well aware of the settlements of the Welsh in America. The very fact that they would have had relatives in this migration probably militated against an interest in the empire. The empire was part of the experience of the schoolroom but the direct connection was much slighter. The modern United States was a beacon of liberty and source of pride to the nation, rather than what was sometimes seen as a dubious imperial mission. Nor did the historiography of colonial America offer much of an encouragement to Welsh historians. British North American history, even when strictly colonial in status, had tended to become the prehistory of the USA, rather than being linked to Britain: 'what was truly important about the colonies was their contribution to American nationhood'.[42] Frederick Jackson Turner in particular had stressed the exceptionalism of America from the 1890s and rejected the older germ theories of American development in which European origins – and connections – were stressed. There was a slight counter-movement of colonial history associated with the work of Charles McLean Andrews who '*invented the colonial period in American history*', but in a heavily institutional form and lacking any grand thesis such as provided much of Turner's attraction. Andrews's stress was on the English connection and he found little room for religion, women, slavery and other ethnic groups.[43] Nor did he create a school; almost half his students were women, who were unlikely to have a large impact on the profession in view of the gender assumptions of that time. Anyway, he had relatively few followers. Turner found the approach a deflection from the mainstream of American history, the view from without rather than from within, though undoubtedly Andrews created a more unified view of the colonial period displacing an antiquarian, colony-by-colony and fragmented approach.[44] Only Perry Miller, with his stress on Puritanism and the European dimension had much historiographical support to offer to Welsh historians, but the hands failed to stretch across the Atlantic.[45]

The second historiographical period starts after the Second World War. After 1950, and through to the mid-1980s, the study of modern history accelerated in Wales and became perhaps the main focus of the work of Welsh historians. The emphasis was upon the history of the people and class analysis,[46] and there was relatively little interest in the wider context of Welsh history, apart from the Welsh in America, a key theme for generations of modern Welsh historians. The general context was far more Atlantic than imperial, an approach underwritten by the influential work of Brinley Thomas and developed by Gwyn Alf Williams.[47]

Welsh people seemed to have little need of empire, anyway, in order to establish a sense of their identity and destiny. There was no need for an earlier generation's spurious claims to the Welshness of famous people – even Edgar Allan Poe on the grounds of his Welsh nanny![48] When historical research began to confront the modern period, the empire was in visible decline and did not seem to be an essential topic for research. Brinley Thomas demonstrated – at least to the satisfaction of that generation of historians – that relatively few Welsh people had emigrated and they had rebuilt Wales and the Welsh language, rather than any new worlds. The Welsh were not the Irish. Indeed the continuance of research on the Welsh abroad could almost be seen as being perverse once Thomas had delivered his statistical verdict on emigration in the period after 1851.[49] The trajectory of modern history was in one famous title 'from empire to welfare state' and Welsh people had more or less created this terminus.[50] Wales's place under the sun lamp was secure, even if it had not secured its place in the sun. Wales was an industrial society and industrial societies seemed the way of the future. That located Wales in the modern world. The empire was in decline and not an appropriate bandwagon to which to be hitched.

Nor did imperial history have such a lot to offer from a Welsh perspective. Much of it was still heavily governmental and constitutional in focus; this had made it difficult to address by the first generation of Welsh historians and there was little encouragement after 1945 either.[51] Some prospect might have been offered by the economic turn which imperial history took from the 1930s. Keith Hancock developed the idea of an imperial economy and showed the process of empire-building to be a social one, based on moving frontiers. Richard Pares influentially reviewed economic interpretations of empire and made his own detailed contributions on the West Indies.[52] But this emphasis was quickly eclipsed by Gallagher's and Robinson's 'historiographical revolution'. That at least was Wm Roger Louis's view of them. Colin Eldridge wittily uses the less reverential description of 'vandals from the Fens' assaulting the venerable old body of scholarship. This, along with the growth of area studies prompted by colonial liberation, shifted the focus of imperial historiography away from the centre and towards the periphery.[53] Beyond this, the hostility towards economic interpretations of imperialism – the whole era was that of the Cold War and economic interpretations were seen as being derived from Lenin – meant that one potential avenue of engagement was more or less closed. Gallagher's and Robinson's work was an alternative view stressing strategy and 'the official mind' when it did engage the imperial core. Welsh historians had more affinity with popular mentalities. Reginald Coupland's last book, a study of Welsh and Scottish nationalism, undertaken as he was dying and with an eye on decolonisation, seems to have had little impact in Wales.[54] It became harder for Welsh historians to engage with empire – even if the thought had crossed their minds. There is no interest in the empire in any of the writings of Glanmor Williams (1920–2005) – the pre-eminent Welsh historian of the period who shaped the direction of modern Welsh historiography – and this includes a published lecture on 'Wales and the world'.[55]

The basic problem was, then, in approach. This can be summed this up by placing two statements side-by-side. One is Ieuan Gwynedd Jones's programmatic statement in his inaugural lecture, that he was 'a social historian – and the historian of Wales can be no other'. The other is David Cannadine's comment that 'there has never been an authoritative social history of the empire.' Cannadine's exception is one which proves the Welsh rule.[56] It is in Asa Briggs's chapter on Melbourne in *Victorian Cities*, and there is distinguished Welsh work on settlements in Australia, where the two approaches can cohere.[57] The categories may be stretched a little here and fit in the distinguished tradition of work on the Welsh in the United States and Patagonia – neither part of the British Empire, though the latter was very much a British settlement.[58] More recently this has expanded into a fair-sized body of work on the Welsh in Canada and a regular conference on the connection.[59] One area where there might have been connection was in religion, a major area of research in Wales in the period where distinguished work was done. But the peripheral turn in imperial history meant diminished concern for missionaries and religion. The gears simply would not mesh.

This period culminated in the multi-volume *Oxford History of the British Empire*, with five volumes published in 1998–99 and

Table 1.2 *References to Wales, Scotland and Ireland in* The Oxford History of the British Empire

Volume	Wales	Ireland	Scotland
I	7	93	63
II	4	108	48
III	3	52	15
IV	0	42	4
V	1	8	1
Race	5[a]	1	0
Gender	2	12	3
Total	18	316	133

Note: [a] These references are to 'Cardiff' rather than 'Wales'. In general, these figures give broad indications only. I have counted only direct references to the countries of their inhabitants. Sometimes there are whole chapters devoted to Ireland. I have tried not to double count; so general references to the country are ignored if they occur again in specific references. Even allowing for the greater significance and size of both Ireland and Scotland the under-representation of Wales is striking.
Source: see note 60.

supplementary companion volumes now coming out so fast that any count would soon be dated.[60] It does little better than *The Cambridge History* in terms of references to Wales – just twenty-two in the main volumes and the first two accompanying collections of essays on race and gender (see Table 1.2).

Other general histories of the empire offer just as little. Lawrence James has no reference to Wales, while managing seven to Scotland and twenty-four to Ireland – thirty if the IRA is counted. Trevor Lloyd similarly has no reference to Wales while getting into double figures for both Scotland and Ireland. Bill Nasson has two references to Wales, eleven to Ireland and oddly just one to Scotland. T. O. Lloyd has six references to Wales, the best total so far, while Peter Marshall's edited volume has a panel on Welsh involvement in the empire, which is perhaps the most valuable source. Indeed many of these references, as for Scotland and Ireland, are to those places as conquered territories rather than to their peoples as conquerors.[61]

Despite this there were certain areas where Welsh historians have engaged with the empire, even if fitfully. These will be little more than listed because of considerations of space but they might be made to add up to something. The most general, was, of course, the work of Gwyn Alf Williams (1925–95) on the Madoc legend and on 'imperial south Wales'.[62] The former is a monumental dissection and far more than a fragment. The latter is a suggestive and stimulating essay, but not backed by the multi-volume collective research that Williams envisaged in the headier days of the Industrial Wales Research unit at Cardiff in the late 1970s and early 1980s.[63] Clearly this cannot be dismissed as rhetoric – it connected with examples and had a coherent argument (though one which could now be probed a little). But it was clearly not the multi-volume study in the manner of Braudel, Chanu or Vives which Williams envisaged it becoming.

Gwyn Williams had two related arguments which ran through his work: the importance of the idea of Britishness, which ultimately derived from Welsh sources, and secondly the centrality of Wales in the British Empire. This latter argument is what concerns us here and it had three key dimensions.

First, the idea of the British Empire – and the very term – derived from Welsh originals, ultimately from the Madoc legend and the way that it was drawn upon by John Dee to justify British claims to North America. The priority of Madoc's landing was an answer to Spanish and Portuguese claims to the New World. There was no such English claim therefore it had to be a *British* empire. Second, the economy of Wales revolved around its imperial connections, from eighteenth-century proto-industrial wool destined for the backs of slaves and soldiers to nineteenth-century minerals – iron, copper, slate and coal – which were all heavily global in orientation. Finally, it was this centrality in empire which produced the prominence of Welsh politicians in government in the early twentieth century – notably Lloyd George's ascent to the top of the greasy pole. This was unthinkable without the prominence given to Wales by the South Wales coal industry.

The derivation of the term 'British Empire' from John Dee does not seem to be widely shared, for instance, though it was later taken up by Southey, for instance.[64] Williams's argument was at least partly inspired by the provocation of Hechter's thesis of internal colonialism and perhaps its flaws are partly explained by these polemical origins. The terms 'imperial' and 'empire' are never defined and there is a slippage between them and the international economy, to which the Welsh exporters were beholden, which was closely related to the British 'informal empire', the so-called 'imperialism of free trade'. Perhaps the slippage is most marked in a phrase from the related work of Dai Smith which portrayed South Wales as 'one of those metropolitan nodes of empire from which British domination radiated. The Atlantic was its lake.'[65]

But in the nineteenth century the Atlantic ceased to be the focus of the British Empire. The 'black Atlantic' of the pre-industrial era, founded on slavery, was very much a part of an imperial nexus but its successor, what we might call the 'white Atlantic', depended on free labour from Europe, including Britain, and united more or less advanced industrial economies and their agricultural bases rather than diverse agricultural systems of free and unfree labour which were the basis of the black Atlantic.[66] Even if the famous shift from the first British empire to the second is exaggerated, it retains some reality and clearly the focus of the British Empire moved significantly to the east after 1783.[67]

'Imperial Wales' is a useful staring point – a much better one than Hechter's 'internal colonialism' – but it needs development. We have to ask how it related to the Atlantic economy and to the realities of British power – which means we need to consider also how it might have changed over time. What role did Wales play within the British impact on the international economy? How was informal empire related to formal? This not to demean what Gwyn Williams achieved – no one has developed the theme better, and any critic should be prepared to offer a more rigorous analysis – but to point out how little we have developed his insights in the twenty-five years since his book was published and the decade and a half since he died. A good deal of his analysis overlaps with Edwardian views of imperial Wales; the Elizabethan origins and the control of the empire by Lloyd George, for instance. But there is none of the celebration of military heroes and there is also the firm insertion of the economic base that might be expected from a Marxist. The imperial connections of the Welsh economy did not figure in Edwardian celebrations of Welsh imperialism[68] and one might imagine the horror of Liberals of that era in having Lloyd George's role rooted in the predominance of South Wales coal, as Gwyn Williams did. For them South Wales was a place of 'metics' – resident aliens who tended to denationalise the territory. In 1939 the poet Saunders Lewis remarked of Dowlais 'here once was Wales', and many of his contemporaries agreed with him, including the geographers involved in thinking about regional boundaries who were prepared to cede industrial South Wales and Anglicised mid-Wales to English regionalism.[69] Gwyn Williams's inclusive and shifting definition of Welshness allowed him to make the imperial connection and he was not distanced from industrial South Wales by cultural or racial nationalism, as were his predecessors. The similarities in views are in the end superficial. The differences are quite profound.

What other fragments might we shore against these ruins of empire? David Quinn gave us a brief account of the (rather marginal) Welsh role in the westward enterprise of the Tudor and Stuart periods.[70] A brief consideration of the application of county government to conquered territories suggests interesting perspectives which might be developed.[71] There is some engagement with early colonisation in North

America and this trend perhaps runs on into Hywel Davies's work on transatlantic Nonconformity.[72] There is a small amount of work on Welsh connections with the so-called 'new' empire of the late eighteenth century onwards, particularly on intellectual and cultural connections. There is work on Sir William Jones and David Samwell, for instance.[73] There has been sporadic work on slavery and anti-slavery and its Welsh connections, with special attention paid to Iolo Morganwg, the Penrhyn estate and Methodism. There is an old thesis – over forty years old – on the Welsh anti-slavery movement of the nineteenth century but it tends to exaggerate the extent of Welsh support.[74] There was a limited amount of research on Welsh relationships with nineteenth-century imperialism, most importantly that conducted by Muriel Chamberlain, but with some attention given to Welshmen involved in imperial administration.[75] The role of empire in Welsh politics is under-explored but some attention is paid to it in the work of Kenneth Morgan and Neville Masterman. Morgan's work extends into the twentieth century and in a fine essay on the Labour Party and decolonisation he brings in many Welsh connections, especially the prominence of Jim Griffiths and Jim Callaghan with Bevan as a brief interregnum between the two.[76] There is some tracing of the imperial in popular culture – the main example is the discussion of the All Blacks match in 1905 in Dai Smith and Gareth Williams's history of the Welsh Rugby Union.[77] Finally there is the imperial connection in settlements within Wales; mainly this means Cardiff's Butetown created in the heyday of the empire and reflecting much of its diversity. All the recent scholars concerned with this community build on the work of Kenneth Little, whose *Negroes in Britain* is a little-recognised classic of urban studies in Wales.[78] But perhaps it says something about recent Welsh history that generally there was little New Commonwealth immigration, and few writers – historians or any other discipline – have pursued the theme.[79]

What of the present? What has gone before is really rather a depressing chronicle for anyone concerned to analyse the place the empire held in Welsh affections and the role that Welsh people played in its development. But it is possible to end in a rather more positive way by arguing that the trends in imperial historiography are now more favourable to work on Wales than at any time in the last hundred and twenty-five years of the subject's existence and that Welsh historians are more open to the subject than has been the case in the past. What has changed?

Perhaps the prime change has been the effort to reintegrate British history (once understood in literally insular ways) with that of the empire.[80] Linda Colley's major interpretation of eighteenth- and early nineteenth-century history in many ways was the starting point, though there were already straws in the wind, including programmatic statements from David Cannadine from within her own household.[81] This has been sustained by a substantial body of detailed research.[82] It is important that there were connections between the so-called 'new British history' and the new emphasis on imperial history. Indeed the birth of the 'new' British history owed much to John Pocock's perspective from New Zealand. This is being pursued at least for the early modern period.[83] Furthermore American colonial history has broken out of the exceptionalist straitjacket of Turner's frontier thesis. It is now a subject viewed within an Atlantic framework – and indeed, increasingly an imperial one. This has been a change long in the making and has involved an engagement with European social history and its approaches and methods, which led to the development of a European and ultimately a wider Atlantic perspective. Ethnic diversity is very much part of the story, as are relations with Native Americans, slavery and local studies which sometimes emphasise transnational links. The nation, which had been the centre of American historiography for a century after 1850, has been dethroned and the dominant image has become that of a mosaic of groups rather than a single people. Studies of Welsh emigration may easily connect with this.[84] One study manages to include the Welsh as one of the diverse peoples who made colonial America, finding persistent 'folkways' within the culture and society of the colonies.[85] Such American colonial studies are now located in a wider Atlantic perspective which includes Africa and the Caribbean and there is a general effort to place American history in a transnational context. This wider context will help locate Welsh migrants and also to address the problem evident in the work of Gwyn Williams of slippage from 'imperial' in his title to the Atlantic economy involving non-imperial trade.

Aled Jones and Bill Jones are already addressing this by comparing the Welsh in America, Australia and India, an approach which promises to isolate just what is imperial in the imperial experience and what is simply the experience of migrants.[86] The excursion of British imperial historians into wider studies of globalisation will also provide context for such studies.[87] And while studies of Welsh emigration have never really abated they have gained added power since Brinley Thomas's statistics on its minimal extent have been overturned. Thomas's claim that after 1850 most Welsh people migrated within Wales and created a new Welsh cultural heartland in the South Wales coalfield has been contradicted by Dudley Baines's demonstration that two Welsh people left the country for every internal migrant. If the earlier figures could support a narrowly class-based and rather insular approach to modern Welsh history the new ones are the legitimation of a transnational perspective.[88] Welsh migrants are now being followed to territories previously unexplored in historical writing, and with a more critical sense of how their identity was formed.[89]

Beyond this, the major work of Cain and Hopkins has altered the landscape in many ways, of which two in particular are significant for Welsh scholars.[90] There is a renewed interest in economic aspects of empire which provides some space for work on Welsh connections. They have also shifted attention back to the metropolis – though very much in relation to the periphery – as opposed to the almost exclusive area studies approach which developed in the wake of decolonisation. Post-colonialism offers a perspective which is anathema to many historians but offers possibilities, if there is critical engagement with it rather than outright rejection. In fact, it chimes with the work of one of its severest critics, John MacKenzie, at least in the sense that there is a focus on the metropolis and on culture. Both agree on the depth of the impression of the imperial experience on Britain. As a variant on this there is the body of work which questions just how deep the impact on Britain really was. The most prominent example of this is Bernard Porter's *The Absent-Minded Imperialists* but it is representative of a wider trend which can be seen in the work of P. J. Marshall and others. Indeed this argument seems to run through current discussion in imperial history at least from the early eighteenth century to the twentieth.[91] Porter has suggested that one way into the debate is to look at regional variations in it. If there were to be a major study of the impact on Wales that would not only be a boost to our understanding of Wales but could contribute to a wider, British, analysis. Cain and Hopkins point in a similar, if economic, direction. Their focus on 'gentlemanly capitalism' is resolutely southern English in orientation and on the surface has little to say about industrial regions like South Wales. But that may be the point. To test the efficacy of the theory it will be necessary to look at industrial areas, too. This is being done elsewhere.[92]

To argue in this way is not simply to project possibilities in existing trends but it is to identify what is beginning to happen. We can already see some of the fruits of that new conjuncture. Rees Davies was the most important interpreter of the English empire of the high middle ages and this is where Wales figures most in recent general works on the British Empire. But the integration of domestic and imperial history which is going on proceeds from this starting point.[93] Chris Evans is producing refreshing work in economic history which takes full account of imperial and overseas perspectives.[94] Aled Jones and Jane Aaron have opened up the area of missionary connections – in the light of post-colonialist work to some extent.[95] We need to complement this with a renewed interest in the social and cultural history of religion at home. This had declined as a topic since the heyday of the 1960s and 1970s and current work in religious history is stronger on theology that on history and context. Aled Jones (again!) and Bill Jones have produced two essays which when read together provide a platform for further work – at least in the age of empire of the late nineteenth century. They can relate to recent developments in the history of the settlement colonies which have broken the homogenous British settler down into English, Scots, Irish and Cornish settlers. This provides a space for Welsh settlers. In the Dominions there is evidence of Welsh communities and a culture and not simply of an aggregation of migrants. Whether or not this is the case in territories less dominated by settlement, such as India, awaits investigation.[96] Finally there is John Ellis's work which links political discussion in late nineteenth-century Wales with the empire.[97]

Perhaps we can exploit the lack of a dominating approach in the present era to our advantage. Welsh historical writing is now more diverse that in the past. It is not obsessed with class or protest and has an aura of pluralism about it. True, it has not embraced the new trends like postmodernism and discourse analysis, though not all think this is an impediment. But it has broadened its agenda to encompass gender, media analysis, ethnic minorities and international connections.[98]

The ideas of rhetoric and fragments have been used to organise this paper. Reviewing the record, there has been very little general analysis, really, but perhaps more fragmentary work than there seems when we list it. The need is to form this into a preliminary analysis, to produce hypotheses which could be tested in the further work that is necessary. What is needed, then, in the words of the title of a radical pamphlet is to go *Beyond the Fragments*. Ever since an influential lecture by David Fieldhouse in the 1980s in which he bewailed the shattering of the old imperial history into shards, Humpty Dumpty after the fall, imperial historians seem to have been obsessed with the idea of broken pieces.[99] In Welsh writing there was never much sustained analysis to shatter. Perhaps now we can see the prospect of pulling things together and even of some invisible mending. As far as Wales is concerned the relationship between its own internal research agenda and those being elaborated in the wider world seems to me the most propitious that it has ever been. To add to this there is the outside world to which scholarship always relates (in addition to its own internal logic and trajectory) and it is difficult to avoid a concern with multiple cultural experiences and social cultural and economic influences stretching beyond the nation-state. Even if much of this trumpeting of globalisation proves to be 'globalony' it is unlikely that historical studies will retreat completely to the protective shell of the nation-state. Welsh historians have never had such a luxury anyway. Going out into the world ought to be easier because of this.

Historiography is far from being a substitute for historical investigation. But it is often a necessary first step in that process, or part of what must be done. It is hard to separate the two things and one scholar has dubbed the decision to do so in *The Oxford History of the British Empire* as bizarre.[100] Historiography is a chart of what we know, a warning of the dangers we might encounter and an indication of the blank spots on the map. But like a chart its main utility is in orienting us towards the relevant archives in helping to make sense of what we find there.

Notes

1 I would like to thank Bill Jones for very helpful discussions and for the use of his amazing teaching bibliographies as well as incisive comments on a draft which I have done my best to incorporate. Paul O'Leary, Huw Pryce and Dai Michael were also very helpful.

2 Ned Thomas, *The Welsh Extremist* (London, 1971), p. 33. For a recent example, by a novelist, see Niall Griffiths, 'Wales: England's oldest colony', *New Statesman*, 23 April 2007.

3 Gregory S. Kealey, 'The writing of social history in English Canada, 1970–1984', *Social History*, 10 (1985), 547.

4 Michael Hechter, *Internal Colonialism: The Celtic Fringe in British National Development, 1536–1966* (London, 1975); Neil Evans, 'Internal colonialism? Colonisation, economic development and political mobilisation in Wales, Scotland and Ireland', in Graham Day and Gareth Rees (eds), *Regions, Nations and European Integration: Remaking the Celtic Periphery* (Cardiff, 1991), pp. 235–64; Jane Aaron and Chris Williams (eds), *Postcolonial Wales* (Cardiff, 2005).

5 Neil Evans, '"When men and mountains meet": historians' explanations of the history of Wales, 1890–1970', *WHR*, 22 (2004), 222–51, and 'Casting nets: modern history', in Geraint H. Jenkins and Gareth Elwyn Jones (eds), *Varieties of Influence: A Tribute to Glanmor Williams* (Cardiff, 2008), pp. 80–95.

6 C. Wright Mills, *The Sociological Imagination* (New York, 1959).

7 *Hwyl* = spirit, enthusiasm, was the term used for the perorations of Nonconformist preachers in the period.

8 Owen M. Edwards, *Wales* (London, 1901), pp. 403–4. This passage is, appropriately, also part of an extract from the book in *Land of My Fathers: A Welsh Gift Book* (London, 1915), pp. 211–12, a volume produced to raise funds for comforts for the troops in the First World War. I can find no reference at all to the empire in Edwards's *A Short History of Wales* (London, 1906), which suggests that the passage in *Wales* was inspired by the Boer War and forgotten in its aftermath.

9 Edwards, *Wales*, p. 381 (the index entry of 398 is incorrect); ch. XXIII. The adherence of most Welsh people to the Crown in the Civil War was an embarrassment to Liberal-Nonconformist historiography, hence Edwards' chapter title.

10 His famous statements about the way in which Welsh history was determined by its geography do not find detailed support in his text, though other Welsh historians did work the arguments out. See Evans, '"When men and mountains meet"'.

11 Reba N. Soffer, *Discipline and Power; The University, History and the Making of an English Elite, 1870–1930* (Stanford, 1994), pp. 79–81, 138–42.
12 Lyn Evans, *Portrait of a Pioneer: A Biography of Howell Thomas Evans* (Llandybie, 1982), pp. 70–82.
13 Howell T. Evans, *The Making of Modern Wales* (Cardiff, n.d., c.1911), p. 147.
14 *Ibid.*, pp. 203–4.
15 *Ibid.*, pp. 206–7.
16 J. E. Lloyd, *A History of Wales* (London, 1930), pp. 74–5.
17 W. Llewelyn Williams, *Making of Modern Wales: Studies in the Tudor Settlement* (London, 1919), pp. 27–8 (quotation on p. 28).
18 W. Llewelyn Williams, 'Sir Henry Morgan, the buccaneer', *Transactions of the Honourable Society of Cymmrodorion*, Session 1903–4, p. 1.
19 Williams, 'Sir Henry Morgan', p. 2.
20 This was Owen M. Edwards's characterisation of Welsh history. But this success was relative; he famously complained that the Welsh people know more of the history and geography of the Holy Land than of their own country. Perhaps the sense of the past has been relatively less developed than in Scotland and many Welsh arguments about nationality revolve around language rather than history.
21 W. Watkin Davies, *Wales* (London, n.d., c.1925). Davies was a barrister – but also a Fellow of the Royal Historical Society.
22 Davies, *Wales*, pp. 241–2.
23 Lloyd, *History of Wales*, pp. 77–8. This thin volume was part of Benn's Sixpenny Library.
24 E. Roland Williams, *Some Studies of Elizabethan Wales* (Newtown, n.d., c.1924), p. 154. The general style of Williams's work is much more like O. M. Edwards's belletrist approach than Lloyd's sober scholarship. The chapters of the book had originally appeared as articles in the journal *The Welsh Outlook*. Williams subsequently turned to a medical career, writing *Work and Rhythm, Food and Fatigue* (London, 1936). He had also been the author of a study of Pontarddulais in the First World War, written for the Carnegie Foundation's unpublished History of Wales in the period (ed. Thomas Jones); Bangor University Archives, Bangor MS, 3196.
25 Williams, *Some Studies*, pp. 29, 30–2.
26 Frederick J. Harries, *The Welsh Elizabethans* (Pontypridd, 1924), *passim*, and especially pp. 142, 279.
27 Williams, *Making of Modern Wales*.
28 Vaughan was a 'cultural nationalist and incorrigible medievalist'. John S. Ellis, 'Reconciling the Celt: British national identity, empire and the 1911 investiture of the Prince of Wales', *Journal of British Studies*, 37 (1998), 395. See also Hywel TEIFI Edwards, *The National Pageant of Wales* (Llandysul, 2009), pp. 29–85.
29 Owen Rhoscomyl, *Flame-Bearers of Welsh History* (Merthyr, 1905), pp. 252–3.
30 Rhŷs, preface to Rhoscomyl, *Flame-Bearers*, p. vii.
31 T. Mardy Rees, *A History of the Quakers in Wales and their Emigration to North America* (Carmarthen, 1925); Richard Jones, *Crynwyr Bore Cymru 1653–1699* (Abermaw [Bormarth], 1931).
32 Gerard Charmley, 'J. Vyrnwy Morgan (1861–1925): Wales in another light', *WHR*, 24 (2008), 120–43.
33 *Cofiant* (pl. *Cofiannau*), literally memoir, referred to biographies/autobiographies of Nonconformist heroes. In Victorian Wales they are more successfully weighed than counted.
34 J. Vyrnwy Morgan, *The Philosophy of Welsh History* (London, 1914), pp. 122–3 (quotation p. 123).
35 H. J. W. Edwards, *The Good Patch* (London, n.d., c.1938), p. 201. Ch. XII is entitled 'Imperial Rhondda'.
36 *Ibid.*, p. 202.
37 J. R. Seeley, *The Expansion of England*, ed. John Gross (Chicago, 1971; originally published London, 1883); Peter Burroughs, 'John Robert Seeley and British imperial history', *Journal of Imperial and Commonwealth History*, 1 (1973), 191–211;

J. G. Greenlee, '"A succession of Seeleys": the "old school" re-examined', *ibid*, 4 (1976), 266–82; Wm Roger Louis, 'Introduction', in Robin W. Winks (ed.), *The Oxford History of the British Empire*, vol. 5: *Historiography* (Oxford, 1999), pp. 1–42; A. P. Thornton, 'The shaping of imperial history', *ibid.*, pp. 612–34.

38 Janet Sondheimer, 'Skeel, Caroline Anne James', *Oxford Dictionary of National Biography* (Oxford, 2004) [http://www.oxforddnb.com/view/article/45663, accessed 7 April 2009]; Bangor University Archives, John Edward Lloyd Papers, Item 468, Caroline Skeel to Lloyd, 6 March 1922; Caroline Skeel, 'The Welsh woollen industry in the 16th and 17th centuries', *Archaeologia Cambrensis* (1922), and 'The Welsh woollen industry in the 18th and 19th Centuries', *ibid.* (1924). Bangor had originally created an independent lectureship in Welsh history and it was elevated to a chair in 1945.

39 Bernard Porter, *The Absent Minded Imperialists: Empire, Society, and Culture in Britain* (Oxford, 2004), pp. xviii, 18.

40 David Fieldhouse, 'Can Humpty Dumpty be put back together again? Imperial history in the 1980s', *Journal of Imperial and Commonwealth History*, 12 (1984), 9–23.

41 William C. Olsen, 'The growth of a discipline', in Brian Porter (ed.), *The Aberystwyth Papers: International Politics, 1919–1969* (Cardiff, 1972), pp. 10, 12; Brian Porter, 'Holders of the Wilson Chair', *ibid.*, pp. 361–9; E. L. Ellis, *The University College of Wales, Aberystwyth, 1872–1972* (Cardiff, 1972), pp. 151–2, 170, 187–8, 222, 244–5; *Calendar of the University College of Wales, Aberystwyth, 1912–13*, pp. 104–7.

42 Joyce Appleby, 'A different kind of independence: the post-war restructuring of the historical study of early America', *William and Mary Quarterly*, 3rd Series, 50 (1993), 245–67 (quotation on 249).

43 Richard R. Johnson, 'Charles McLean Andrews and the invention of American colonial history', *ibid.*, 43 (1986), 519–41 (quotation on 528; italics in original).

44 *Ibid.*; Gordon S. Wood, 'A century of early American history: then and now compared; or how Henry Adams got it wrong', *American Historical Review*, 100 (1995), 678–96, esp. 680–3.

45 Appleby, 'A different kind of independence', 264–5.

46 Neil Evans, 'British history: past, present – and future?', *Past and Present*, 119 (1988), 194–203, and 'Writing the social history of modern Wales: approaches, achievements and problems', *Social History*, 17 (1992), 479–92.

47 Brinley Thomas, *Migration and Economic Growth: A Study of Great Britain and the Atlantic Economy* (London, 1954).

48 Bill Jones, 'The Welsh experience in Scranton, PA', *Papers in Modern Welsh History*, 1 (no date), 1. The original source is Frederick J. Harries, *Welshmen in the USA* (Pontypridd, 1927).

49 Brinley Thomas, 'Wales and the Atlantic economy', in Brinley Thomas (ed.), *The Welsh Economy: Studies in Expansion* (Cardiff, 1962). Thomas concluded that Wales had very low levels of emigration after 1850, far below any of the other countries of the UK in per capita terms.

50 T. O. Lloyd, *Empire to Welfare State: English History, 1906–1967* (Oxford, 1970).

51 The classic work was, of course, Ronald Robinson and John Gallagher (with Alice Denny), *Africa and the Victorians: The Official Mind of Imperialism* (London, 1961). For the controversy it generated see Wm Roger Louis (ed.), *Imperialism: The Robinson and Gallagher Controversy* (London, 1976).

52 Ronald Hyam, 'The primacy of geopolitics: the dynamics of British imperial policy, 1763–1963', *Journal of Imperial and Commonwealth History*, 27 (1999), 27–52 (at 27–8); Wm Roger Louis, 'Sir Keith Hancock and the British Empire: the Pax Britannica and the Pax Americana', *English Historical Review*, 120 (2005), 937–62.

53 Henk Wesserling, 'Overseas history', in Peter Burke (ed.), *New Perspectives on Historical Writing* (London, 1991), pp. 67–92; C. C. Eldridge, 'Introduction', in C. C. Eldridge (ed.), *British Imperialism in the Nineteenth Century* (London, 1984), p. 3; Louis, 'Introduction', in Louis (ed.), *Imperialism*, p. 38.

54 Reginald Coupland, *Welsh and Scottish Nationalism* (London, 1954).

55 Neil Evans, 'Professor Sir Glanmor Williams, 1920–2005', *Llafur*, 9 (2006), 5–10; Jenkins and Jones, *Varieties of Influence*; Glanmor Williams, *Wales and the World* (Cardiff, 1984).

56 Ieuan Gwynedd Jones, *Explorations and Explanations: Essays in the Social History of Victorian Wales* (Llandysul, 1981), p. 296; David Cannadine, *Ornamentalism: How the British Saw their Empire* (London, 2001), pp. xviii, 202 (note 12).

57 Asa Briggs, *Victorian Cities* (London, 1963), ch. 7; Deirdre Beddoe, *Welsh Convict Women* (Barry, 1979); 'The Welsh in Australia: a bibliography' at www.llgc.org.uk/index.htm; Bill Jones, 'Welsh identities in Ballarat, Australia, during the late nineteenth century', *WHR*, 20 (2000), 283–307; Robert Llewellyn Tyler, 'Gender imbalance, marriage patterns and cultural maintenance: the Welsh in an Australian gold town, 1850–1900', *Llafur*, 9 (2006), 14–28, 'Occupational mobility and cultural maintenance: the Welsh in a nineteenth-century gold town', *Immigrants and Minorities*, 24 (2006), and 'The Welsh language in a nineteenth-century Australian gold town', *WHR*, 24 (2008), 52–66; Lesley Walker, '"Two jobs for every man": the emigration decision from Wales to New South Wales, 1850–1900', *Australian Studies*, 13 (1998), and 'Finding the Welsh in New South Wales', in W. Ross Johnston, 'Acquiring emigrants: the information chain in Wales 1860s–1870s', *Proceedings of the University of Queensland History Research Group*, 2 (no date).

58 Gareth Alban Davies, 'Wales, Patagonia and the printed word: the missionary role of the press', *Llafur*, 6 (1995), 44–5 'The Welsh Press in Patagonia', in Philip H. Jones and Eiluned Rees (eds), *A Nation and Its Books: A History of the Book in Wales* (Aberystwyth, 2001); Robert Owen Jones, 'The Welsh language in Patagonia', in Geraint H. Jenkins (ed.), *Language and Community in the Nineteenth Century* (Cardiff, 1999); Glyn Williams, *The Desert and the Dream: A Study of Welsh Colonisation in Chubut, 1865–1915* (Cardiff, 1975), and *The Welsh in Patagonia: The State and the Ethnic Community* (Cardiff, 1991).

59 Muriel Chamberlain (ed.), *The Welsh in Canada* (Lampeter, 1986); Muriel Chamberlain, 'The Welsh in Canada: historical sources', *WHR*, 19 (1998), 265–88; Wayne K. D. Davies, 'Falling on deaf ears? Canadian promotion and Welsh emigration to the Prairies', *WHR*, 19 (1999), 679–712, and '"Send a thousand Welsh farm labourers to Canada!": The crow's nest pass scheme and damage control', *WHR*, 20 (2001), 466–94; W. Ross Johnston, 'The Welsh diaspora: emigrating around the world in the late nineteenth century', *Llafur*, 6 (1993), 368–98; Peter Thomas, *Strangers From a Secret Land. The Voyages of the Brig 'Albion' and the Founding of the First Welsh Settlements in Canada* (Toronto, 1986).

60 The five-volume series was produced under the General Editorship of Wm Roger Louis: vol. 1: Nicholas Canny (ed.), *The Origins of Empire* (Oxford, 1998); vol. 2: P. J. Marshall (ed.), *The Eighteenth Century* (Oxford, 1998); vol. 3: Andrew Porter (ed.), *The Nineteenth Century* (Oxford, 1999); vol. 4: Judith M. Brown and Wm Roger Louis (eds), *The Twentieth Century* (Oxford 1999); vol. 5: Robin Winks (ed.), *Historiography* (Oxford, 1999). The first companion volumes were Philip D. Morgan and Sean Hawkins (eds), *Black Experience and the British Empire* (Oxford, 2004), and Philippa Levine (ed.), *Gender and Empire* (Oxford, 2004).

61 Lawrence James, *The Rise and Fall of the British Empire* (London, 1994); Trevor Lloyd, *Empire: The History of the British Empire* (London, 2001); Bill Nasson, *Britannia's Empire: Making a British World* (Stroud, 2004); T. O. Lloyd, *The British Empire, 1558–1995* (Oxford, 2nd edn, 1996); P. J. Marshall (ed.), *The Cambridge Illustrated History of the British Empire* (Cambridge, 1996), p. 265.

62 Neil Evans, 'Gwyn Alfred Williams (1925–1995)', *Llafur*, 7 (1996), 7–11.

63 Gwyn A. Williams, *Madoc: The Making of a Myth* (London, 1979), *The Search for Beulah Land: The Welsh and the Atlantic Revolution* (London, 1980), *The Welsh in Their History* (London, 1982), and *When was Wales? A History of the Welsh* (London, 1985).

64 Linda Colley does not consider such arguments in her influential *Britons: Forging the Nation, 1707–1837* (New Haven and London, 1992). David Armitage, *The*

Ideological Origins of the British Empire (Cambridge, 2000) spends a good deal of time on Dee and locates the idea in (essentially Welsh) Arthurian and Galfridan origins but has only one reference to Madoc, and this in the eighteenth century (p. 183). See also Caroline Franklin, 'The Welsh American dream: Iolo Morganwg, Robert Southey and the Madoc legend', in Gerard Carruthers and Alan Rawes (eds), *English Romanticism and the Celtic World* (Cambridge, 2003), pp. 69–84. The recent tendency to date the British Empire from the mid-seventeenth century, rather than the Elizabethan period, as in the Victorian age, tends to rule out much consideration of this angle.

65 David Smith, 'Tonypandy, 1910: definitions of community', *Past and Present*, 87 (1980), 160.

66 The term 'black Atlantic' was popularised by Paul Gilroy in his book of that title published in 1993. But it is a much wider idea and there has been no very effective engagement with the later Atlantic economy. See Walter T. Nugent, *Crossings: The Great Transatlantic Migrations, 1870–1914* (Bloomington, 1992) (an expanded first chapter of an abandoned Braudelian account); Daniel Rodgers, *Atlantic Crossings: Social Politics in a Progressive Age* (Cambridge, Mass., 1998), ch. 1.

67 P. J. Marshall, 'The first British empire', in Winks (ed.), *Historiography*, pp. 43–53.

68 Empire is not mentioned in D. A. Thomas, 'The growth and direction of our foreign trade in coal during the last half century', *Journal of the Royal Statistical Society*, 66 (1903), 439–533.

69 Alun R. Jones and Gwyn Thomas, *Presenting Saunders Lewis* (Cardiff, 1973), p. 177; Lloyd, *History of Wales*; W. T. R. Pryce, 'Region or national territory? Regionalism and the idea of the country of Wales, c.1927–1998', *WHR*, 23 (2007), 99–152.

70 David B. Quinn, 'Wales and the West', in R. R. Davies *et al.* (eds), *Welsh Society and Nationhood: Historical Essays in Honour of Glanmor Williams* (Cardiff, 1984), pp. 90–107.

71 Myron C. Noonkester, 'The third British Empire: transporting the English shire to Wales, Scotland, Ireland and America', *Journal of British Studies*, 36 (1997), 251–84.

72 Hywel Davies, '"Very different springs of uneasiness": emigration from Wales to the USA in the 1790s', *WHR*, 15 (1991), 368–98, 'Goronwy Owen, the parsons' cause and the College of William and Mary in Virginia', *Transactions of the Honourable Society of Cymmrodorion*, new series, 1 (1995), 40–64, and *Transatlantic Brethren: Rev. Samuel Jones (1735–1814) and His Friends: Baptists in Wales, Pennsylvania, and Beyond* (Bethlehem, Penn., 1995), ch. 1; A. H. Dodd, *The Character of Early Welsh Emigration to the United States* (1953); David Hackett Fischer, *Albion's Seed: Four British Folkways in America* (New York, 1989); Edward George Hartmann, *Americans from Wales* (Boston, 1967), ch. 3; Boyd Schlenther, '"The English is swallowing up their language": Welsh ethnic ambivalence in colonial Pennsylvania and the experience of David Evans', *Pennsylvania Magazine of History and Biography*, 114 (1990), 201–28.

73 E. G. Bowen, *David Samwell (Dafydd Ddu Feddyg) 1751–1798* (Cardiff, 1974); Michael J. Franklin, *Sir William Jones* (Cardiff, 1995); Michael J. Franklin (ed.), *Sir William Jones: Selected Poetical and Prose Works* (Cardiff, 1995); D. J. Ibbetson, 'Sir William Jones (1746–1794)', *Transactions of the Honourable Society of Cymmrodorion*, new series, 7 (2001), 66–82; Garland Cannon and Michael J. Franklin, 'A Cymmrodor claims kin in Calcutta: an assessment of Sir William Jones as philologer, polymath, and pluralist', *ibid.*, new series, 11 (2005), 50–69.

74 Jean Lindsay, 'The Pennants and Jamaica, 1665–1808', *Transactions Caernarvonshire Historical Society* (1982), 37–82, and *ibid.* (1983), 59–93; Clare Taylor, 'Edward Williams (Iolo Morganwg) and his brothers: the Jamaican inheritance', *Transactions of the Honourable Society of Cymmrodorion* (1980), 35–43; Andrew Davies, '"Uncontaminated with human gore"? Iolo Morganwg, slavery and the Jamaican inheritance', in Geraint H. Jenkins (ed.), *A Rattleskull Genius: The Many Faces of Iolo Morganwg* (Cardiff, 2005).

75 Muriel Chamberlain, 'Lord Aberdare and the Royal Niger Company', *WHR*, 3 (1966), 45–62, and 'Lord Dunraven and the British Empire', *Morgannwg*, 15 (1971), 50–72; Ralph A. Griffiths, 'Governor Richard Philipps and the province of Nova Scotia', *Transactions of the Honourable Society of Cymmrodorion* (1968), 265–92; W. R. Owain-Jones, 'The contribution of Welshmen to the administration of India', *ibid.*, (1970), 250–62; D. E. Lloyd Jones, 'David Edward Evans: a Welshman in India', *ibid.*, (1967), 132–41.

76 Kenneth O. Morgan, *Wales in British Politics, 1868–1922* (Cardiff, 2nd edn, 1970); 'Tom Ellis *versus* Lloyd George: the fractured consciousness of *fin de siècle* Wales', in Geraint H. Jenkins and J. Beverley Smith (eds), *Politics and Society in Wales, 1840–1922: Essays in Honour of Ieuan Gwynedd Jones* (Cardiff, 1988); 'Imperialists at bay: British labour and decolonization', in Robert D. King and Robin Kitson (eds), *The Statecraft of British Imperialism: Essays in Honour of Wm Roger Louis* (London, 1999), pp. 233–54; Neville Masterman, *The Forerunner: The Dilemmas of Tom Ellis, 1859–1899* (Llandybie, 1972).

77 David Smith and Gareth Williams, *Fields of Praise: The Official History of the Welsh Rugby Union, 1881–1981* (Cardiff, 1980).

78 Kenneth Little, *Negroes in Britain: Race Relations in English* [sic] *Society* (London, 1948, 2nd edn, 1972); Neil Evans, 'The South Wales race riots of 1919', *Llafur*, 3 (1980), and 'Regulating the reserve army: Arabs, blacks and the local state in Cardiff, 1919–1945', *Immigrants and Minorities*, 4 (1985); Marika Sherwood, 'Racism and resistance: Cardiff in the 1930s and 40s', *Llafur*, 5 (1991).

79 But see Charlotte Williams, Neil Evans and Paul O'Leary (eds), *A Tolerant Nation? Exploring Ethnic Diversity in Wales* (Cardiff, 2003).

80 A. G. Hopkins, 'Back to the future: from national history to imperial history', *Past and Present*, 164 (1999), 198–243.

81 Colley, *Britons*.

82 Kathleen Wilson, *The Sense of the People: Politics, Culture and Imperialism in England, 1715–1785* (Cambirdge, 1995), and *The Island Race: Englishness, Empire and Gender in the Eighteenth Century* (Cambridge, 2003); Kathleen Wilson (ed.), *A New Imperial History: Culture, Identity, and Modernity in Britain and the Empire, 1660–1840* (Cambridge, 2004); Catherine Hall, *Civilising Subjects: Metropole and Colony in the English Imagination, 1830–1867* (Cambridge, 2002); Catherine Hall (ed.), *Cultures of Empire: Colonisers in Britain and the Empire in the Nineteenth and Twentieth Centuries* (Manchester, 2000); Catherine Hall, Keith McClelland and Jane Rendall, *Defining the Victorian Nation: Class, Race, Gender and the British Reform Act of 1867* (Cambridge, 2000).

83 Many of Pocock's essays are conveniently collected in J. G. A. Pocock, *The Discovery of Islands: Essays in British History* (Cambridge, 2005). See the forum entitled 'The new British history in Atlantic perspective' in *American Historical Review*, 104 (1999), 426–500.

84 Wood, 'A century of early American history'; Appleby, 'A different kind of independence'; John Higham, 'The future of American history', *Journal of American History*, 80 (1994), 1289–1309; Ian K. Steele, 'Exploding colonial American history: Amerindian, Atlantic and global perspectives' in Louis P. Masur (ed.), *The Challenge of American History* (Baltimore, 1999), pp. 70–95. Ronald L. Lewis, *Welsh Americans: A History of Assimilation in the Coalfields* (Chapel Hill, 2008), confronts such issues for post-colonial US history.

85 Fischer, *Albion's Seed*.

86 Bernard Bailyn, *Atlantic History: Concept and Contours* (Cambridge, Mass., 2005); Thomas Bender (ed.), *Rethinking American History in a Global Age* (Berkeley, 2002), and *A Nation Among Nations: America's Place in World History* (New York, 2006); Aled Jones and Bill Jones, 'The Welsh world and the British Empire, c.1851–1939: an exploration', *Journal of Imperial and Commonwealth History*, 31 (2003), 57–81. The forum 'Entangled empires in the Atlantic world', *American Historical Review*, 112 (2007), 710–99, takes a broad approach and includes a case-study of a Welsh aristocrat in James Epstein, 'Politics of colonial sensation: the trial of Thomas Picton and the cause of Louisa Calderon', 712–41.

87 A. G. Hopkins (ed.), *Globalization in World History* (London, 2002).

88 Dudley Baines, *Migration in a Mature Economy: Emigration and Internal Migration in England and Wales, 1861–1900* (Cambridge, 1985), ch. 10.

89 Heather Hughes, 'How the Welsh became white in South Africa: immigration, identity and economic transformation from the 1860s to the 1930s', *Transactions of the Honourable Society of Cymmrodorion*, new series, 7 (2001), 112–27.

90 P. J. Cain and A. G. Hopkins, *British Imperialism: Innovation and Expansion 1688–1914* (London, 1993), and *British Imperialism: Crisis and Destruction 1914–1990* (London, 1993).

91 Porter, *The Absent-Minded Imperialists*; P. J. Marshall, 'Imperial Britain', *Journal of Imperial and Commonwealth History*, 22 (1994); Marie Peters, 'Early Hanoverian consciousness: empire or Europe?', *English Historical Review*, 122 (2007), 632–68.

92 Sheryllynne Haggerty, Anthony Webster and Nicholas J. White, *The Empire in One City? Liverpool's Inconvenient Imperial Past* (Manchester, 2009).

93 R. R. Davies, *Domination and Conquest: The Experience of Ireland, Scotland and Wales, 1100–1300* (Cambridge, 1990), and *The First English Empire: Power and Identities in the British Isles: 1093–1343* (Oxford, 2000). See the absorption of this approach in Philippa Levine, *The British Empire: Sunrise to Sunset* (London, 2007).

94 See his contribution to this volume.

95 See their essays in Williams *et al.*, *A Tolerant Nation?*; Aled Jones, 'Welsh missionary journalism in India, 1880–1947', Currents in World Christianity Position Paper No. 123 (Cambridge, 2000), and 'Gardens of Eden: Welsh missionaries in British India', in R. R. Davies and Geraint H. Jenkins (eds), *From Medieval to Modern Wales: Historical Essays in Honour of Kenneth O. Morgan and Ralph A. Griffiths* (Cardiff, 2004). See also Nigel Jenkins, *Gwalia in Khasia: The Biggest Overseas Venture Ever Sustained by the Welsh* (Llandysul, 1995).

96 Jones and Jones, 'The Welsh world'; Aled Jones and Bill Jones, 'Empire and the Welsh press', in Simon Potter (ed.), *Newspapers and Empire: Ireland and Britain, c.1857–1921* (Dublin, 2004), pp. 75–91.

97 John S. Ellis, '"The methods of barbarism" and the "rights of small nations": war propaganda and British pluralism', *Albion*, 30 (1998), 49–75.

98 Andy Croll, '"People's remembrancers" in a post-modern age: contemplating the non-crisis of Welsh labour history', *Llafur*, 8 (2000), 5–18, and 'Holding onto history: modern Welsh historians and the challenge of postmodernism', *Journal of Contemporary History*, 38 (2003), 323–32. The best and most up-to-date survey of recent Welsh historical writing is Paul O'Leary, 'Masculine histories: gender and the social history of modern Wales', *WHR*, 22 (2004), 252–77. The fact that a study centred on gender is an effective survey of the subject as a whole speaks volumes for the changes in Welsh historiography since the early 1990s.

99 Fieldhouse, 'Can Humpty Dumpty be put back together again?'; Douglas M. Peers, 'Is Humpty Dumpty back together again? The revival of imperial history and the *Oxford History of the British Empire*', *Journal of World History*, 13 (2002), 451–67; Andrew Thompson, 'Is Humpty Dumpty together again? Imperial history and the *Oxford History of the British Empire*', *20th Century British History*, 12 (2001), 511–27.

100 Angus Calder cited in Stephen Howe, 'The slow death and strange rebirth of imperial history', *Journal of Imperial and Commonwealth History*, 29 (2001), 131.

CHAPTER 2

Wales, Munster and the English South West: contrasting articulations with the Atlantic world

Chris Evans

Between 1600 and 1760 the British acquired an empire that was substantially – although by no means exclusively – Atlantic in nature. Large volumes of capital and much political energy were expended in Asia, but in terms of territorial acquisition, the settlement of migrant populations or the volume of commercial traffic, the Atlantic was the principal imperial theatre for the English and (after 1707) the British. Indeed, in the seventeenth century the English (and therefore Welsh) were effectively restricted to the Atlantic. The Portuguese and the Dutch were far more important players in the Indian Ocean. As for the Pacific, the inhabitants of half-a-dozen sizeable colonial Spanish cities stared out across that ocean. The Spanish even essayed a transpacific presence, and even though it was nothing more than the gossamer-thin connection between Acapulco and the Philippines, it was something that the English could not hope to match.

Yet, despite the Atlantic orientation of the English/British empire before 1760, relatively little attention is given to the Atlantic borderland of the British archipelago, of which Wales was part. Although historians are increasingly interested in the impact that imperial endeavour had on the British Isles themselves, the focus of attention is very often metropolitan – on London as the organising centre of a 'gentlemanly capitalism', for example. The cultural turn taken by the 'new imperial history', with its professed concern for the marginal and the subaltern, promises something different, but here too a metropolitan bias resurfaces. The new imperial historians tend to interest themselves with the ways in which empire was presented on the London stage, or reflected in metropolitan literary culture, or paraded in the capital's fashionable salons. For all their efforts to 'de-centre' the empire, the centre obstinately reimposes itself.

Scotland is the only part of the Atlantic frontier to have received sustained attention from historians of empire, for reasons that are easily stated. With Glasgow, Scotland could boast one of the most dynamic Atlantic entrepôts of the age. North Britain was also a major source of imperial personnel after the Act of Union. Scottish soldiers, administrators, merchants, doctors and plantation managers played a disproportionately large role in the drive to empire and have been accorded matching scholarly attention. By comparison, the Welsh are scarcely visible in the historical literature. It may be that this historiographical obscurity is justified. Did pre-industrial Wales have the critical mass – economic, political or cultural – to affect imperial endeavour in a way worthy of note? Put simply, are the historical actors too few in number for meaningful conclusions to be drawn? Or is the evidence too exiguous? This is a particular difficulty when considering the place of Wales within the system of Atlantic commerce which was the most tangible expression of Stuart and Hanoverian imperial effort. This is an era for which statistical data are not abundant and those that are available seldom permit the Welsh experience to be detached from that of 'England and Wales'.

There is no wholly satisfactory response to this problem, but one is to place Wales in a comparative framework alongside other regions that share some of its structural features. If the British Isles are quartered on the map, the south-west quadrant, broadly speaking, is occupied by the English South West, the province of Munster and Wales.[1] Between the 1650s, when the first of the Navigation Acts began to give shape to England's Atlantic trade, and the 1770s, when the Atlantic empire fell apart, these three peninsular obtrusions into the western ocean can be considered side by side. A comparative approach, bringing three adjacent parts of Britain's Atlantic frontier into analytical alignment, can disclose the peculiarities of the Welsh contribution. It can also guard against an overemphasis on Welsh singularity. While a comparative perspective on Wales, Munster and the South West can bring to light commonalities (in topography and environment) and distinctions (in political and social structure), it can also highlight interconnections between the three regions. These interconnections gathered dialectical strength as the eighteenth century wore on, only to wither as the Atlantic world was transformed in the revolutionary age. The waxing of commercial ties between the three regions tells us something about the nature of the Atlantic empire in its heyday. Their waning, part of a process of 'de-Atlanticisation', points to the divergent paths that Wales, Munster and the South West followed in the nineteenth century.

The peninsulas of the archipelagic south-west shared a mild, damp climate. Large parts were given over to upland moors, unsuitable for cereals production but ideal for pastoralism. That said, there were important variations. Some parts had a greater acreage in tractable, fertile valleys (Devon with the Taw–Torridge basin emptying into the Bristol Channel, or County Cork with the valleys of the Blackwater, Lee and Bandon); others had rather less (most of Wales, Cornwall and Kerry). Some parts enjoyed a considerable urban tradition; others did not. Devon could boast Exeter, a commercial and ecclesiastical centre of note since the middle ages, which had perhaps 14,000 inhabitants in 1700. And both Plymouth and Tiverton could show populations of between 5,000 and 10,000. Daniel Defoe rhapsodised about Devon's urban plenitude. The county, he wrote, was 'so full of great towns, and those towns so full of People, and those People so universally Employ'd in Trade and Manufactures, that not only it cannot be equall'd in England, but perhaps not in Europe.'[2] Munster could not equal it, but the province still made a respectable urban showing. Cork, the regional capital, was home to about 6,000 people at the time of the Restoration, growing very rapidly in the century that followed to top 44,000 by 1760. The lesser maritime centres of Kinsale and Youghal were far smaller, but even they exceeded anything that Wales had to offer.[3] The Welsh urban tradition before the nineteenth century was notoriously feeble. Welsh towns were shabby affairs: 'small, modest, and unprepossessing'.[4] Those in search of urban facilities had to travel to Chester, Shrewsbury or Bristol. The strength or otherwise of urban development can stand as a broad measure of whether a region was capital-rich and an exporter of capital, like Devon, or capital-deficient and reliant on inward investment, as was the case with Cornwall or, still more so, Wales.

Our three regions were also, of course, marked by differing political conditions. Munster stands out in this respect. Its status was painfully ambivalent: it was at once a colony and a platform for further imperial endeavour in the Atlantic world. The Munster experience was one of prolonged disorder in the seventeenth century. The devastation brought about by the Confederate Wars in the 1640s was compounded by the recurrent brigandage that continued long after the Cromwellian conquest of the early 1650s. The calm of the 1660s and 1670s was no more than relative, and the 1680s terminated in the Williamite War, ushering in another brutal pacification, one that underscored the colonial relationship between Britain and Ireland. It is, of course, the colonial character of Munster that sets it apart from Wales and the South West. The wave of expropriations and expulsions that revolutionised Munster society in the seventeenth century had no parallel in the other regions under discussion. The Irish province was also exceptional in experiencing a major loss of human capital during these upheavals. The thousands of Confederate prisoners who were shipped off to the West Indies and an early death represented an absolute and irredeemable loss. Another major outflow followed the Treaty of Limerick of 1691, which led to the exodus of the Jacobite forces, mostly recruited in Munster, which had been cornered in the city. Twelve thousand sailed off to enter French military service, and the region continued to supply surreptitious recruits to the armies of Europe's Catholic powers for years thereafter. The export of military personnel, which remained significant down to the 1730s, was an index of economic uncertainty for the province's rural poor.[5]

The English South West was not free of political violence – it was the scene, after all, of the Monmouth Rebellion in 1685 and the Dutch invasion of 1688 – but these were not events that retarded commercial development. Indeed, the Glorious Revolution, by transforming Britain from a client state of France to a key adversary of Louis XIV, was a direct stimulus to economic growth in the South West. It did so by virtue of a lavish expansion and reorientation of military spending by the new regime. The naval bases of the restored monarchy had been along the Thames and the Medway, facing east against the Dutch. The naval apparatus of the post-1688 era faced south and west; it was intended to thwart a French invasion of England or a descent on Ireland. The royal dockyard at Plymouth, begun in 1692 on a green-field site, embodied this new outlook. Its workforce and attendant population soon eclipsed those of Chatham and Deptford, and by the time of the American War 'Dock', as it was prosaically known, employed over 2,400 workers. With this, Plymouth edged past Portsmouth to become Britain's premier naval base.

There was nothing in Munster or Wales to match this. Ships of the line could find a sheltered anchorage beneath the guns of Fort Charles at Kinsale, but Kinsale had no shipbuilding capacity. The building of naval depots around Cork Harbour came later. It was a feature of the American War, still more of the Napoleonic period. The same can be said of developments along Milford Haven. The yard and fortifications did not rival, even remotely, the installations at Plymouth. 'Dock' was in a league of its own. As such, it relied upon a procurement system of corresponding scale. In times of war, the western squadron sailing out of Plymouth was crewed by upwards of 20,000 sailors, every one of whom would receive, in addition to the pound of bread and gallon of beer that was issued daily, 1 lb of pork on Sunday, 2 lb of beef on Tuesday, 1 lb of pork on Thursday and a further 2 lb of beef on Saturday.[6] During the dockyard's early decades victualling was somewhat improvised, but by the middle of the eighteenth century the naval authorities had dedicated on-site facilities for the brewing of beer, the baking of biscuit, and the production of salted provisions. The last of these required the slaughter, disassembly, salting and packing of hundreds of beasts. The peacetime requirement in 1738 was 230 beef oxen weekly. War with Spain in 1739 sent demand rocketing, with the yard's butchers cleaving their way through between 500 and 800 oxen a week, plus a proportionate number of hogs.[7]

This was a mighty undertaking, but it was paralleled and greatly exceeded by the salted provisions industry of Cork, which furnished Munster's principal point of articulation with the Atlantic world. During the heyday of the trade – roughly speaking, the 1680s to the 1760s – Cork's slaughterhouses processed between 50,000 and 80,000 cattle annually. This was, as one authority has stated, 'the most highly developed provisions industry in the Atlantic economy'.[8] It was not always so. Until the 1660s Ireland had been a major exporter of *live* cattle. That export collapsed when the Westminster parliament passed the Cattle Acts of 1665 and 1667 that banned the commerce in livestock between Munster ports and England. Thwarted by this prohibition, Munster's graziers and merchants redirected their efforts westwards and outwards to what soon proved to be highly lucrative Atlantic markets.

It is the historic fate of wet uplands to supply animal protein to more prosperous neighbouring regions. When Daniel Defoe travelled through Cardiganshire he found the county 'so full of cattle, that tis' said to be the nursery, or breeding place, for the whole kingdom of England . . . but this is not a proof of its fertility, for tho' the feeding of cattle requires a rich soil, the breeding them does not, the mountains and moors being as proper for that purpose as richer land.'[9] It was a function fulfilled with equal success by Munster and Wales in the early seventeenth century. Cattle were reared in Kerry or Cardiganshire, driven to lowland pastures for fattening, and then slaughtered. For Welsh cattle the route lay along drovers' roads that terminated at Smithfield. Irish cattle were shipped from Cork or Youghal and disembarked at Bideford or Minehead before recommencing their long march to the shambles of urban England.

When the Cattle Acts put paid to Irish imports Wales was unaffected, allowing Welsh drovers to continue along their accustomed tracks well into the nineteenth century.[10] The Irish, clearly, were disadvantaged, just as was intended. But their ejection from the English market had paradoxical effects; they were compelled to develop all the value-added operations – the butchering, the dressing, the salting of the meat; the packing and cooperage; the rendering of the carcass and the manufacture of by-products such as tallow and glue – that had once been surrendered to English towns and cities. Although Welsh graziers and drovers enjoyed privileged access to the free-trade area at the empire's core from which the Irish were excluded, it is their lot that appears rather more 'colonial'. The Welsh exported an unadorned commodity; they added no value and therefore enjoyed meagre returns. Had Welsh producers been penalised as their Irish counterparts were, who is to say that Carmarthen, Swansea or Haverfordwest might not have sprouted a provisions industry to rival Cork's?

Cork's provisions bonanza was contingent, however, on Atlantic developments. Had they not been favourable, the outcome of the Cattle Acts would have been ruinous. Needless to say, Cork's success rested upon Atlantic slavery. The beginning of the provisions trade correlates closely with the rise of sugar in the Caribbean. The so-called 'sugar revolution' that swept the West Indies in the mid-seventeenth century has been defined succinctly by one of its leading historians as 'a swift shift from diversified agriculture to sugar monoculture, from production on small farms to large plantations, from free labour to slave labour, from sparse to dense settlement, [and] from white to black populations'.[11] Barbados supplies the classic example. European planters there in the 1630s had comprised a modest gentry, supported by indentured white servants; they had practised a mixed husbandry that allowed them to sustain themselves without an over-reliance on food imports. The transformed social structure of the 1670s, one rooted in sugar monoculture, was far more volatile and contradictory: large populations of enslaved Africans could not survive unaided on islands on which every eligible acre was dedicated to the growing of sugar cane. Their viability as a workforce depended upon the importation of food on a colossal scale.

It was here that Cork merchants were well placed to intervene. Soaring demand from the West Indies allowed Irish drovers and graziers to compensate for their exclusion from the English market in the 1660s. The suburb of Shandon, across the river Lee from Cork's medieval centre, grew into a dedicated and malodorous meat-packing district. The city was home to an army of butchers and coopers, augmented during the autumn killing season by hordes of wagoners, porters and labourers. Exports of salt beef from Cork hovered around 30,000 barrels annually in the first years of the eighteenth century. After the coming of peace in 1713 they lurched upwards, and between the 1730s and 1760s the export seldom slipped below 100,000 barrels per annum.[12] Much of this went to the English sugar islands. Much also went to France.[13] That, at least, was the destination listed in the official record; in reality, La Rochelle or Nantes served as mere staging posts. Irish beef was re-routed to the French Caribbean, the most dynamic plantation complex of the eighteenth century.[14] Fewer than 3,500 slaves were held in Saint-Domingue, later France's largest sugar colony, in 1690, but growth was exponential over the next century. By the late 1780s there were 460,000 slaves crowded on to Saint-Domingue's fertile and well-irrigated plains, almost half the total captive population of the Caribbean.[15]

It was an immense market for Irish provisions, for the eating of beef was mandatory for French bondsmen: Louis XIV's *Code noir* of 1685 required planters to include two pounds of beef in the weekly ration of every slave over the age of ten.[16] Not that it was appetising: French slaves gnawed on so-called 'small beef' cut from the shanks and stringier quarters of slaughtered beasts. The better cuts were reserved for the British islands, where beef was more popular among Europeans. This points to a significant dietary division in the Caribbean: Africans enslaved by the French took much of their protein in the form of beef; those enslaved by the British were more likely to chew salted cod. Cod was generally supplied by New England merchants, who shipped in low-quality fish from Newfoundland to exchange for molasses and rum. This 'refuse' cod was a product of the Grand Banks. It was therefore a *de facto* product of the English South West, for the Grand Banks fishery was essentially a Devonian enterprise.

The early modern importance of the Grand Banks, where fish stocks are now irreparably depleted, is often lost on us. But for seventeenth- and eighteenth-century commentators the fishery appeared as an inexhaustibly fecund source of riches. Malachy Postlethwayt, when identifying the world's most lucrative centres of wealth creation in his *Universal Dictionary of Trade and Commerce* (1751), focused on precious metals and exotic luxury foods: the immense Andean silver mine at Potosí, the coffee-growing hinterland of the Arabian port of Mocha, and the East Indian spice island of Amboina. He added: 'the banks of Newfoundland'.[17] Newfoundland was, to be sure, unalluring. As a colonial official of the 1670s confessed, 'the Country itself is but a . . . Rocky barren soyle incapable of cultivation and consequently not capable of improvement'; but that mattered little when the surrounding ocean teemed with fish.[18] Here, where the continental shelf lunged eastwards and the icy waters of the Labrador Current collided with warmer waters from the south, were ideal feeding-grounds for cod. Cod's value lay not just in its superabundance, but in its capacity to be transformed into a form of protein that could be transported for thousands of miles without perishing. Having a low fat content, the flesh of cod would not, if properly dried and salted, turn rancid.

Breton and Iberian fisherman were exploiting these happy conditions from the fifteenth century onwards. English endeavour was tentative until the later sixteenth century when the Wars of Religion and the Dutch Revolt absorbed the energies of the French and Spanish respectively. It was then that the so-called 'English Shore', Newfoundland's most easterly coast, began to host large and regular fleets of fishing vessels from the ports of the South West. Capital for the Newfoundland fishery came largely from Devon, the personnel overwhelmingly so.

Devonian merchants and mariners built upon experience gained in the late medieval fishing bonanza that swept the South West.[19] At first Cornish and Devonian seafarers restricted themselves to their own coastal waters, but they also experimented with longer-range expeditions, ones involving summer encampments on the west coasts of Cork and Kerry. These were the prototypes for the migratory settlements that began to flourish along the English Shore of Newfoundland in the seventeenth century. Only 2,000 people over-wintered at the coves and inlets of the English Shore in the seventeenth century; at least twice that number arrived in April and May for the fishing. They left from Dartmouth and Topsham, Barnstaple and Bideford. Many were experienced mariners; others were landsmen hoping to make big money at this piscine Klondike. The daily routine was arduous. The fishing shallops, each with four or five men, were rowed out several miles every morning. The day was spent spinning out and reeling in the baited lines, then back to the shore stations where cod by the thousand were headed, eviscerated, salted and dried.[20]

By the 1680s a distinctive triangular trade, originating in Devon, was well-established. The fishing fleet would leave the South West's ports in the spring, calling at Waterford or Dungarvan to pick up salted provisions. (Time was not wasted trying to grow or gather food in Newfoundland; the long summer days were better spent fishing.) As cheap labour as well as salt pork was available on the quaysides, the Devon shipmasters acquired the habit of hiring additional hands for the summer season. In the 1730s the habit became ingrained, and by the 1760s as many as 5,000 Irish labourers may have made the crossing to the English Shore every year. The Devon-based fishery was now at its height. The ejection of the French from the bays to the west of the English Shore under the terms of the Treaty of Utrecht in 1713 allowed West Country venturers to dominate the offshore waters as well as the inshore stretches.

English hegemony on the Grand Banks coincided with the upsurge of slave imports into the Caribbean, creating a major new market for salt fish. It was the most unpalatable fish, of course, which was sold off to New Englanders for shipment to the sugar islands. Fully cured fish was carried back across the Atlantic to the Iberian Peninsula and the western Mediterranean, the traditional markets served by Devonian ships. There, cod was exchanged for wine and other foodstuffs of southern Europe, and for industrial raw materials that were in demand in Devon. Chief among these was wool, Spanish wool for the serge manufacture that overspread the south of the county, what Defoe called 'the great Serge Manufacture of *Devonshire*'. At the start of the eighteenth century Devon was the single most important centre of woollen production in England and Wales, accounting for about a quarter of all woollen exports in Anne's reign.[21] So buoyant was the industry in the seventeenth century that it outran local supplies of wool from Dartmoor and the Blackdown Hills.

Serges were woven from a mix of short- and long-combed wools. Spanish wool from Bilbao supplied the one, fleeces from Munster the other. In the 1670s and 1680s cargoes of raw Irish wool were shipped to Barnstaple, Minehead and other Bristol Channel ports and put out to rural spinners in north Devon. The yarn they produced was carried south to Tiverton, Crediton and other manufacturing towns in the hinterland of Exeter. Irish wool was also consumed within Ireland, however. Indeed, the native woollen industry was expanding fast in the late seventeenth century, boosted by the Dutch and Huguenot communities planted by magnates such as the Duke of Ormond in south Tipperary towns like Clonmel and Carrick-on-Suir.[22] But the new draperies of Munster, which held out so much promise in the 1670s and 1680s, suffered in the new century. Serge manufacturers in the South West were determined to nullify Irish competition, which was proving troublesome for them in north European markets. They clamoured for protective legislation; they got it with the Woollen Act, passed by the Westminster parliament in 1699, which prohibited the export of Irish woollens to the continent.

The logic of the 1699 act was this: the makers of light woollens in Bandon, Clonmel and other weaving towns were to be excluded from overseas markets, allowing wool from Irish sheep-walks to be aggrandised by the serge makers of the South West. The processing of yarn could still be performed in Munster, of course, even if weaving was now disadvantaged. So it proved. Spinners multiplied across rural Cork in the two decades after the 1699 Act. Perhaps 12,000 were active in the 1710s, working up materials put out to them by the master combers of Cork city. By the 1720s the shipment of raw wool had effectively ceased but 'woollen yarn spinning and its export to England . . . [was] one of the central features of the regional economy'

– to the grief of the West Country spinners who had once processed Munster wool and now found themselves idle.[23]

Yet the 1699 act was not quite the lethal blow that its architects in Exeter had intended. Just as the Cattle Acts of the 1660s forced the processing of livestock into new channels, so the Woollen Act pushed Munster textiles into less obtrusive, clandestine routes. And just as Munster beef found distinctively Atlantic outlets, so did the fabrics of Munster's textile towns. Cloth from Bandon and Tallow found its way to Lisbon, and from Lisbon to the vast colonial market of Brazil, which was undergoing massive expansion as successive gold rushes in the Minas Gerais opened up the interior to settlement. As an illegal trade, this is impossible to document fully or even to estimate, but the panicky reaction in Cork to the Lisbon earthquake of 1755 reveals something of the importance of the Portuguese Atlantic to Munster's business community.[24]

The serge industry of Devon was the intended beneficiary of the discriminatory legislation of 1699 but it did not lead an untroubled existence. Indeed, the trade underwent a sharp contraction between the 1710s and 1740s as Devon serges lost ground on the all-important German market. Although there was a period of renewed growth in the 1760s and 1770s with new sales in Italy and Spain compensating for the collapse of north European demand, Devon's textile industry failed to demonstrate the technological dynamism that distinguished some other English regions, most notably Yorkshire. Manufacturers and merchants in the West Riding also proved organisationally nimble in a way that their rivals in the South West were not. In particular, Yorkshire manufacturers paid court to consumers in British North America, whose population grew more than eightfold in the three-quarters of a century before the Revolution.[25]

Devonshire worsteds did not 'Atlanticise' in the same way. In fact, they may even have receded on Atlantic markets in the middle decades of the eighteenth century. Hard-wearing Devon perpetuanas had been an enormously popular trade good in West African slave marts at the end of the seventeenth century when the Royal African Company's exports sometimes exceeded £10,000 annually in value.[26] 'Perpets' were still a feature of English slaving in the 1720s when private traders, largely from Bristol, had usurped the position of the African Company, but by 1750 this variety of serge no longer appeared on the manifests of Bristol ships bound for Guinea. African tastes had shifted in ways that were mysterious to contemporaries and remain so to historians.[27] In the years after the American Revolution the serge industry of Devon was in a parlous condition. A sluggish and uneven performance on European markets was compounded by a failure to take advantage of Atlantic opportunities. Succour came from the east, not the west, when the East India Company became an important buyer of serge for export to China.[28]

Woollen textiles from Wales, by contrast, found a ready market in the Atlantic slave empire. At the end of the Middle Ages the Welsh woollen industry, such as it was, had been concentrated in the small urban centres of the south. There followed a shift into the countryside of mid-Wales. The 'ruralisation' of industry in the early modern period was not unusual; indeed, it was a commonplace across Europe as peasant households, typically in pastoral regions, sought ways of boosting their incomes. The production of low-quality textiles was a characteristic response – and so it was in mid-Wales. Cloth manufactured in Montgomeryshire and Merionethshire was carried to Shrewsbury where the powerful Drapers Company controlled the finishing processes. The final product was exported via London, usually to France.[29] There was, however, in the later seventeenth century a switch in the nature of the product and its destination. Welsh producers concentrated more on lighter flannels and plains rather than heavy broadcloth, and these were exported to the slave societies of the New World. 'The exportation of flannels to America and the West-Indies, by the Merchants of London and Liverpool, is much more considerable than the home consumption', one eighteenth-century observer wrote.[30] Another elaborated: the coarse local cloth was for 'covering the poor Negroes in the West Indies'.[31]

Wales became the principal source, in other words, of 'Negro cloth', the woollen fabric that, in conjunction with low-grade German linens, made up the basic uniform of enslaved Africans in the British sugar islands and British North America.[32] Colonial slave-owners wrote every year to their agents in the metropolis for fresh supplies, usually specifying 'Welsh plains' or 'Welsh cottons'.[33] There were rival products – like 'Kendall cottons' from the Lake District, an equally inhospitable and impoverished area – but the Welsh fabric appears to have been dominant. When Elias Ball, an exiled American loyalist, investigated the source of the 'Negro cloth' in which the slaves of his native South Carolina were clad he discovered that 'the great Markett for that article . . . is at Shroesberry [sic] the Capital of Shropshire'.[34] The actual production zone, of course, was further to the west, in Wales.

The export of Welsh plains has evaded statistical capture, but the volumes must have been considerable. British North America had a captive population of over 240,000 at mid-century, and the British sugar islands a further 255,000, so the market was potentially immense.[35] By the conventional reckoning of the time five yards of plains were required per slave: 'You know', a southern planter told his London supplier in 1764, 'that 5 yds of Plains usually makes a mans jacket & Breeches or a womans gown'.[36] It was also understood that a new set of clothes would be required every autumn, as a year's labour would reduce the old suit to rags.

The changing organisation of the Welsh woollen industry in the eighteenth century is poorly understood, and so too the means by which the product was marketed, but what is beyond doubt is that increasing numbers of rural dwellers in Montgomeryshire and Merionethshire came to be harnessed to the Atlantic economy.[37] The labouring poor resorted to industrial by-employments in response to their 'growing dependence on the returns of day-labour and . . . the faltering cottage economy'. They were joined by small hill farmers who, faced by an 'economic terrain [that] became increasingly unyielding as the various demands of rents, taxes, rates and tithes outpaced returns from agriculture . . . looked to resolve their material difficulties through participation in the woollen industry'.[38] Parishes in the mountainous woollen-producing heartland swarmed with spinners and weavers.

Much of the export went by London, as it had done when Welsh woollens served European markets, but as the slave plantations became the chief destination so Bristol and Liverpool became more prominent ports of dispatch.[39] As one Virginia planter told his London correspondent in 1735, 'we want our Cloathing early for our slaves . . . wch will force us to correspond wth ye out ports; or let our slaves perish; or sit all ye winter by ye fire . . . besides all coarse woollens come Cheaper from thence'.[40] Indeed, factors from the out-ports usurped the position of dominance once enjoyed by the Drapers Company of Shrewsbury. Once, pack horses from the weaving districts had converged on Shrewsbury; now, the agents of international cloth merchants roamed the upland parishes. 'The Liverpool Merchants have now persons on the spot, to purchase of the makers; and to assist the poorer manufacturers with money to carry on their trade.'[41] Cash advances were very welcome to the 'poorer manufacturers'; they were also a mechanism through which the factors could take control of the commodity. By enabling the makers to buy wool on credit, the factors had a stake in the cloth before it had been woven and a say in how it was finished. Ownership of the product had shifted from the weaver to the merchant capitalist. Abject proletarianisation came next.

Although it may not always have seemed so to the direct producers who were governed by the clatter of shuttles, the circulation of 'Negro cloth' through the Atlantic world was a major success story for eighteenth-century Wales. There was another, one achieved in conjunction with the far South West: copper. At the end of the seventeenth century British copper, hitherto marginal to European markets, became quite suddenly of pivotal importance. 'British copper' is something of a misnomer, however, for this was a specific product of the Atlantic borderlands: a meeting of Cornish ore and Welsh coal. Explaining the sensational rise of Cornish copper in the last years of the seventeenth century requires a consideration of several issues: changes in mining practice, changing market conditions, and abrupt technological change in the smelting of ores.[42]

Let us take mining first. It was tin, not copper, which was mined on a substantial scale in Cornwall and west Devon in the early modern period. Only in the final decades of the seventeenth century, as tinners drove their workings deeper underground, were appreciable deposits of copper found mixed in with those of tin. The presence of copper galvanised mining speculators, for the ore lodes of the German lands were in decline. And in 1687 the enormous mine at Falun in Sweden, Europe's principal source of supply in the Baroque age, suffered a catastrophic cave-in, suspending production completely for a number of years.

The shrivelling up of rival supplies opened a new era for deep-mined Cornish ore. Still more important was the application of coal to smelting. Ore extraction could only flourish if there was fuel with which to smelt. In Sweden, with its abundant forests and a state-imposed conservation programme, this was not a problem. In wood-depleted Cornwall it was – hence the efforts made in the late seventeenth century to employ mineral fuel in the smelting of copper ore. The viability of coal-fired smelting methods was unequivocally demonstrated at Redbrook in the lower Wye valley in the 1680s by John Coster. The availability of coal-smelted copper stimulated in turn a burst of investment in brass production in the Bristol area. There was a compelling spatial logic at work here. When copper could be had from the Forest of Dean to the north and calamine (zinc carbonate) brought in from the Mendips to the south, the Avon valley was ideally placed for brass manufacture. That the monopoly rights to copper and brass manufacture that had long been vested in the Society of Mineral and Battery Works were annulled in 1689 can only have helped. Bristol-based entrepreneurs like the Coster family now had free rein to deploy their pioneering coal-fired techniques.[43]

Bristol remained an important organisational centre for the copper and brass trades throughout the eighteenth century, but copper production facilities soon started to slip westward into Wales.[44] This relocation is readily explained. Seaborne Cornish ores could be brought directly to the abundant, outcropping coal of the Swansea–Neath district. Sir Humphry Mackworth, that ever-busy late Stuart gentleman-industrialist, had a smelting plant up and running on his estate at Neath in the mid-1690s, and in 1713, as the head of a joint-stock company called the Mineral Manufacturers of Neath, he expanded into brass-making. Bristol's copper and brass manufacturers soon took note. A Bristol man, Dr John Lane, had been one of those involved in the Mineral Manufacturers of Neath. In 1717 he moved on to build the first dedicated copper-smelting plant in the Swansea valley: a massive, streamlined works at Llangyfelach. The sons of John Coster, the pioneer in smelting with coal of the 1680s, who had built up extensive mining interests in Cornwall and Devon, followed suit, shifting their smelting operations from Bristol to South Wales. They took over premises at Melincryddan in the Neath valley in *c.*1730, then huge, purpose-built works at White Rock in the Swansea valley in the late 1730s. The Coster family are worthy of special note, not just because they embody copper's shift to coal technology and to Wales at the turn of the eighteenth century, but because they exemplify a specific articulation with the Atlantic – Welsh copper's intimate link to Atlantic slavery.

There was a disturbing symmetry between the smelting of copper in South Wales and Bristol slaving. The 'golden' age of Bristol slaving coincided with Swansea's emergence as Europe's foremost centre of copper-smelting. It was no accident. Bristol merchants had been quick to respond to the revocation of the Royal African Company's monopoly of trade on the Guinea Coast in 1698. These Bristol men were soon making incursions into the Bight of Biafra, well to the east of the trading areas that had been exploited by the London-based Company in the late seventeenth century. The Bight was the new frontier of British slaving, and its traders were interested in particular types of trade goods – metallic ones.

One of the key findings of the last generation of slave-trade scholarship has been the complexity of African demand. Different parts of the coast served different hinterlands, and each of these had particular demands to make on the international market. If Europeans were to procure slaves they had to attend closely to the shifting contours of African demand. So, whereas indigenous merchants along the Loango Coast were most interested in Indian-made textiles, their early eighteenth-century counterparts on the Gold Coast requested Devon-made perpetuanas. At Ouidah it was the cowrie shell that was the prime article of exchange, but along the Bight of Biafra copper rods were indispensable, as were brass vessels such as 'Guinea kettles'.[45]

It was this appetite for copper and copper-based wares that drew copper masters like the Costers into the Guinea trade. Thomas Coster (1684–1739), the head of the family in the 1720s and 1730s, was an enthusiastic slaver. He was part-owner of the 85-ton *Amoretta*, purpose-built in New England to carry captive Africans from the Bight of Biafra. His co-owners included Joseph Iles and Isaac Hobhouse, two of Bristol's most eminent slave-merchants. And the *Amoretta* was no isolated experiment. In the mid-1730s, as the Costers prepared to launch the White Rock smelting works, they also ploughed capital into slaving expeditions. Thomas Coster was part-owner of the *Mary*, launched in 1735 and promptly set to work running slaves to Jamaica. And in 1737 he joined once more with Iles and Hobhouse to fit out the *Squirrel*, which joined the *Amoretta* in carrying slaves to the Carolina Lowcountry, British North America's most brutal slave society.[46]

The Costers, whose White Rock works boasted a 'Manilla House', were not alone in embracing both copper and slavery. From the very beginning Welsh copper and brass makers paid close attention to African wants. The proprietors of the Llangyfelach works complemented the smelting plant built in 1717 with battery works at which pans and kettles for the Guinea trade could be manufactured. The same concern for satisfying African consumers was shown in Flintshire, the other great centre of copper and brass manufacture in Wales. The Swedish traveller Reinhold Angerstein, who stopped there in the early 1750s, watched copper rods being prepared. The rods were drawn out under a trip hammer. Angerstein was a little surprised to see the work done in this way. 'The production would take much less time', he wrote, 'if the rods were drawn through holes in an iron plate, as is done with heavy brass wire, but I was told that this way of processing would not give the copper the same degree of ductility'. And ductility was an essential quality because, Angerstein added, the 'Negroes in Guinea use the rods as ornaments and wind them around arms and legs'. Indeed, these lengths of copper had a simple and expressive trade name: 'Negroes'.[47]

Still more Welsh copper went to the West Indies, where sugar, molasses and rum were made on an industrial scale, using methods that that required huge copper vessels. The sap obtained from crushed sugar cane was collected in copper pans called clarifiers. 'Of these, there are commonly three; and their dimensions are generally determined by the power of supplying them with liquor.' Clarifiers of 300 or 400 gallons were commonplace, and a capacity of 1,000 gallons not unheard of.[48] The copper utensils needed for distilling rum were no less impressive. 'The still-houses on the sugar-plantations in the British West Indies, vary greatly in point of size and expence, according to the fancy of the proprietor, or the magnitude of the property', it was reported, with the largest stills holding between 'one to three thousand gallons of liquor'.[49]

The explosive growth of the market for clarifiers and stills over the course of the eighteenth century is illustrated readily enough by the statistics for sugar exports from the British islands. At the start of the century some 22,000 tons of sugar were shipped annually to English ports. By 1748 exports had nearly doubled, reaching 41,425 tons. Growth thereafter was still more dramatic: exports were touching 165,000 tons at the end of the Napoleonic Wars.[50] A huge quantity of Welsh copper stood behind these spiralling figures.

The years between the first Navigation Acts and the American Revolution saw each of the three regions under discussion become more Atlantic and more imperial in aspect. Trading links with Britain's Atlantic settlements – especially those that were most heavily implicated in slavery – grew in strength and frequency. Irish beef fed the captive workers of the Caribbean and British North America; 'Welch Cotten' clothed them. Sometimes, Exeter serges and Welsh copper helped to acquire them. Very often, this Atlantic thrust was achieved through interaction between the different peninsulas of the archipelagic south-west. Devon's worsteds incorporated Irish yarn, Welsh copper embodied Cornish ore, and the South West's long-range fishing fleet sailed for the Grand Banks via the ports of Munster, where salted provisions could be loaded.

Nevertheless, the extent of commercial integration between Wales, Munster and the South West should not be exaggerated. Each followed an individual trajectory. Only Devon could boast a long-range Atlantic fishing industry. Munster's ports played no more than a supporting role in the fishery on the Grand Banks, and Cornwall's pilchard fishery was a more modest inshore affair, one that served European rather than Atlantic markets.[51] As for Wales, the weakness of long-range maritime endeavour when compared with the South West is striking. There was an attempt to establish a whaling fleet at Milford Haven in the 1790s, employing refugee American loyalists from Nantucket, but the initiative quickly came to grief.[52]

Munster's uniqueness lay in its devotion to the salted provisions trade – a uniqueness highlighted by the contrast with Ulster, a province that specialised in the export of linen and Presbyterians instead.[53] Munster's attachment to beef and pork stemmed from the colonial status imposed on Ireland by the Navigation Laws and other restrictive regulations. Yet the restrictions placed on Irish trade did not always have the cramping effect anticipated by those who had framed them. Instead of confining Munster's export commodities to a subaltern role within Britain's Atlantic empire, the Cattle Acts of the 1660s and the Woollen Act of 1699 caused a leakage into rival empires. Beef packed in Cork went to the French Caribbean in massive volumes; illicit Munster textiles penetrated the Portuguese Atlantic.

The transoceanic connections of the archipelagic south-west waxed in the century following the restoration of the monarchy, but from the 1770s, as Britain's Atlantic empire cracked apart amid revolution and war, the different regions disengaged in one way or another from the Atlantic economy. To start with, Devon's dominance of the Grand Banks fishery fell away sharply in the aftermath of the American Revolution. The surge in transatlantic migration that followed British victory in the Seven Years' War had sent tens of thousands to the colonies, most of them heading for the Appalachian back country; but significant numbers of settlers sailed for more northerly destinations, so that by the time of the American Revolution there was at last a permanent population on the English Shore of sufficient size to throw off Devon's tutelage. A migratory workforce no longer left Dartmouth or Bideford. The English South West continued to furnish supplies for the cod fishery, but organisational control was a thing of the past.[54] In fishing, as in the serge trade, Devon 'de-Atlanticised' in the late eighteenth century.

Munster's export of salted provisions was also in decline by the 1770s. Population growth in England pushed up grain prices, encouraging Irish landlords to put more of their land under the plough. The result was that shipments of beef to the Caribbean tumbled as grain exports across the Irish Sea multiplied. (The switch from grass to tillage also, it should be said, hastened the decline of woollen textiles in Munster: shrinking pasturelands meant fewer sheep; and fewer sheep, more expensive fleeces.) Growing competition from New England was a further problem for Cork's merchant houses: Connecticut-packed beef was considered an inferior product, but it enjoyed a price advantage in the West Indies by the revolutionary era.[55] The deterioration of Atlantic markets continued apace in the 1790s as the Haitian Revolution removed Saint-Domingue from the commercial equation. Exports of raw sugar from the ravaged colony fell from 93,573 tons in 1789 to 18,519 tons in 1800–1; refined sugar exports plunged from 47,516 tons to just 17 in the same period.[56] The export of beef through Cork sank in tandem, back to the levels of Queen Anne's reign. Had it not been for heightened military demand in this era of war, the decline would have been worse.[57]

Changes in Wales's articulation with the Atlantic world were less clear-cut. Just as the rise of Welsh-made 'Negro cloth' requires further investigation so does its fall. There are references enough to suggest that 'Welsh plains' continued to clothe slaves in the Antilles and the American South in the early nineteenth century. Seven yards of the fabric were issued to every male inmate on the Cannon's Point plantation in coastal Georgia as a winter clothing ration in 1821, for example; the women got six yards.[58] Yet by the middle decades of the nineteenth century the domestic woollen industry of mid-Wales was no longer spoken of as being either thriving or export-driven. The reasons why have to be surmised. It may be that Welsh weavers were out-flanked by rivals from Yorkshire or from industrialising New England, whose innovations in the making and marketing of cloth proved too competitive.[59] It may also be the case that plantations, especially in the American South, became more self-sufficient in the ante-bellum era. What is certain is that the mountain communities of Merionethshire and Montgomeryshire where domestic textile-making was prevalent were plunged into misery. By the time of Victoria's accession the woollen-producing district that girdled mid-Wales recorded some of the highest levels of pauperism in Britain.[60]

If 'Welsh plains' were of dwindling importance, Welsh copper continued to prosper. Indeed, Swansea was the *global* centre of copper-smelting by the early nineteenth century. And the connection with Cornwall held firm. Ores from Parys Mountain on Anglesey rivalled those from the South West in the 1780s and 1790s, but the deposits there were quickly worked out. Mines in Cuba and Chile began to ship ore to Swansea Bay in the 1830s and 1840s, but it was not until the 1860s that Cornish producers were eclipsed.[61] The Atlantic markets that the Welsh copper industry had once served, on the other hand, sank in relative importance. The post-emancipation sugar islands occupied a much diminished place in the imperial pantheon, and so too the trading stations on the West African coast. Even so, of all the trades of the south-west quadrant that had enjoyed success in the imperial Atlantic, Welsh copper was the only one that survived into the nineteenth century in full health.

The fundamental contribution of Wales, Munster and the South West to Britain's Atlantic empire of the late Stuart and Hanoverian era lay in protein and fibre: fish, animal flesh, woollen textiles. It was a contribution that foundered in the late eighteenth century amid revolutionary turmoil, agrarian crisis and the intertwined processes of industrialisation and de-industrialisation that swept all three regions. Copper was exceptional. It alone negotiated these switchback changes. Significantly, it was the only sector that rested upon mineral energy; the others exploited fauna and flora. They trusted, ultimately, to the caprice of nature. They depended on the ability of the soil to support herds of cattle, flocks of sheep, stands of timber or fields of grain. Nature could be bounteous, but it was not inexhaustible. The fixed acreage of land available to people in the Atlantic borderlands imposed limits on what could be done. Land that was devoted to grazing sheep could not simultaneously be put under the plough to plant grain, or turned over into potato beds. Copper-smelting and refining exploited a fossil fuel and seemed therefore able to leap beyond the resource restrictions that the land imposed. Copper-makers delved beneath the surface of the earth to access what appeared to be inexhaustible subterranean resources.[62] Coal was the key, even at the threshold of Welsh modernity. It poses the question: does all of modern Welsh history, imperial as well as domestic, have to be traced in coal dust?

Notes

1 Wales is defined here, as in the volume as a whole, as the twelve historic counties subject to the jurisdiction of the Great Sessions, plus Monmouthshire. Munster comprises the six counties of Cork, Kerry, Clare, Limerick, Tipperary and Waterford. The South West (capitalised), for the purposes of this essay, is taken as Cornwall, Devon and those parts of western Somerset that were structurally connected to Devon's textile trade and fisheries. The adjectival form 'south-west' (not capitalised), when used in this essay, does not carry this restrictive sense. The expression 'British Isles' is used in a geographical rather than a political sense. This essay draws on work generously supported by the Institute for Southern Studies at the University of South Carolina, the Pasold Research Fund and the Virginia Historical Society. I am grateful to Huw Bowen, Sharif Gemie, Göran Rydén and Gareth Williams for their comments on an earlier draft.

2 Daniel Defoe, *A Tour Through the Whole Island of Great Britain* ed. Pat Rogers (London, 1986), p. 217.

3 David Dickson, *Old World Colony: Cork and South Munster 1630–1830* (Cork, 2005), p. 662. See also Mark McCarthy, 'The forging of an Atlantic port city: socio-economic and physical transformations in Cork, 1660–1760', *Urban History*, 28 (2001), 25–45.

4 Geraint H. Jenkins, *The Foundations of Modern Wales 1642–1780* (Oxford, 1993), p. 116.

5 L. M. Cullen, 'The Irish diaspora of the seventeenth and eighteenth centuries', in Nicholas Canny (ed.), *Europeans on the Move: Studies in European Migration, 1500–1800* (Oxford, 1994), pp. 112–49, especially pp. 123–5.

6 N. A. M. Rodger, *The Wooden World: An Anatomy of the Georgian Navy* (Glasgow, 1986), p. 83.

7 A. J. March, 'The local community and the operation of Plymouth Dockyard, 1689–1763', in Michael Duffy, Stephen Fisher, Basil Greenhill, David J. Starkey and Joyce Youings (eds), *The New Maritime History of Devon*, vol. 1: *From Early Times to the Late Eighteenth Century* (London, 1992), p. 203. See also Jonathan Coad, 'The development and organisation of Plymouth Dockyard, 1689–1815', in the same volume, pp. 192–200, especially 197–8.

8 Thomas M. Truxes, *Irish-American Trade, 1660–1783* (Cambridge, 1988), p. 147.

9 Defoe, *A Tour*, p. 382.

10 Richard J. Colyer, *The Welsh Cattle Drovers: Agriculture and the Welsh Cattle Trade before and during the Nineteenth Century* (Cardiff, 1976).

11 B. W. Higman, 'The sugar revolution', *Economic History Review*, 2nd series, 53 (2000), 213.

12 Dickson, *Old World Colony*, p. 657, table XI.i.

13 In the 1730s the export of Irish beef to the English plantations averaged 54,000 barrels annually. The export to France averaged 71,000 barrels. See Joseph Leydon, 'A study of the Irish cattle and beef trades in the seventeenth and eighteenth centuries', *Journal of History and Politics*, 11 (1993–94), 23.

14 Bertie Mandelblatt, 'A transatlantic commodity: Irish salt beef in the French Atlantic world', *History Workshop Journal*, 63 (2007), 18–47.
15 Robin Blackburn, *The Making of New World Slavery: From the Baroque to the Modern, 1492–1800* (London, 1997), p. 295; Herbert Klein, *The Atlantic Slave Trade* (Cambridge, 1999), p. 33.
16 By way of comparison, on the eve of the Revolution per capita consumption of meat in France was less than 1 lb per week. See Fernand Braudel, *Civilisation and Capitalism 15th–18th Century. The Structures of Everyday Life* (London, 1981), p. 196.
17 Malachy Postlethwayt, *The Universal Dictionary of Trade and Commerce: With Large Additions and Improvements* (London, 4th edn, 1774), *sub* 'Manufacturers'.
18 John Mannion, 'Victualling a fishery: Newfoundland diet and the origins of the Irish provisions trade, 1675–1700', *International Journal of Maritime History*, 12 (2000), 4.
19 Marianne Kowaleski, 'The expansion of the south-western fisheries in late medieval England', *Economic History Review*, 2nd series, 53 (2000), 429–54.
20 Peter E. Pope, *Fish into Wine: The Newfoundland Plantation in the Seventeenth Century* (Chapel Hill, 2004).
21 W. G. Hoskins, *Industry, Trade and People in Exeter 1688–1800* (Manchester, 1935), pp. 39–40.
22 L. A. Clarkson, 'The Carrick-on-Suir woollen industry in the eighteenth century', *Irish Economic and Social History*, 16 (1989), 23–41.
23 Dickson, *Old World Colony*, p. 133.
24 *Ibid.*, p. 129; A. J. R. Russell-Wood, 'The gold-cycle, *c.*1690–1750', in Leslie Bethell (ed.), *Colonial Brazil* (Cambridge, 1987), pp. 190–243.
25 John Smail, *Merchants, Markets and Manufacture: The English Wool Textile Industry in the Eighteenth Century* (Basingstoke, 1999).
26 K. G. Davies, *The Royal African Company* (London, 1957), p. 352.
27 David Richardson, 'West African consumption patterns and their influence on the eighteenth-century English slave trade', in Henry A. Gemery and Jan S. Hogendorn (eds), *The Uncommon Market: Essays in the Economic History of the Atlantic Slave Trade* (New York, 1979), pp. 319–20.
28 H. V. Bowen, 'Sinews of trade and empire: the supply of commodity exports to the East India Company during the late eighteenth century', *Economic History Review*, 2nd series, 55 (2002), 472–3, 476–7.
29 T. C. Mendenhall, *The Shrewsbury Drapers and the Welsh Wool Trade in the Sixteenth and Seventeenth Centuries* (Oxford, 1953); C. A. J. Skeel, 'The Welsh woollen industry in the sixteenth and seventeenth centuries', *Archaeologia Cambriensis*, 7th series, 2 (1922), 220–58.
30 J. Evans, *A Tour Through Part of North Wales, in the Year 1798* (London, 1800), p. 33.
31 Thomas Pennant, *A Tour in Wales. MDCCLXX* (2 vols, London, 1778–83), vol. 2, p. 351.
32 For a general account see Chris Evans, *Slave Wales: The Welsh and Atlantic Slavery, 1660–1850* (Cardiff, 2010), pp. 46–54.
33 'Cottons' were woollen goods that had undergone 'cottoning'; that is, the nap had been teased upwards to give a fuller depth to the cloth.
34 South Carolina Library, University of South Carolina, Ball family papers, box 1, folder 7, Elias Ball to Elias Ball junior, 21 April 1786.
35 Ira Berlin, *Many Thousands Gone: The First Two Centuries of Slavery in North America* (Cambridge, Mass., 1998), pp. 369–70; Richard B. Sheridan, 'The formation of Caribbean plantation society, 1689–1748', in P. J. Marshall (ed.), *The Oxford History of the British Empire*, vol. 2: *The Eighteenth Century* (Oxford, 1998), p. 400.
36 'A Georgia planter buys negro clothes in London', in Ulrich B. Phillips (ed.), *Plantation and Frontier Documents: 1649–1863. Illustrative of Industrial History in the Colonial and Ante-Bellum South* (2 vols, Cleveland, 1909), vol. 1, p. 294. A similar allowance is stipulated in *American husbandry* (2 volumes, 1775), vol. 1, p. 407.

37 J. G. Jenkins, *The Welsh Woollen Industry* (Cardiff, 1969), is the basic source but unhelpful in this respect.

38 Melvin Humphreys, *The Crisis of Community: Montgomeryshire, 1680–1815* (Cardiff, 1996), p. 7.

39 The continued importance of London is conveyed in the correspondence of Henry Laurens, the South Carolina planter and merchant, who visited the capital in the early 1770s: 'parcels of Plains are hourly expected from Wales', he told one associate back in Charleston; 'a large Supply by Sea from Wales' was imminent, he told another. George C. Rogers and David R. Chesnutt (eds), *The Papers of Henry Laurens*, vol. 9: *April 19, 1773–Dec. 12, 1774* (Columbia, SC, 1981), pp. 330, 352–3.

40 Virginia Historical Society, MSS 1 C9698a, John Custis to Micajah Perry, 1735. A contemporary concurred: 'Bristol is by much ye best place for such woolings they are 20 per Ct better' (College of William and Mary, Earl Gregg Swem Library, Special Collections, MSS 39.1 J47, William Johnston to Neill Buchanan, 16 [month unclear] 1738).

41 Quoted in M. J. Jones, 'Merioneth woollen industry from 1750 to 1820', *Transactions of the Honourable Society of Cymmrodorion* (1940), 193.

42 John Rowe, *Cornwall in the Age of the Industrial Revolution* (Liverpool, 1953), chs 1 and 2, provides the classic account from a Cornish perspective. The view is broadened in J. R. Harris, *The Copper King: A Biography of Thomas Williams of Llanidan* (Liverpool, 1964).

43 Joan Day, 'Coster family (*per. c.*1685–1764)', *Oxford Dictionary of National Biography* (Oxford 2004) [http://www.oxforddnb.com/view/article/47489, accessed 14 July 2008].

44 R. O. Roberts, 'The smelting of non-ferrous metals', *Glamorgan County History*, vol. 5: *Industrial Glamorgan from 1700 to 1970* (Cardiff, 1980), pp. 47–96.

45 For the consumption of copper and brass in Africa see Stanley B. Alpern, 'What Africans got for their slaves: a master list of European trade goods', *History in Africa*, 20 (1995), 5–43, especially 13–16, and Eugenia W. Herbert, *Red Gold of Africa: Copper in Pre-Colonial History and Culture* (Madison, 2003), ch. 6.

46 Information on the Costers' slaving has been extracted from *Voyages: The Trans-Atlantic Database*, available online at http://www.slavevoyages.org/tast/index.faces. Ten voyages fitted out by Thomas Coster (sometimes as Caster and sometimes in the guise of Costin) are recorded.

47 Torsten Berg and Peter Berg (eds), *R. R. Angerstein's Illustrated Travel Diary, 1753–1755: Industry in England and Wales From a Swedish Perspective* (London, 2001), p. 324; Joan Day, *Bristol Brass: A History of the Industry* (Newton Abbot, 1973), p. 199.

48 Bryan Edwards, *The History, Civil and Commercial, of the British Colonies in the West Indies* (Dublin, 2 vols, 1793), vol. 2, pp. 220–1.

49 *Ibid.*, vol. 2, p. 229.

50 Sheridan, 'The formation of Caribbean plantation society', p. 401; J. R. Ward, 'The British West Indies in the age of abolition, 1748–1815', in Marshall (ed.), *The Eighteenth Century*, p. 429.

51 Tony Pawlyn, 'The Cornish pilchard fishery in the eighteenth century', *Journal of the Royal Institution of Cornwall*, 2nd series, 3 (1998), 67–90.

52 Edouard A. Stackpole, *Whales and Destiny: The Rivalry Between America, France, and Britain for Control of the Southern Whale Fishery, 1795–1825* (Amherst, 1972), pp. 197–247.

53 A twin process caught in Patrick Griffin's *The People with No Name: Ireland's Ulster Scots, America's Scots Irish, and the Creation of a British Atlantic World, 1689–1764* (Princeton, 2001).

54 David J. Starkey, 'Devonians and the Newfoundland trade', in Duffy, Fisher *et al.*, *New Maritime History of Devon*, vol. 1, 163–71.

55 Truxes, *Irish-American Trade*, pp. 156–7; R. C. Nash, 'Irish Atlantic trade in the seventeenth and eighteenth centuries', *William and Mary Quarterly*, 3rd series, 42 (1985), 352.

56 Robin Blackburn, *The Overthrow of Colonial Slavery, 1776–1848* (London, 1988), p. 241.
57 Dickson, *Old World Colony*, p. 657, table XI.i.
58 John Solomon Otto and Augustus Marion Burns III, 'Black folks and poor Buckras: archaeological evidence of slave and overseer living conditions on an antebellum plantation', *Journal of Black Studies*, 14 (1983), 193.
59 One Rhode Island manufacturer exulted in overcoming Welsh plains: 'The Sea Island Planters in Carolina & Georgia who used Welsh Plains at from sixty to ninety cents that have tried our goods give [us] the prefference and our orders for them this year are now nearly double the last years & last year more than double the year before – we intend making them as low as possible and selling them at small proffits to regular customers' (Rhode Island Historical Society, Peace Dale Manufacturing Company Records, MSS 483 sg 36, Box 1, folder 3., I. P. Hazard to D. W. Urquhart & Co., 6 June 1826). My thanks to Dr Seth Rockman of Brown University for this reference and advice on US textile manufacturers.
60 Ian Levitt, 'Poor law and pauperism', in J. Langton and R. J. Morris (eds), *Atlas of Industrialising Britain, 1780–1914* (London, 1986), p. 161.
61 Edmund Newell, '"Copperopolis": the rise and fall of the copper industry in the Swansea district, 1826–1921', *Business History*, 32 (1990), 75–97.
62 I draw here on a distinction, between 'organic' economies that are reliant on vegetable energy and 'mineral energy' economies that exploit fossil fuels, made in E. A. Wrigley, *Continuity, Chance and Change: The Character of the Industrial Revolution in England* (Cambridge, 1988).

CHAPTER 3

Celtic rivalries: Ireland, Scotland and Wales in the British Empire, 1707–1801

Martyn J. Powell

In 1992 Linda Colley published *Britons: Forging the Nation*, an exceptionally important work of eighteenth-century British, and imperial, history.[1] In the course of this book Colley did much to demonstrate the ways in which the inhabitants of England, Scotland and Wales came together as Britons after the Scottish Act of Union, forging a new identity through warfare – chiefly with France – and anti-Catholicism. Whenever historians try to make sense of the convergence of the British Isles' four nations, England is often the lynch-pin, and the exercise then becomes a series of bi-national case-studies – Anglo-Scottish, Anglo-Welsh or Anglo-Irish. Colley is guilty of this to a certain degree, and there is also different weighting to the connections. In *Britons* there is certainly more on England and Scotland than England and Wales. Of course there is nothing on England and Ireland. Much to the chagrin of Irish historians, Colley opted to leave out Ireland rather than deal with its complicating features – its quasi-colonial status, its Catholic majority – though it does not stop her piling up evidence from Ireland in later chapters when this advances her case.[2]

Arguably another facet missing from Colley's study is the way in which the subsidiary nations, Wales, Scotland and Ireland, related to one another. When bonding agents are discussed they invariably relate to the whole polity or to England. Rarely is there a sense that the three 'Celtic' regions might have peculiar tensions in their own relationships that might influence the forging of a British nation. There are good reasons for this. The Celtic areas of the British Isles do not have common land borders. More importantly England provided the centripetal force. Nevertheless an analysis of what could be called inter-Celtic relations might shed additional light on Colley's model. This essay seeks to explore the connections between these countries, with Ireland replacing England as the locus, paying particular attention to periods of imperial crisis in the second half of the eighteenth century

– the American War of Independence and the French Revolutionary Wars. The imperial angle here is inescapable, and it is central to Colley's study. There is good reason to believe that Ireland itself was treated as an imperial problem in the second half of the eighteenth century, along with India and America.[3] English governmental preoccupations during this period, plus Ireland's *de facto* colonial position, must therefore mean that inter-Celtic rivalries were informed by the imperial framework.

Filling the inter-Celtic historical *lacuna* does not in any way suggest an incompatibility with the Colley model. Indeed within Colley's study there is a hint of the broad line of argument put forward in this essay: that Scotland was transformed from a rebellious, Jacobite thorn in England's side, to the empire's driving force, a repositioning that could not but have an impact upon Wales and Ireland. At the same time Wales and Ireland were experiencing shifts in the nature of their political cultures, and some of these shifts can be teased out by looking, in turn, at commercial, political and military developments.

Because of the vast scope of this topic, some of these thoughts are necessarily impressionistic, and clearly more can be said, and indeed has been said about, say, trade and economic links[4] and religious connections. There can be no doubt that the Irish and Scottish Presbyterian communities were closely entwined as part of 'a transatlantic subculture'.[5] There are also difficulties with sources: this piece is based upon books, pamphlets, periodicals and newspapers, yet Wales had no newspaper press until the early nineteenth century. Analysis of Irish and Scots newspapers cannot take account of Gaelic language feeling. Vincent Morley rightly notes the resulting 'failure of historians to comprehend the political culture of the majority of the Irish poulation'.[6] Yet an assessment of Celtic rivalries through the medium of Irish print culture remains a worthwhile task, and can offer a corrective to the all too common binary studies focusing upon England, and to nationalist historiographies eager to depict that same England as the hegemonic oppressor of brother Celts.

In the second half of the eighteenth century prominent Scottish commentators and intellectuals made a conscious effort to place themselves at the centre of imperial ambitions. The failure of the Darien scheme marked the end of any Scottish national pretensions to colonial expansion, and Smith, Hume and friends moved to the centre – intellectually and occasionally physically – of a British empire. According to Colley, for some Scots 'it was less the job and trading opportunities that empire provided, than the idea of empire that proved so compelling'. It was a means of being treated as equals with the English. Colley even goes as far as to suggest that Scots with Jacobite backgrounds were more likely to uphold royal authority, and, indeed 'take a strong line in suppressing colonial disorder'.[7] From the Bute administration onwards Scottish politicians and commentators became proponents of imperial reform. It was Bute rather than George Grenville who began an ambitious plan to reform the financing of the colonies.[8] William Murray, later Lord Mansfield, was no friend to the Americans, and after all interested parties agreed on the need to concede Irish legislative independence in 1782 it was Mansfield whose intervention in the Lords threatened to destroy the settlement.[9]

The commercial nature of the Scottish Enlightenment has been stressed by Roy Porter and others.[10] But it is worth dwelling on the way in which many Scottish writers sought to foster improvement and commercial success in the other Celtic regions. Adam Smith was an influential proponent of Irish free trade and corresponded with key members of the government who were to deliver this concession.[11] In the 1760s John Campbell acted as a domestic and imperial propagandist for Lord Bute as well as his secretary, and was agent for the colony of Georgia. He fought a rearguard action against the Wilkites on behalf of his paymaster and wrote a pamphlet defending the unpopular Peace of Paris.[12] But he also did his bit to emphasise the key roles that Wales, Scotland and Ireland could play in the development of nation and empire. His *A Political Survey of Britain* reads something like a tour, the exception being that he was irrepressibly positive about all parts of Britain, no doubt a straightforward proposition if one refrains from leaving one's house.[13] Campbell avoided snide remarks – unlike Irish Lord Shelburne who when visiting Wales described the inhabitants of mountainous areas as 'little, cunning, and crafty'[14] – and laid out the commercial and imperial possibilities that awaited Wales, Scotland and Ireland if the right kind of improvement was achieved.[15]

Wales was praised for its mineral waters and springs, and Campbell urged their development as a means of persuading the Welsh gentry away from Bath and Tunbridge and attracting company from the borders, 'in order to share not only the Benefits of the Waters, but in the Conversation and Amusement'. This was about stimulating politeness as well as the economy. Elsewhere he noted that Carmarthen was 'justly esteemed the politest Place in South Wales'. Wales was also urged to foster its own markets, and Milford Haven championed as an imperial port for the future. Campbell sententiously added: 'I had rather be of real service to one Welch Village, than receive the Applause of this whole Island'. His ultimate aim, for Wales, as in Scotland and Ireland, was to stimulate domestic Trade and 'a larger Proportion of foreign Commerce, than the Inhabitants of this valuable Country at present possess'.[16] In Scotland it was access to imperial markets that he said had brought about an economic transformation. Like Smith he argued for the reduction or removal of duties to facilitate commercial development, and to undermine smuggling. Campbell pointed to the unjust restrictions on Irish trade in particular, a line that was taken not only by Adam Smith but also the Welsh-born political economist Josiah Tucker. Campbell saw Irish trade with 'all parts of the known World, and more especially with America' as 'a matter of the utmost Importance', which would result in it 'contributing exceedingly to the Support of the British Empire in that Part of the World'. Above all the message in this mighty – and tedious – tract was improving, commercial and imperial, but also one that stressed a uniting vision, 'a uniform System of Policy that renders their Inhabitants in Effect but one People'.[17]

Another Bute propagandist, the author Tobias Smollett, editor of the Butite organ the *Briton*, was similarly upbeat about the Celtic periphery in his novel *The Expedition of Humphrey Clinker*. The lead tourist Matthew Bramble, was happiest in his homelands in the Welsh borders near Abergavenny and in Scotland's Trossachs. The only cities from which he gained any enjoyment – he hated Bath and London – were the economically dynamic Glasgow and Edinburgh.[18] The Welsh Thomas Pennant returned the favour in 1771 with a Scottish tour deliberately designed 'to conciliate the affections of the two nations, so wickedly and studiously set at variance by evil designing people.'[19] Pennant was critical of the violence meted out by the Duke of Cumberland's soldiers after Culloden, though he thought that the pacification had brought benefits, and welcomed the disintegration of the clan system.[20] Even so, it is difficult to imagine a similarly generous assessment coming from an Irish patriot during this period. From Swift's *Story of the Injured Lady* onwards, the Irish looked jealously at the commercial gains that Scotland had made through the Union of 1707.[21] Irish requests for a Union in the same decade had been rebuffed, and the rebellions of 1715 and 1745 only served to rub salt into the wound. When an Anglo–Irish Union was discussed at the highest levels in 1779 the Scots were again the target of Irish resentment.[22] The same themes emerged during the Union debates of 1799–1800. William Ogilvie's plan for a federal Union, originally drawn up in 1782, was raised as a precedent, and the patriot Henry Grattan and his friends did little to hide their contempt for this Scotsman, second husband of the Duchess of Leinster.[23]

The Scots' determination to reposition themselves, and in the process make them guilt-free members of the Union, led to a number of attacks on the Irish. David Hume was critical of both the native Irish and Scottish highlanders. He claimed that the Irish, 'from the beginning of time, had been buried in most profound barbarism and ignorance'.[24] From a different angle James Macpherson sought to rehabilitate the Scottish highlanders by making them the original Britons, and this required downgrading any Irish claim to the title. The nature of his Ossianic ballads threatened to undermine Irish cultural prowess, and it provoked replies from both Catholics and Protestants, some of whom had already been exercised by Hume's comments.[25] There was no pan-Celticism here. As Dafydd Moore notes: 'For Scottish historians of Macpherson's ilk, Ireland bashing seems to have been the preferred option, and the possibility of making common cause against the acquisitive ambitions, cultural or otherwise, of the English does not seem to have been entertained.'[26] The Irish Protestant writer Thomas Campbell thus directed one of his works against the Scottish historian John Dalrymple, who had also slighted the Irish national character.[27] Macpherson may have been accused of forgery, and had certainly got the dander of the Irish up by juxtaposing barbarous Irish against civilised Celt, but the tone of articles in the *Hibernian Journal* suggests that his Scottishness – and the Scottishness of his patron Lord Bute – was as much of a problem as his myth-making and his approach to source material.[28] There was also a wider imperial dimension. A series of anti-Macpherson pieces appeared in the *Hibernian Journal* in 1776, the year of the Dublin edition of his *The Rights of Great Britain Asserted against the Claims of America.*

These cultural tensions were replicated – at least in some quarters – when it came to Irish commercial development, and any assessment of commercial interaction between the Celts should not underestimate petty jealousy. Glasgow merchants campaigned vigorously in the British Parliament for trade restrictions on Ireland to be retained, preventing it from accessing imperial markets. As a result, the Irish free trade crisis of 1779 saw as much ire poured upon the Scots as upon the English. When this issue returned in 1784 the *Volunteers Journal* reported meetings of foreign riders and importers desperate to outfox Irish tar and feather bands, and they apparently met at the Welsh ale house in White's Lane.[29] Though such tittle-tattle often lacked veracity, it is worth noting that there was a public house called the Old Established Welsh Ale House on Dublin's George's Quay.[30] Commercial and economic rivalry was clearly very potent. Irish and Welsh commentators spent a good deal of time railing against the other's addiction to smuggling. The *Volunteers Journal*, when listing the sins of the viceroy, Lord Northington, included the fact that he had supported 'a grant for accommodating our Welsh neighbours with a bridge'.[31] The *Limerick Chronicle* could not, it seems, recognise that the evils of absenteeism worked both ways when it praised the

Tipperary baronet Sir Cornwallis Maude for spending the income from his Welsh estate in Ireland.[32] In more general terms there was perhaps an awareness of Wales's backwardness in politeness and print. The Irish-born Master of Ceremonies for Bath, Samuel Derrick, found that the only means of provoking the Welsh to speak was 'to whip their horses hard'.[33] Elsewhere, the Irish *Volunteer Evening Post* had plenty of fun with a rather gauche and peculiarly lengthy advertisement placed by a hairdresser in a Welsh market town.[34]

All three Celtic nations underwent political transformations during the eighteenth century, in broadly similar ways. Each would see the retreat of Jacobitism and the firm embrace by political elites of a very Protestant variety of Whiggism, at least until the 1790s. Peter D. G. Thomas has discussed the survival of Jacobitism in eighteenth-century Wales, and Philip Jenkins goes further, seeing life in Jacobitism up until the 1770s, albeit in a new format: freemasonry.[35] Yet even in the early eighteenth century a commitment to Jacobitism, at least for the elite, seemed to mean nothing more proactive than the drinking of toasts. John Glynn was arrested after giving the Pretender's health on the bowling green at Hawarden in 1746. Private houses were thus a better bet, and the leading Cardiganshire squire Lewis Pryse and his friends 'drank to the Pretender's health and return upon their knees' at a house in Aberystwyth.[36] It is noteworthy that this so-called 'Jacobite firebrand' became a close friend of John Wilkes, as did another ex-Jacobite Robert Jones of Fonmon. Given Wilkes's violent anti-Scottishness the Jacobitism of these two Welshmen was either put aside, or else seen simply as a variant of High Toryism.[37]

More toasting was done in Welsh Jacobite clubs such as the Cycle of the White Rose club in North Wales, founded on White Rose Day, the birthday of 'James III'. There were two Jacobite clubs in Montgomeryshire and another in south-west Wales, the Society of Sea Serjeants. This latter club certainly had Jacobites within its leadership, and it acted against government in electoral contests. Whether it was genuinely seditious is another matter; although the members did drink a toast to 'the northern star' and his 'bonny highland lads'.[38] Jacobitism had also infected the lower orders. There was an attack on two Dissenter meeting-houses in Wrexham in 1715, and a Jacobite mob assaulted Lord Lisburne in Llanidloes in 1721.[39]

Wales's most famous Jacobite, Sir Watkin Williams Wynn, toasted the Pretender's health in public in Shewsbury, burned a picture of George II and plotted in the lead-up to the '45: however, he failed to show up for the rough stuff.[40] Prince Charles Edward Stuart seemed to sum up Welsh Jacobite commitment when he allegedly remarked: 'I will do as much for my Welsh friends as they have done for me;

I will drink their healths.'[41] By the mid-eighteenth century the only remnants of Jacobitism in Wales were dining clubs like the Sea Serjeants, the odd ill-considered toast, and some private memorabilia – the Viscounts Bulkeley had a bust of Charles Edward in their Baron Hill home, but even this had disappeared from public display by the 1760s. Peter Thomas's summation that 'Jacobitism in Wales was always a sentiment rather than a practical cause' seems apposite.[42]

The Irish political elite were much quicker to abandon Jacobitism, quite simply because the Protestant land grab depended upon the Williamite settlement. Eamonn Ó Ciardha and Vincent Morley play up the survival of Jacobitism in Gaelic culture, both domestically and in the Irish regiments active in France and Spain.[43] Morley argues that the lower orders did not follow the example of the Catholic elite and shy away from the Jacobite connection.[44] But David Hayton, Sean Connolly and James Kelly, among others, have their doubts about any real political significance.[45] The wearing of white cockades, the playing of Jacobite airs, toasts to the Old and Young Pretenders and the rage and anguish present in vernacular poetry are indicative of a sentimental attachment,[46] but played no part in the politicisation that took place from mid-century onwards. Whether or not one agrees with Louis Cullen's view that an aisling was 'a literary form; not a message for the people',[47] it is another leap to suggest that a poem may have caused a riot, as was certainly true of newspapers and hand-bills. Morley, for example, has little evidence to link popular protest in Dublin during the American War with aisling poetry. It can be argued that the tenor of Dublin protest in the 1770s and 1780s – with its focus upon parliamentary reform and the liberty of the press – had moved far beyond the Jacobite creed and into radical territory. Even where white cockades were still in evidence in the last quarter of the century it surely said more about disaffection with the political status quo than any real hankering for a Stuart restoration. Pro-American, even pro-revolutionary French, feeling was simply a continuation of sectarianism using whichever political language was current. The Protestant Ultra Patrick Duigenan felt that pro-Stuart feeling in Catholic Ireland had only ever been an attachment of convenience.[48] And if we come back to the theme of anti-Scottishnesss, then it is also clear that Gaelic poets had no great love of English-speaking lowland Scots, on a number of occasions seeing the American War of Independence as a civil war that would, happily, weaken both England and Scotland.[49] Similarly Catholic Defenders associated their Protestant enemies with the Scottish Covenanters who had given up Charles I.[50]

The Duke of Cumberland ensured that Scottish abandonment of Jacobitism would be quick, and long-lasting. The appointment of

Lord Bute, first as Secretary of State and then as Prime Minister, brought the Scots to the heart of the political system barely fifty years after union, but as Colley, John Brewer and, most recently, Adam Rounce have pointed out, this development was far from welcome, and the success of the Wilkites owed much to their anti-Scottish rhetoric.[51] Yet there has perhaps been a tendency to see the Wilkite phenomenon as peculiarly English – partly because it was so anti-Scots in nature. As yet no substantial studies have been done on support for Wilkes in Ireland and Wales, but there was, it seems, widespread backing, at least among Protestants, which complicates any attempt to see Wilkes's campaign as a resistance to Britishness.[52] Welsh Wilkites were not thin on the ground. Ten out of twenty-seven Welsh MPs voted against the decision to expel Wilkes from the Commons in 1769. Robert Morris was the first secretary of the Bill of Rights Society, formed to support Wilkes and help pay his debts. Addresses were drawn up by Cardigan, Carmarthen and Pembroke on the Wilkite issue of parliamentary reporting, though these probably owed as much to the lobbying of the local politician Watkin Lewes as to popular Wilkite feeling.[53] Similarly the illumination of the bridge of Llangollen to celebrate Wilkes's re-election as MP for Middlesex was encouraged by the MP Richard Myddleton.[54] The bridge was apparently lit with 136 lamps to celebrate the number of healths drank to key supporters of the Wilkite cause. In this case there did seem to be more widespread support in Denbighshire. Taking the lead from the lighting of a bonfire on Dinas Brân hill, a total of forty-five hills in the county were set alight in Wilkes's honour.[55] Such celebrations were widely reported – they made the Irish press – and secured a positive reputation for the Welsh.[56] One Wilkite journalist wrote that the Welsh and the Scots 'are very opposite in their principles. The former are hot, generous, and great lovers of liberty. The latter violent and tyrannical.'[57] There remains a pub in Llandysul, in West Wales, called the Wilkes Head.

Thanks to a flourishing newspaper industry, Wilkite opinion in Ireland is much easier to gauge, and though some parliamentary politicians had their doubts, popular political sentiment was firmly behind Wilkes. The nature of the Wilkites' Whiggism certainly suited. No doubt Irish Protestants would have approved of the choice of venue for a procession of Wilkite Middlesex voters in 1768: a tavern named after William of Orange.[58] Sniping by Wilkes's ally Charles Churchill at Macpherson would also have amused Irish readers.[59] The Wilkite agitations resulted in the formation of a number of clubs in Dublin sympathetic to John Wilkes, including the Liberty Tree Blues, the Old Nol Club and the 45 Club.[60] The Free Citizens of Dublin drank to

'John Wilkes' and included the anti-Butite 'may his Majesty confide in the old supporters of his Family, and no longer place a confidence in those who attempted to deprive his Grand-father of the Throne'.[61] To celebrate John Wilkes's restoration to liberty the *Freeman's Journal* published their top forty-five toasts.[62] There are plenty of other examples of Irish Wilkite coverage that was anti-Scottish in tone, including a report that Scots newspapers had refused to print advertisements placed by the Society of the Bill of Rights,[63] and a more casual remark that the arrest of the printer John Almon was a measure worthy of the Stuarts.[64]

Yet, though general warrants and the freedom of the press doubtless concerned leading Irish Whigs like Charles Lucas and Sir Edward Newenham, support for Wilkes in Ireland was also shaped by hostility towards a Scottish-driven imperial mission. With the support of the Chatham and North ministries Lord Townshend, as Irish viceroy, launched a largely successful attempt to reassert British control over the Irish political system. His personal connections with Lord Bute, and those of his chief secretary Sir George Macartney, Bute's son-in-law, meant that his venture was perceived as an attempt to export Butite, Scottish influence over Ireland.[65] Consequently during Townshend's Castle party-building and public relations exercises, the coaches of government peers were daubed with potato; Ireland's favourite tuber being used to write the number 45.[66] In Parliament there was a concerted attempt to stymie the award of a pension on the Irish establishment to Jeremiah Dyson, the procedural expert who had schemed against Wilkes.

Linda Colley correctly notes that this anti-Scots feeling survived into the American War of Independence. Indeed the inward gaze, the soul-searching, provoked by the war probably drew the Scots back into sight. Such was the strength of the notion of a double cabinet as delineated by Edmund Burke – with the likes of Bute and Mansfield as powers behind the throne – that the conflict would be referred to as a 'Scotch war'. There was perhaps a little truth in terms of sentiment. The Scots did send proportionally more addresses supporting armed coercion than England or Wales.[67] William Drennan was scornful of loyalist sentiment while a student in Edinburgh: 'Nothing is going on here at present but raising regiments, to be devoted to destruction in America.'[68] In contrast with Ireland, anti-war feeling was slow to get off the ground, and, when it did develop, metamorphosed into a very moderate campaign for parliamentary reform.[69] Earlier battles were clearly in the mind of John Witherspoon, a leading Scottish supporter of American independence, as he blamed Scotland's loyalty to the crown upon John Wilkes.[70]

Anti-Scots feeling in Ireland was, if anything, strengthened by the outbreak of hostility with the colonies. When threatened with invasion Cork gentlemen decided to call their armed society the Culloden Volunteers.[71] A writer in the *Dublin Evening Post*, with a jealous eye on the Americans, bemoaned the fact that 'since the accession of George III we are debilitated by luxury, and governed by Scotchmen'.[72] As for the Scots nation: 'it is too obvious', said the *Hibernian Journal*, 'that the Adulation of a B[ut]e and a M[ansfiel]d precedes the worship of their God'.[73] With this in mind the Free Citizens added 'A speedy downfall to the present Jacobite administration' to their litany of toasts.[74] Bute and the alleged double cabinet were simply the highest-profile examples of Scottish political corruption. Joseph Pollock, a leading Volunteer writer, commented upon the 'potent body of corruption' emanating from Scots MPs since the Union. And the like-minded Frederick Jebb agreed that 'the principles of these Scotchmen have contributed very much to the ruin of the Britsh empire'.[75]

Irish newspapers delighted in fashioning fictional stories to provoke their enemies, and the Scots were a favourite butt during the American war. It was alleged that 'some Scots lords have employed their interest to have the Names of sundry of his Majesty's Ships changed. The Culloden to the New-York; The Boyne to the White Plains; the Sterling Castle to the Hell-gates.'[76] Another vitriolic anti-Scottish letter in the *Hibernian Journal* suggested that the Caledonians 'seem to vie with each other in the cruel, ruinous, and destructive Business of fettering our fellow Subjects in America; of Subjugating a brave and loyal, and a free People to absolute Slavery and Bondage'. The enemy was dancing reels, 'their Daggers fresh reeking from the Sacrifice of Freedom'. And, in a final rather marvellous piece of hyperbole: 'The Groans of Liberty are sweeter and more melodious now to *Scotchmen*, than even the grunts of their favourite *Bagpipe*.' In contrast 'every Whig in England and Ireland' sympathised for 'the sufferings of the innocent, injured, insulted Sons of Liberty in America'. Common cause was effectively being made with Whigs throughout the empire: Americans, Englishmen and Irishmen were cut from the same political cloth.[77]

This letter may well have been taken from the English press, but plenty of other examples had a particularly Irish inflection. Disagreements over the American War in his local coffee-house with Scottish physicians led a Dublin barber to call, somewhat facetiously, for the medics to be forced to pay the anti-Catholic quarterage tax.[78] Indeed there were plenty of jibes directed at migrant Scots. The Volunteer writer Frederick Jebb inveighed against the vices that the Scots brought with them: '[r]eligious hypocrisy, servility of manners, and political depravity'.[79] A section of government supporters associated with Bute and the Duke of Bedford, whose supporters were regarded as pro-war, were actually termed 'the Scotch' and the patriotic *Hibernian Journal* expressed its delight at the fact that 'the Scotch are not in favour at the Castle – alas poor Sawney!'[80] When the Irish press launched an attack on the tourist Richard Twiss, for, among other slights, claiming that native Irish women had fat legs, and that the inhabitants of Connaught were savages, a method of tainting his character was to claim that his father was Scottish, 'Sawney Twiss'.[81] Although here it is worth re-emphasising that, in terms of Irish-Scottish relations, Ulster was always likely to be of a different view, and when similar pieces were published in the *Londonderry Journal* the word 'Sawney' was omitted.[82]

The survival of anti-Scottish feeling among the Irish Protestant political elite was in part a logical adjunct of the 'old' Whiggism that played such a key part in patriotic life. Many Irish MPs who were sympathetic to the American colonies were rabidly opposed to the Quebec Act allowing toleration for Canadian Catholics. The 1770s would see a dimming of anti-Catholic feeling, culminating in relief acts of 1778 and 1782, and this period allowed Irish reformers to point to their disciplined, liberal programme in contrast to the dominant popular movement emerging in Scotland. Referring to Lord George Gordon's Protestant Association a letter in the *Limerick Chronicle* noted that 'the Scotch are playing the enthusiastic pranks of John Knox's days'. In the riots 'neither eminence of station or dignity of character were regarded by people, armed with enthusiastic fury and religious madness'.[83] Another writer in the same newspaper boasted that, in relation to the Irish Catholic relief bill of 1778, 'most of the Protestants throughout the kingdom thought the relaxation of the popery laws a liberal, harmless, and expedient measure; and those who differed in opinion with them, though they strenuously opposed it, did it in a Christian, manly, and constitutional manner. How different is the conduct of the Scottish nation?' After noting that the inquisition was falling out of favour in Spain and Portugal, and that Malta allowed a Turkish mosque in its capital, the piece went on: 'Is it then in Scotland alone, among the most favoured subjects of an indulgent Monarch, that the bloody standard of persecution is unfurled; outrage, violence, fury, and all the horrid concomitants of religious fury let loose; houses rifled, temples for divine service raised, and libraries, with more than Saracenic rage destroyed?'[84] Long uncomfortable with the tag of being the most uncivilised of Celtic regions, Irish writers, with more than a degree of smugness, were casting Scotland as the savage 'other'.

It was not surprising, perhaps, that during the American War Ireland was developing the confidence to move towards a more independent status. Yet even the end of the war would not shake suspicion of the Scots. The *Volunteer Evening Post*, ultra-loyalist, and hostile to both Irish Catholics and Presbyterians, attacked the University of Edinburgh for opposing a prospective Irish college of medicine. The Scots intended to scupper the scheme by petitioning the spiritual members of the House of Lords. Apparently the Irish medical school would be open to Catholics, so the tack was to use the bishops' hatred of popery, which, so the Scottish minute went, 'we heartily applaud'. The Scottish medics lambasted the notion of 'permitting Roman Catholics, those pests of society, dupes of superstition, and enemies of all good government, to become Professors of Physic'. The letter ended with a reference to the violence sparked by Scotland's Protestant Association: 'We have lately in this country set a splendid example of our abhorrence of such abominations.'[85] Little wonder that in a later issue the same newspaper, at least partly motivated by its fear of Irish Dissenters, described Lord George Gordon as 'that bigoted lunatic'.[86] Patriotism in 1780s Ireland was a complicated credo with both sides – radical and loyalist – laying claim to the enlightened tag. Yet if we are searching for common threads then it is clear that neither side showed much love for the Scots. One of Burke's key charges against Warren Hastings during his impeachment in 1785 was the manner in which he distributed a fount of corruption to thirsty Scottish contractors and placemen. And he was of course allied with another Irishman, Richard Brinsley Sheridan.[87]

Welsh political development had much less of an impact in Ireland, though the progress of the Watkin Williams Wynn family – from Jacobites, to apathetic Foxites, before ending the century as supporters of religion and constitution – would doubtless have met with approval and recognition in many quarters. The one Welshman who was much admired achieved the feat through opposition to the American War. In March 1784 the *Dublin Evening Post* described Dr Richard Price as 'that revered and most respectable character', a man 'who so often has distinguished himself in asserting the rights of mankind, and maintaining the true dignity of civil liberty'.[88] In that year Price, along with other British radicals, had entered into correspondence with Volunteers in the vanguard of the Irish parliamentary reform movement.[89] John Jebb, educated at Trinity College Dublin and in contact with the Irish reformers, was also feted in the radical pockets of Wales and elected as a member of the Association Committee for Caernarvon.[90]

There was a Welsh contribution to the Dublin paper war of the late 1780s, sparked by a pamphlet by the Bishop of Cloyne, Richard Woodward, *Present State of the Church of Ireland* that propounded the need to secure the status of the Protestant Ascendancy. Daniel Thomas, resident in Ireland, but with experience in America, focused on Woodward's scornful treatment of the Gaelic language: he had urged government 'to take measures to bring it into entire disuse'. Thomas responded: 'What! Should a language confessedly derived from one of the first tongues which subsisted amongst polished nations, be abolished, merely to make room for another compounded of all the barbarous dialects which imperfectly communicated the thoughts of savages to each other?' He continued: 'the natives of Ireland must ever be instructed in their vernacular tongue, were it only to prevent the country from being overflowed by an inundation of foreigners, equally ignorant of their language, and estranged from their manners'.[91] He concluded that any design 'to destroy the vernacular tongue, is an attempt to annihilate the nation'. In his support he cited the survival of the Irish language among northern Presbyterians into the early eighteenth century, and the efforts of antiquarians, including Colonel Vallancy and Sylvester O'Halloran.[92] The latter had crossed swords with Macpherson over his uncomplimentary remarks about Irish Gaelic.[93]

Thomas's Welsh background clearly influenced the linguistic thrust of his piece. He urged the Irish to look to the example of 'the Welsh parsons, who instruct their flocks in their primitive language'. In another passage he suggested that the bishop of Cloyne 'cannot be surprised that a person of Welsh origin, should glow with the sympathetick fire of insulted Aborigines; for as we are doomed to poverty, we should be left (at least) the support of our pride'.[94] By finding linguistic common cause with the native Irish – in an explicitly anti-English tone – this pamphlet was unusual, although it should be noted that elements within the Volunteer movement from 1784 onwards had begun to display proto-nationalistic sentiments.[95] In any case there were other elements in Thomas's Hiberno-Cymric political credo that allowed him to ally comfortably with political radicalism. He vehemently defended the admission of Catholics into Volunteer regiments, rubbishing any suggestion that this may have been a contributory factor in the spread of Rightboyism. This seemed to rise from his sympathy towards Dissent: Thomas wrote positively on Presbyterianism and Methodism and was particularly enamoured with life in Philadelphia, 'where there are at least sixty different sects'. To Thomas any diminution of Presbyterianism was destructive to democracy in Ireland and would allow the aristocracy – 'this many-headed tyrant' – to increase its influence. As might be expected he was also an opponent of the tithe system. But much of his language on this issue was couched in terms of improvement; an issue much beloved of Irish patriots. So we also find an attack on the Irish grazier, a keeper of racehorses and cocks, whose house 'is generally crouded with bucks, players, pimps, and buffoons'. In the same pamphlet Thomas pre-empted the Edgeworths by defending the Irish against the charge that they frequently committed the linguistic errors commonly termed bulls.[96]

In *Britons* Linda Colley refers to the importance of participation in imperial military ventures in the forging of Britishness.[97] The Scots were ubiquitous in the British army, and Thomas Bartlett has noted the increasing significance of Irish troops – no longer wild geese – by the end of the century; Wellington, of course, was Irish.[98] Less has been said of the Welsh, though Colley does include some valuable information on Welsh recruitment during the American and French Revolutionary Wars.[99] Such information can tell us a little about the relative enthusiasm for army life, even for the imperial cause, with the Irish and Scots trouncing the Welsh, but a more interesting example, if we are looking for evidence of inter-Celtic relations would be to look at an imperial conflict much closer to home: the rebellion that engulfed Ireland in 1798. Marianne Elliott, Kevin Whelan and others have convincingly argued that this was a rebellion with an international dimension. Even Wexford has been Frenchified – no longer the peasant jacquerie depicted by Thomas Pakenham and R. B. McDowell, according to Whelan's research.[100]

Work on Irish–Scottish relations in the context of the 1790s has tended to focus upon radicalism – the missionary work done by the United Irishmen in Scotland, and the attempts to succour United Scotsmen and United Britons. Drennan, Archibald Hamilton Rowan and Simon Butler were all involved in forging contacts with Scottish reformers, and the oaths, resolutions and Masonic links used by the United Scotsmen were frequently Irish imports; as indeed were some of the migrant members.[101] Yet Irish migrants were not universally welcomed, and were greeted on the government side with a suspicion that bordered upon hysteria. Even among radicals it is doubtful whether a sense of common identity or political community was particularly strong; Scottish reformers did not warm to the language of nationalism and republicanism in Drennan's 'Address to the Scottish Radicals'.[102] Far more attractive to some were the English Society for Constitutional Information and London Corresponding Society.[103]

In a recent work on Scotland and the 1798 rebellion Emma Macleod notes that 'Scottish responses – whether supportive or hostile – were in general lukewarm'. Bob Harris suggests that the brutal measures adopted by Irish government forces were seen by many Scots as justified in the circumstances.[104] But if we are looking at Scotland's position in the British Isles in an imperial context, then the one dimension that pushes Scottish involvement beyond the pockets of interest in radicalism and predictable loyalist proclamations is the commitment to military service – and more particularly willingness to serve in Ireland. The same can be said for the Welsh in the form of the Ancient Britons fencible cavalry regiment.

Both Scottish and Welsh troops played a major role in putting down the 1798 rebellion, and the fact that they have become caught up in the mythology of 1798 is as interesting as the fact that many fought in volunteer-type regiments. When the rebellion erupted thirteen out of the twenty regiments in Ireland were Scottish, and during its course reserve regiments were also sent from Scotland. When the Royal Scots and the Sutherland fencibles left they did so with no little enthusiasm: the widespread violence provoked by the Scottish Militia Act occurred after many soldiers had already left for Ireland. However in some regiments a willingness to serve was artfully contrived – convivial dinners helped.[105] When in Ireland there was an appetite for action against the rebels. Along with the Ancient Britons, Scottish troops were active in disarming Ulster in 1796–97; one Belfast United Irishman claimed that the three things his men feared most were 'a bad harvest, the exportation of victuals, and the importation of Scotch soldiers'.[106]

The United Irishmen had another reason to be disappointed at such a high level of Scottish involvement. Scots soldiers proved to be remarkably immune to the United Irish message, and very few took their oath. One exception may have been the Breadalbane fencibles – a regiment that had initially refused to go to Ireland – who were accused of giving the United Irishmen at Ballynahinch firearms training.[107] As for their conduct, they were disciplined when under good leadership, but, as McFarland points out, 'where this was less certain, the Scotch could rival the Ancient Britons and the Hessians in their undisciplined conduct'.[108] According to Luke Cullen at Knightstown an honourable surrender was not an option when faced with the Scottish dragoon regiment: 'there was no mercy for us because we were Irishmen and Catholics'.[109] Elsewhere the Dunbartonshire regiment were involved in the raping of camp followers after Vinegar Hill and the Fraser fencibles went on the rampage after the defeat of government forces at Castlebar.[110] If we are looking at the formation of new types of British identity, it is noteworthy that an Irish–Scots radical alliance failed to materialise in 1798 – though Irish migrants would add something of a spur to the United Scotsmen – and that it was soldiers returning from Irish service in 1799 who brought the Orange Order to Scotland.[111]

In 1811 Irish soldiers stationed in Scotland to counteract a potential anti-eviction uprising relished the prospect of revenging themselves upon the Sutherlanders for their brutality at Ballinamuck.[112]

When referring to 'free quarters and pillage', Lord Cloncurry mentioned the Ancient Britons and the Fraser fencibles in the same breath.[113] The Ancient Britons were raised in 1794 by Sir Watkin Williams Wynn, and contained men from Chester along with a sizeable Welsh contingent. On this occasion it seems that the Welsh were eager to be imperial enforcers. Charles Williams Wynn took on Richard Brinsley Sheridan in the Commons over the need to send the militia to Ireland, and served alongside his brother in the Ancient Britons. The Ancient Britons were active in Ulster in 1797 searching for weapons, and this phase, broadly known as Lake's dragooning of Ulster, has become notorious. From May 1797 Lake had ordered his generals to 'make war upon property until the surrender can be made'.[114] The Welsh regiment, along with the local yeomanry, who were eager to settle local scores, were thus partly an instrument of policy. This was not only about discovering United Irish weapons, but about strengthening loyalism. Nevertheless, the Ancient Britons' charge list was lengthy and, out of many regiments involved in the counter-terror, the Ancient Britons were marked out for particular mention. Indeed A. T. Q. Stewart notes that the Ancient Britons' actions around Newry 'were not characteristic of the disarming of Ulster as a whole'.[115] Seemingly motivated by a British patriotic zeal, Major Gwilliam Wardle and Captain John Burganey destroyed a number of houses in Newry that had failed to illuminate their windows in celebration of Duncan's victory at the battle of Camperdown; an incident reported by the *Press*, a United Irish newspaper.[116] They were also involved in indiscrimate action on Lord Charlemont's estate in Co. Armagh, wrecking, beating, and seizing all arms, even those registered by Protestants.[117] In the House of Commons Lord Moira recounted ninety-one householders evicted from his estate in Co. Down, many wounded, their houses plundered.[118] He described men being picketed and half-hanged by 'troops that have been sent full of prejudice'.[119] Even a staunch Orangeman like John Giffard was shocked, and described the Britons firing at random, killing between ten and twenty, burning houses and taking prisoners who were eventually all found to be innocent. He said that the Ancient Britons' route could be traced by 'the smoke and flames of burning houses, and by the dead bodies of boys and old men'.[120] Presumably these activities put some weapons out of use, but a further consequence was increased Catholic involvement in the areas where the Ancient Britions were active when the rebellion began.[121]

The reputation of the regiment did not improve during the course of the rebellion. Arms searches in and around Bray were conducted with characteristic ferocity.[122] However it was through their activity in and around Newtownmountkennedy in Co. Wicklow that they became most notorious. Floggings, half-hangings and picketing were regular occurrences, and one case of picketing – the suspension of an individual with foot impaled upon a wooden spike pointing upright from the floor – was detailed in *Saunder's News-Letter* and *Faulkner's Dublin Journal*. On other occasions they were accused of ignoring promises of immunity or protection, and setting fire to wounded rebels taking refuge in a thicket.[123] Thomas Parsons, a Protestant, informed his brother, the MP, Sir Lawrence, that the Welsh regiment when in Newtownmountkennedy had taken 'six of the inhabitants selected indifferently from those they met in the street and without any trial whatsoever or previous suspicion of guilt, hung them'. Others, he said, were half-strangled, beaten and wounded.[124] The Ancient Britons also took part in the execution of more than forty-three prisoners on the fair green at Dunlavin.[125]

Shortly afterwards the Ancient Britons came to grief at Ballyellis, in one of the most spectacular defeats for government forces of the war. Such was the notoriety of the regiment that the reversal was seen as a defeat for the Britons, although other corps had borne twenty-four out of the forty-nine casualties.[126] One account suggested that after Ballyellis it was difficult to persuade the rebels to move on to the next engagement: 'the men felt such a satisfaction in the overthrow of the Ancient Britons, to whom they had an insuperable hatred for their inhuman conduct'.[127] No quarter was given by the rebels – the Britons's black trumpeter was tortured and his ears cut off before he died, his body being left to rot in a hedgerow.[128] Ruán O'Donnell notes that the 'conduct of the Britons in Wicklow before the Rebellion and during its early weeks was deemed to be the principal reason for the slaughter of virtually every member who fell into the hands of the rebels'.[129] Charles Apperley, later famous as a writer on British sporting pursuits under the pseudonym 'Nimrod', held the rank of cornet, and recounted that 73 out of 264 men were killed during the campaign. The *Times* claimed that the numbers in the regiment had been reduced to forty due to its high casualty rate.[130]

The unsavoury reputation of the Ancient Britons built steadily following the rebellion, as memoirs were published. The United Irishman Miles Byrne in Spain in 1812 claimed not to be stunned by the English sack of Badajoz 'from the knowledge I have had of the cruelties committed by the regiment of Ancient Britons in my own unfortunate country, Ireland, in 1798'.[131] In Australia the United Irish general Joseph Holt could only compare the inter-tribal warfare that he saw near Sydney to 'the Ancient Britons cutting the haunches and eyes off of the young women in the fair of Newtownmountkennedy in the year of ninety eight'; and there were, it seems, attacks on women in this Irish village who had dared to sport dresses made with green cloth.[132] At Arklow the Britons were said to have seized the burned body of the rebel Father Michael Murphy, after which they helped themselves to some of the fat that had leaked out, and then used it to polish their boots;[133] an accusation described by Wynn as 'a gross calumny, totally destitute of any foundation'.[134] Henry Grattan's son called them 'a savage and a sanguinary crew', noting that they actually sawed a man's head off.[135] This may perhaps relate to Captain John Deakin of Gelly, who has a monument in his honour in Llansanffraid. Seeing an Irish rebel aim to take Watkin Wynn's head off during a skirmish, Deakin apparently responded and cut the head off the Irishman.[136] There is another memorial in the form of an ornamental building in the park at Wynnstay, built by Wynn in memory of those members of his fencible regiment who fell in Ireland.[137] In this light it is perhaps worth noting that Wynn's character sits uneasily with the reputation of his regiment. He was a patron of the arts and in politics a Grenvillite Whig well-versed in Ireland's political troubles. Indeed in 1783 he produced a hand-written newspaper, 'The Breakfast Courant: Or, Bread and Butter Chronicle', in part for his friend William Wyndham Grenville who was the Irish chief secretary. This satirical journal was replete with Irish political gossip.[138]

As Colley has pointed out, the 1790s did much to unite the country around the person of George III against the French revolutionary threat.[139] Welsh and Scottish soldiers travelling to Ireland were clearly not disinclined towards fighting, and doubtless those with a more radical bent had their minds concentrated by talk of sectarian atrocities. One Welsh soldier quickly adapted to calling the Catholic rebels 'croppies'.[140] Broader Welsh sentiment on 1798 is not easily found, but most commentators seemed to call for strong measures. Others expressed concern over the Irish settling in Wales, fearing that they might be United Irishmen.[141] Paul O'Leary calculates that as many as 2,000 people may have fled to Pembrokeshire, and for these, and those landing in the north, there was only suspicion and hostility from the native inhabitants.[142] The earliest issues of the *Cambrian* newspaper, printed in Swansea, offered clear support for firm measures against Robert Emmett's rebellion, including the suspension of habeas corpus, and an increase in the size of the army reserve.[143]

The same of course could be said for Ireland's loyalist newspapers. The Irish press – including some broadly patriotic newspapers – did not vilify the Britons, even when reporting their most notorious episodes. *Saunders' News-Letter* described the picketing of a member of the Long family as a 'slight punishment'.[144] The *Freeman's Journal* reported that forty rebels were killed by the Britons in an episode in Wicklow, and 'like treacherous, murdering assassins [they] fled before them'.[145] At Arklow Wynn and his regiment were said by the *Freeman's Journal* to have 'charged the rebels most gallantly'.[146] The *Limerick Chronicle* lamented the 'unfortunate affair at Ballyellis' and then enthusiastically reported the arrival of reinforcements: 'some very fine recruits from Wales, for the cavalry regiment of Ancient Britons'.[147] British accounts of their actions also failed to mention atrocities. A history of Chester referred to 'their gallant conduct'.[148] Askew Roberts in his 1885 book on Wynnstay seemed unfazed by their nickname 'The Bloody Britons' and happily recounted that for many years the sound of the Welsh air 'Sir Watkin's Delight' could infuriate Irishmen.[149]

In this sense, therefore, there is a broader significance behind the narrative of Scots and Welsh involvement in 1798. Just as England, Wales and Scotland were forging a new British identity, any hope that Ireland could be embraced within this was undermined, not only by rebellion and Union, but by the myths that would be built around them. The type of inclusiveness found by Jim Shanahan in his work on the depiction of the Welsh in Irish novels of the 1790s – particularly *The History of Ned Evans* (1796) – was largely wishful thinking on the part of conservatives and proto-Unionists. For these Irish writers Wales was useful 'as a place of refuge and succour and as a more benign and controllable version of Ireland'. The sober religiosity of Wales was frequently stressed, though always the sensible Anglican variant rather than anything enthusiastic or Nonconformist. None of these novels were particularly sympathetic towards radicalism and it is notable that the eponymous Welshman in *The Soldier of Pennaflor* (1810) was of the honourable (non-Ancient Briton) type.[150]

This brand of Welshman would have been unfamiliar to those reading early nationalist accounts of the rebellion. More recently in many of the bicentennial works, particularly those by post-revisionists like Kevin Whelan and Ruán O'Donnell, the Ancient Britons have improved upon their position as the leading bogeymen. Along with the North Cork militia not only were they the chief culprits of atrocities, but it has been shown that their behaviour paved the way for sectarianism to enter an arena that until that point, had been political, enlightened and revolutionary. Evidence of their enduring villainy was shown in a novel published in 2006, *The Devil's Anvil* by Christopher Kavanagh, in which Patrick Kelly, son of a blacksmith, sought revenge after his father and brother were tortured and killed by Cornet Billy Evans of the Ancient Britons. Another modern reference can be found in the oral testimony of a Carnew schoolmaster. It seems that Carnew Protestants in the years after the battle of Ballyellis would leave flowers on the graves of the Ancient Britons. In turn their Catholic neighbours would retaliate by letting their cattle into the field to chew them up.[151]

There is no doubt that the second half of the eighteenth century witnessed the development of a phenomenon that might be described as Celtic one-upmanship, as each region or nation sought to demonstrate its loyalty – and by extension its Whiggery – to the crown. This desire to move from periphery to centre, shaking off rebellious, Jacobite and Catholic baggage was thus a road travelled by all three Celtic regions. The '45 meant that the Scots had most to prove, and they did so a little too enthusiastically in 1780. Welsh religious revivalism meant that Wales soon became the most staunchly Protestant of the three, and after ignoring Lord George Gordon they petitioned against Catholic emancipation in 1829, partly because of Irish men and women in their midst. Ireland was fastest to first-base in the love affair with the Georgians, but it was monarchy rather than ministers that became the key attraction.

Having shaken off the rebellious tag, the Irish enjoyed taking the moral high ground. During the American War they saw their beloved Volunteers as a truly patriotic body of Whigs, unsullied by old English (and more to the point new Scottish) corruption. The American War was a crucial phase in this period of nascent nation-building, and one which, had Colley felt able to include Ireland, would have pulled her model apart, such was the strength of Irish parliamentary and popular patriotism. It was the French Revolution, however, that altered the trajectory of Ireland, making any notion of independence from Britain and its parliament a chimera. After 1789, and particularly 1798, the Irish Protestant elite had to catch up the Scots and Welsh, and competitive Whiggism was abandoned in favour of pan-loyalism. Yet the events of the late 1790s, and the mythology that grew around them would play a key role in ensuring that this was a hopeless quest.

Notes

1 Linda Colley, *Britons: Forging the Nation, 1707–1837* (New Haven and London, 1992).

2 Works addressing Ireland's absence include S. J. Connolly (ed.), *Kingdoms United?: Ireland and Great Britain from 1500 – Integration and Diversity* (Dublin, 1998); Jim Smyth, *The Making of the United Kingdom, 1660–1800* (London, 2001); and Tony Claydon and Ian McBride (eds), *Protestantism and National Identity: Britain and Ireland, c.1650–c.1850* (Cambridge, 1998).

3 Martyn J. Powell, *Britain and Ireland in the Eighteenth-Century Crisis of Empire* (Basingstoke, 2003). Also see Stephen Conway, *The British Isles and the American War of Independence* (Oxford, 2002); P. J. Marshall, *The Making and Unmaking of Empire: Britain, India and America c.1750–1783* (Oxford, 2005).

4 See especially the work of Louis Cullen: L. M. Cullen and T. C. Smout (eds), *Comparative Aspects of Scottish and Irish Economic and Social History, 1600–1900* (Edinburgh, 1978); L. M. Cullen, 'Incomes, social classes and economic growth in Ireland and Scotland, 1600–1900', in T. Devine and D. Dickson (eds), *Ireland and Scotland, 1600–1850: Parallels and Contrasts in Economic and Social Development* (Edinburgh, 1983), pp. 248–60; L. M. Cullen, 'Scotland and Ireland, 1600–1800: their role in the evolution of British society', in R. A. Houston and I. D. Whyte (eds), *Scottish Society, 1500–1800* (Cambridge, 1989), pp. 226–44.

5 Ian McBride, 'The school of virtue: Francis Hutcheson, Irish Presbyterians and the Scottish Enlightenment', in D. G. Boyce, R. Eccleshall and V. Geoghegan (eds), *Political Thought in Ireland* (London, 1993), p. 74.

6 Vincent Morley, *Irish Opinion and the American Revolution, 1760–1783* (Cambridge, 2002), p. 3.

7 Colley, *Britons*, p. 131.

8 P. D. G. Thomas, *British Politics and the Stamp Act Crisis. The First Phase of the American Revolution, 1763–1767* (Oxford, 1975), p. 34.

9 Powell, *Britain and Ireland*, pp. 223–4.

10 Roy Porter, *Enlightenment: Britain and the Creation of the Modern World* (London, 2000), pp. 242–57.

11 Powell, *Britain and Ireland*, pp. 177, 179.

12 John Campbell, *Candid and impartial considerations on the nature of the sugar trade* (London, 1763). See John Brewer, 'The misfortunes of Lord Bute: a case-study in eighteenth-century political argument and public opinion', *Historical Journal*, 16 (1973), 14.

13 For this phenomenon see Percy Adams, *Travellers and Travel Liars 1660–1800* (Berkeley, 1962).

14 BL, Bowood MS B46A, Shelburne's Irish travel journal, fol. 51, 6 Aug. 1775–26 Aug. 1775.

15 The significance of improvement in the Irish context is explored in Toby Barnard, *Improving Ireland?: Projectors, Prophets and Profiteers 1641–1786* (Dublin, 2008).

16 John Campbell, *A Political Survey of Britain* (London, 2 vols, 1774), vol. 1, pp. 86, 178, 412–3, 188–9.

17 *Ibid.*, vol. 1, pp. 22–4, 233, 237, 711, 721.

18 Tobias Smollett, *The Expedition of Humphrey Clinker*, ed. L. M. Knapp (Oxford, 1988).

19 Quoted in Colley, *Britons*, p. 116.

20 See Robert Clyde, *From Rebel to Hero: Image of the Highlander, 1745–1830* (Edinburgh, 1994), pp. 98–105.

21 Jonathan Swift, *The Story of the Injured Lady. Being a True Picture of Scotch Perfidy, Irish Poverty, and English Partiality* (London, 1746).

22 Joseph Pollock, *The Letters of Owen Roe O'Neill* (Dublin, 1779), p. 35.

23 Powell, *Britain and Ireland*, pp. 215–16.

24 Quoted in Clare O'Halloran, *Golden Ages and Barbarous Nations: Antiquarian Debate and Cultural Politics in Ireland, c.1750–1800* (Cork, 2004), p. 141.

25 O'Halloran, *Golden Ages*, pp. 28–39.

26 Dafydd Moore, 'James Macpherson and "Celtic Whiggism"', *Eighteenth-Century Life*, 30 (2005), 8.

27 O'Halloran, *Golden Ages*, p. 86.

28 *Hibernian Journal*, 16–18 October 1776.

29 *Volunteers Journal*, 23 August 1784.

30 *Dublin Evening Post*, 27 January 1784.

31 *Volunteers Journal*, 27 February 1784.

32 *Limerick Chronicle*, 6 August 1779.

33 Samuel Derrick, *Letters from Leverpoole, Chester, Corke . . . and Bath* (Dublin, 2 vols, 1767), vol. 1, p. 47.
34 *Volunteer Evening Post*, 22–7 March 1784.
35 P. D. G. Thomas, 'Jacobitism in Wales', *WHR*, 1 (1960), 279–300; Philip Jenkins, 'Jacobites and freemasons in eighteenth-century Wales', *ibid.*, 9 (1978–79), 391–406.
36 Thomas, 'Jacobitism in Wales', p. 298; P. D. G. Thomas, *Politics in Eighteenth-Century Wales* (Cardiff, 1998), p. 135.
37 Jenkins, 'Jacobites and freemasons', 399–400.
38 Thomas, 'Jacobitism in Wales', 287–92; Jenkins, 'Jacobites and freemasons', 393–5; Thomas, *Politics in Eighteenth-Century Wales*, p. 139.
39 Thomas, *Politics in Eighteenth-Century Wales*, pp. 136–7.
40 *Ibid.*, pp. 138–47.
41 Quoted in *ibid.*, p. 147.
42 *Ibid.*, p. 148.
43 Eamonn Ó Ciardha, *Ireland and the Jacobite Cause, 1685–1766: A Fatal Attachment* (Dublin, 2002); Morley, *Irish Opinion*, pp. 6, 46–7, 64–5, 110–13.
44 Morley, *Irish Opinion*, pp. 46–7.
45 Ó Ciardha, *Ireland and the Jacobite Cause*; Eamonn Ó Ciardha, 'The Stuarts and Deliverance in Irish and Scots-Gaelic Poetry, 1690–1760', in Connolly (ed.), *Kingdoms United?*, pp. 78–94; S. J. Connolly, 'Jacobites, Whiteboys, and Republicans: varieties of disaffection in eighteenth-century Ireland', *Eighteenth-Century Ireland*, 18 (2003), 63–79; David Hayton, review of Ó Ciardha, *Ireland and the Jacobite Cause*, in *Eighteenth-Century Ireland*, 18 (2003), 154–60; James Kelly, *The Liberty and Ormond Boys: Factional Riot in Eighteenth-Century Dublin* (Dublin, 2005), p. 48. For a response by Morley see 'The continuity of disaffection in eighteenth-century Ireland', *Eighteenth-Century Ireland*, 22 (2007), 189–205.
46 Morley, *Irish Opinion*, p. 11.
47 Morley, 'The continuity of disaffection', 189.
48 *Ibid.*, 203.
49 Morley, *Irish Opinion*, pp. 108–9.
50 Morley, 'The continuity of disaffection', 201.
51 Brewer, 'The misfortunes of Lord Bute', *passim*; Adam Rounce, '"Stuarts without End": Wilkes, Churchill, and anti-Scottishness', *Eighteenth-Century Life*, 29 (2005), 20–38.
52 Rounce, '"Stuarts without End"', 21, 27.
53 Thomas, *Politics in Eighteenth-Century Wales*, pp. 219–20.
54 *Ibid.*, pp. 237–8.
55 *Freeman's Journal*, 4 March 1769.
56 *Ibid.*
57 Quoted in Colley, *Britons*, p. 139; *Middlesex Journal*, 29 April 1769.
58 Colley, *Britons*, p. 111.
59 Rounce, '"Stuarts without End"', 29–30.
60 Peter Clark, *British Clubs and Societies 1580–1800* (Oxford, 2000), p. 99.
61 *Hibernian Journal*, 14–16 October 1776.
62 *Freeman's Journal*, 21 April 1770.
63 *Ibid.*, 13 June 1769.
64 *Ibid.*, 19 June 1770.
65 Powell, *Britain and Ireland*, ch. 4.
66 *Freeman's Journal*, 20 March 1770.
67 Colley, *Britons*, p. 140.
68 Drennan to McTier, 20 Jan. [1778], *The Drennan–McTier Letters, 1776–1793*, vol. 1, ed. J. Agnew (Dublin, 1998), p. 32.
69 Elaine W. McFarland, 'Scotland and the 1798 Rebellion: The limits of "common cause"', in Thomas Bartlett, David Dickson, Dáire Keogh and Kevin Whelan (eds), *1798: A Bicentenary Perspective* (Dublin, 2003), p. 566.

70 Morley, *Irish Opinion*, p. 32.
71 *Limerick Chronicle*, 22 March 1779.
72 *Dublin Evening Post*, 4 August 1778.
73 *Hibernian Journal*, 17–19 February 1777.
74 Quoted in Morley, *Irish Opinion*, p. 126; *Hibernian Journal*, 19 July 1775.
75 Pollock, *Roe O'Neill*, p. 35; [Frederick Jebb,] *The Letters of Guatimozin* (Dublin, 1779), p. 41. I am very grateful to Dr Michael Brown for these references.
76 *Hibernian Journal*, 10–12 March 1777.
77 *Ibid.*, 17–19 February 1777.
78 *Freeman's Journal*, 27–30 July 1776.
79 [Jebb,] *Letters of Guatimozin*, p. 41.
80 *Hibernian Journal*, 5–7 March 1777.
81 *Ibid.*, 28–30 August 1776.
82 *Londonderry Journal*, 20 September 1776.
83 *Limerick Chronicle*, 1 March 1779.
84 *Ibid.*, 25 February 1779.
85 *Volunteer Evening Post*, 22–24 April 1784.
86 *Ibid.*, 23–25 September 1785.
87 Colley, *Britons*, p. 130.
88 *Dublin Evening Post*, 11 March 1784.
89 R. B. McDowell, *Irish Public Opinion, 1750–1800* (London, 1944), p. 99.
90 Anthony Page, *John Jebb and the Enlightenment Origins of British Radicalism* (Westport, 2003), p. 260.
91 Daniel Thomas, *Observations on the Pamphlets Published by the Bishop of Cloyne, Mr Trant, and Theophilus, on One Side; And on Those by Mr O'Leary, Mr Barber, and Doctor Campbell, on the Other* (Dublin, 1787), p. 23.
92 Thomas, *Observations*, pp. 28, 31–3.
93 O'Halloran, *Golden Ages*, p. 112.
94 Thomas, *Observations*, pp. 35, 45.
95 Breandán MacSuibhne, 'Whiskey, potatoes and Paddies: volunteering and the construction of the Irish nation in Northwest Ulster, 1778–1782', in Peter Jupp and Eoin Magennis, *Crowds in Ireland, c.1720–1920* (Basingstoke, 2000), pp. 45–82.
96 Thomas, *Observations*, pp. 57, 69, 81, 70–2, 14.
97 Colley, *Britons*, pp. 126–32.
98 Thomas Bartlett, '"This famous island set in a Virginia sea": Ireland in the British Empire, 1690–1801', in P. J. Marshall (ed.), *The Oxford History of the British Empire*, vol. 2: *The Eighteenth Century* (Oxford, 1998), p. 273.
99 Colley, *Britons*, pp. 139, 293–300.
100 Thomas Pakenham, *The Year of Liberty: The Great Irish Rebellion of 1798* (London, 1968); R. B. McDowell, *Ireland in the Age of Imperialism and Revolution, 1760–1801* (Oxford, 1979); Marianne Elliott, *Partners in Revolution: United Irishmen and France* (New Haven, 1988); Kevin Whelan, *The Tree of Liberty: Radicalism, Catholicism and the Construction of Irish Identity 1760–1830* (Cork, 1996).
101 Emma Vincent Macleod, 'Scottish responses to the Irish Rebellion of 1798', in Terry Brotherstone, Anna Clark and Kevin Whelan (eds), *These Fissured Isles: Ireland, Scotland and British History, 1798–1848* (Edinburgh, 2005), p. 126.
102 *Ibid.*, p. 131.
103 *Ibid.*, p. 130.
104 *Ibid.*, pp. 124, 129; Bob Harris, *The Scottish People and the French Revolution* (London, 2008), p. 2. For more on radical connections between Ireland and Scotland see John Brims, 'Scottish radicalism and the United Irishmen', in David Dickson, Dáire Keogh and Kevin Whelan (eds), *The United Irishmen: Republicanism, Radicalism and Rebellion* (Dublin, 1993); Elaine W. McFarland, *Ireland and Scotland in the Age of Revolution: Planting the Green Bough* (Edinburgh, 1994), and 'Scottish radicalism in the later eighteenth century: "The

social thistle and shamrock"', in T. M. Devine and J. R. Young (eds), *Eighteenth-Century Scotland: New Perspectives* (East Linton, 1999).

105 McFarland, 'Scotland and the 1798 Rebellion', p. 568; Macleod, 'Scottish responses', p. 134.

106 Quoted in McFarland, 'Scotland and the 1798 Rebellion', p. 569.

107 *Ibid.*, p. 569; Ruán O'Donnell, *The Rebellion in Wicklow, 1798* (Dublin, 1998), p. 167; Macleod, 'Scottish responses', p. 134.

108 McFarland, 'Scotland and the 1798 Rebellion', p. 569.

109 Luke Cullen, *Personal Recollection of Wexford and Wicklow Insurgents of 1798* (Enniscorthy, 1959), p. 59.

110 Kevin Whelan, 'Reinterpreting the 1798 Rebellion in County Wexford', in Dáire Keogh and Nicholas Furlong (eds), *The Mighty Wave: Aspects of the 1798 Rebellion in Wexford* (Dublin, 1996), p. 28.

111 McFarland, 'Scotland and the 1798 Rebellion', p. 569.

112 Clyde, *From Rebel to Hero*, p. 172.

113 Valentine Cloncurry, *Personal Recollections of the Life and Times, With Extracts From the Correspondence of Valentine Lord Cloncurry* (Dublin, 1849).

114 Quoted in Allan Blackstock, *An Ascendancy Army: The Irish Yeomanry 1796–1834* (Dublin, 1998), pp. 240–1.

115 A. T. Q. Stewart, *The Summer Soldiers: The 1798 Rebellion in Antrim and Down* (Belfast, 1995), p. 37.

116 O'Donnell, *Rebellion in Wicklow*, p. 143.

117 Blackstock, *An Ascendancy Army*, p. 241.

118 William Cobbett, *Parliamentary History of England from 1066 . . . to . . . 1803* (London, 36 vols, 1806–20), vol. 33, p. 134, 21 March 1797.

119 *Ibid.*, vol. 33, pp. 1059, 1061.

120 Quoted in Marianne Elliott, 'Religious polarization and sectarianism in the Ulster rebellion', in Bartlett *et al.* (eds), *1798: A Bicentenary Perspective*, p. 283.

121 *Ibid.*, p. 284.

122 O'Donnell, *Rebellion in Wicklow*, pp. 137–43.

123 *Ibid.*, pp. 147, 165, 188.

124 *General Joseph Holt's Personal Account of 1798*, ed. Peter O'Shaughnessy (Dublin, 1998), p. 44 n.

125 O'Donnell, *Rebellion in Wicklow*, p. 176.

126 *Ibid.*, p. 259.

127 Cullen, *Personal Recollection*, p. 46.

128 This episode reveals the flexibility of popular memory, in that there are competing tales involving the most notorious of the government's regiments. O'Donnell has the hedgerow named Drummer's Corner after the black soldier, while Pádraig Ó Tuathail's account contends that Drummer's Corner was named after a sergeant in the North Cork militia known as 'Tom the Devil', who was killed after the Battle of Rednagh Bridge. See *Holt's Personal Account*, pp. 44 and n.; O'Donnell, *Rebellion in Wicklow*, p. 259; Ó Tuathail, 'Wicklow traditions of 1798', in *Béaloideas*, 5:2 (1935), 161–3.

129 *Ibid.*, p. 259.

130 *The Times*, 29 August 1799.

131 Thomas Bartlett, 'Miles Byrne, United Irishman, Irish Exile, Beau Sabreur', in Keogh and Furlong (eds), *The Mighty Wave*, p. 124.

132 *Holt's Personal Account*, p. 44n; O'Donnell, *Rebellion in Wicklow*, p. 144.

133 Daniel Gahan, *The People's Rising: Wexford, 1798* (Dublin, 1995), p. 162.

134 Quoted in O'Donnell, *Rebellion in Wicklow*, p. 222.

135 *Memoirs of the Life and Times of the Rt Hon Henry Grattan by his son Henry Grattan Esq. MP* (4 vols, London, 1839–46), vol. 4, p. 378n.

136 Askew Roberts, *Wynnstay and the Wynns: A Volume of Varieties* (Oswestry, 1885), p. 101.

137 *Gentleman's Magazine*, April 1840.

138 NLW, Wynnstay MS 115, 'The Breakfast Courant: Or, Bread & Butter Chronicle'.
139 Colley, *Britons*, pp. 204–36.
140 NLW, Glansevern MS 3897, [?] to Dr Jones, 8 August 1799.
141 NLW, D. T. M. Jones MS 9644, J. Williams to Edward Jones, 23 March 1799.
142 Paul O'Leary, *Immigration and Integration: The Irish in Wales – 1798–1922* (Cardiff, 2000), p. 16.
143 *Cambrian*, 28 January 1804.
144 O'Donnell, *Rebellion in Wicklow*, p. 147.
145 *Freeman's Journal*, 31 May 1798.
146 *Ibid.*, 19 June 1798.
147 *Limerick Chronicle*, 14 July 1798, 6 February 1799.
148 Joseph Hemingway, *History of the City of Chester, from its Foundation to the Present Time* (2 vols, Chester, 1831), vol. 2, p. 255.
149 Roberts, *Wynnstay and the Wynns*, p. 20.
150 Jim Shanahan, '"The fostering aid of a sister country: Wales in Irish novels, 1796–1810', in Damien Walford-Davies and Lynda Pratt, *Wales and the Romantic Imagination* (Cardiff, 2007), pp. 127–9, 131.
151 *Holt's Personal Account*, pp. 44n–45n.

CHAPTER 4

Welsh evangelicals, the eighteenth-century British Atlantic world and the creation of a 'Christian Republick'

David Ceri Jones

In an anonymous letter published in the evangelical magazine *The Weekly History* during the summer of 1741, Howel Harris, one of the pioneers of the Welsh Methodist movement, wrote: 'I would advise every one of them [the members of the Methodist movement] for the general good of the Christian Republick, to send you an account of what they have experienced of the work of God upon their souls, which you may insert in your weekly paper.'[1] The 'Christian Republick' of which Harris spoke was an international community that had grown up in the wake of the dramatic religious revivals that had occurred in parts of Germany, Switzerland, Austria, France, England, Wales, Scotland and the American colonies spanning a twenty-year period from the later 1720s to the closing years of the 1740s.[2] Benefiting from population increases and enhanced demographic mobility, the opening up of new trade routes and markets, the growth of consumer demand and the extension of the reach of the tentacles of empire, these religious awakenings brought like-minded evangelicals into contact and interaction with one another in ways that would simply not have been possible fifty years earlier.[3] Revivalists like George Whitefield, John Wesley, Count Zinzendorf, Jonathan Edwards and Howel Harris travelled, preached, established networks of religious societies, wrote letters and published books creating and sustaining a trans-national and trans-Atlantic evangelical movement.

The Welsh Methodist Revival, which had its origins in the separate, but simultaneous, religious awakenings begun by Daniel Rowland and Howel Harris in 1735,[4] was a fully signed-up member of this 'transatlantic community of saints'.[5] In an earlier study I attempted to establish the case for an internationalist perspective on early Welsh Methodism, writing the Welsh perspective and contribution into the story of the early phase of evangelicalism's international expansion.[6]

But that work did not develop the concept of internationalism beyond establishing that an international dimension existed, and that it was something which the Methodists exploited for their own benefit. The Welsh Methodists' involvement in what David Hempton has recently called an 'empire of the spirit'[7] meant that they did not just benefit from British imperial expansion almost by default but became, as much as any merchant, naval officer, slave-trader or traditional cross-cultural missionary, some of its most active agents. This essay, therefore, attempts to explore two closely related questions: it examines how some eighteenth-century Welsh evangelicals took advantage of their involvement in the imperial project, and reflects on the role which that participation played in the expansion of evangelicalism in Wales itself.

Historical writing on Wales and empire has been both thematically and chronologically restricted; where there has been extended study it has tended to focus on the nineteenth and early twentieth centuries, on the second British empire in other words, and, with some notable recent exceptions,[8] it has been largely preoccupied with the movement and settlement of Welsh people overseas. The further back chronologically one goes the more circumscribed the historiography of Wales and the wider world becomes. Part of the reason for this is undoubtedly the dark shadow cast by the presence of a large imperially minded neighbour next door, with the consequence that much of the historical writing dealing with Wales in the centuries following the passing of the Acts of Union (1536 and 1543) has been understandably preoccupied with Welsh relations with England and the English in all their multilayered complexity.[9] Where there has been an attempt to place Wales in a wider context the focus has tended to be upon those marginal religious groups like the South Wales Baptists or Merionethshire Quakers who migrated to the American colonies in the aftermath of the English Civil War and the Restoration of the Monarchy in 1660.[10] In many respects this limited approach is indicative of a way of doing imperial and colonial history that equates the involvement of the constituent nations of the British archipelago in the imperial programme with the activities of ambitious and speculative individuals who carved out a new life or career for themselves in the colonies.

The relatively recent innovation that is Atlantic history, or the history of the Atlantic world, presents the historian with an alternative way of configuring the history of Britain's overseas empire.[11] Peter Marshall's observation that the early eighteenth-century empire could mean just as easily 'power or dominant interests outside Britain' as control over territory, hints at the need of a historiographical paradigm more all-encompassing than those provided by either imperial or colonial approaches.[12] Atlantic history takes the physicality of the Atlantic Ocean seriously, positing that it was a body of water which brought four continents, Europe, North America, South America and Africa, and three races, Europeans, Americans and Africans, into creative engagement with one another.[13] As first the Spanish and Portuguese, but then the British, the French and the Dutch, tried to establish interests in the New World, they were brought into creative tension with one another, with the indigenous peoples of the New World, and with those who were transplanted there against their wills.

Initially inspired by the study of the Atlantic slave-trade, Atlantic history, in the words of J. H. Elliot, is the study of the 'creation, destruction and recreation of communities as a result of the movement, across and around the Atlantic basin, of people, commodities, cultural practices and ideas'.[14] While not uninterested in war and the acquisition and defence of territory, the traditional preoccupations of imperial and colonial historians, Atlantic historians tend to be more concerned with the movement of people groups and commodities, the interaction of peoples and the transference of cultures and ideas around the Atlantic basin.[15] Religious belief was just one of the cultural expressions that fostered bonds of association throughout the British Atlantic world. Treating the Atlantic Ocean, in David Armitage's words, as a 'zone of exchange and interchange, circulation and transmission',[16] has the effect of encouraging historians to write much more finely textured accounts of the engagement of different nations, people groups and socio-cultural communities with the world beyond their immediate shores.

When Gwyn Alf Williams tantalisingly talked about Great Britain and its Atlantic province in *When was Wales?*,[17] he limited his discussion of Welsh engagement with the Atlantic world to the period following Britain's loss of the American colonies after 1776 when, inspired by the revolutionary ideas of the Americans, political radicals in Wales began to espouse 'democratic' ideas themselves.[18] This essay attempts to bring an Atlantic perspective to the study of early and mid-eighteenth-century Welsh evangelicalism; it is, in essence, a study of cultural transference.[19] It does so by looking at three layers of Welsh evangelical identity, all of which were informed by a strong Atlantic dimension. In this it uses Benedict Anderson's notion of imagined communities,[20] to argue that some early eighteenth-century Welsh evangelicals saw their primary identities not in solely national terms. It begins with the Welsh evangelicals' identification with the concept of the 'Protestant interest', before looking at the extent of the stake which many of them had in Britain's ever-expanding empire through their support and communication with missionaries who had left Wales to serve overseas. It then proceeds with a detailed examination of the Welsh Methodists' participation in the international evangelical community that grew from the evangelical revivals, and suggests that the development of evangelical Protestantism in Wales was informed by involvement in a spiritual empire that brought co-religionists from around the Atlantic basin into contact with and mutual dependence upon one another.[21]

The first and, therefore, foundational layer of Welsh religious identity was the worldwide Protestant enterprise. In the fifty years between the Glorious Revolution and the evangelical revival, Protestantism faced formidable challenges. The threatening spectre of a rejuvenated Roman Catholicism, and the determination of many European states to extirpate Protestant minorities within their borders in the search for confessional conformity following the Revocation of the Edict of Nantes in 1685,[22] forced Protestants to come together and at least attempt to present a united front.[23] Thomas Kidd has shown that what became known as the 'Protestant interest' was made possible by the rapid expansion of Britain's Atlantic possessions.[24] As the British Atlantic world was being revolutionised by a commercial and communications revolution, better postal services and the proliferation of cheap print,[25] Protestants were enabled to keep in touch with each other and therefore identify much more readily with one another. Once the full scale of the crisis facing international Protestantism began to become apparent in the final decades of the seventeenth century, residual antipathy to Britain was, according to Kidd, to some extent laid aside, particularly in New England, as Britain increasingly came to be looked upon as the bastion of Protestantism and the first line of defence against European Catholicism.[26]

The most readily observable way in which an awareness of the threats being faced by the Protestant enterprise can be traced is in the prevalence and virulence of anti-Catholicism in early eighteenth-century Britain.[27] In Wales the fear of Catholicism can be seen operating on two levels. Concerned over the perceived spiritual ignorance of the Welsh in the late seventeenth century, Anglican groups such as the Welsh Trust and the Society for Promoting Christian Knowledge (SPCK) attempted to raise the temperature of religious devotion in Wales through the provision of a system of elementary schools and the publication of large quantities of earnest devotional literature. The schools had a definite Anglicising agenda; they used the English language almost exclusively and so their impact was fairly limited,[28] but the SPCK's publication programme bore considerably more fruit. The number of books published in Welsh between 1660 and 1730 mushroomed,[29] the majority of them consisting of practical theology and down-to-earth devotional advice designed to stimulate piety in Wales. The popularity of this literature is indicative of the impact which Pietist ideas were having in Wales. Since its emergence in the 1670s, Pietism had stressed the centrality of heart religion that consisted of individual conversion and the meticulous cultivation of the inner spiritual life, both of which were worked out through a life of practical charity and good works.[30] While not solely a response to the threatening sight of a revitalised Catholicism, making religion an inward matter rather than one of external allegiance enabled many Pietists to operate in a more clandestine fashion, as they sought to endure persecution and arrest the declining fortunes and low morale of the Protestant enterprise.

However, the most popular works to be published in Wales during these years were not the devotional manuals or theological treatises, but the more than eighty almanacs produced by individuals such as Thomas Jones, John Jones and Sion Rhydderch.[31] In early eighteenth-century Wales, almanacs played an important role in educating readers in contemporary political and religious affairs and in helping them interpret events taking place on the world stage. Those produced annually between 1680 and 1713 by Thomas Jones, a Corwen-based printer, were by far the most politicised and virulently anti-Catholic of all of the Welsh almanacs. Jones's almanacs also had a journalistic edge, as he reported on the course of Britain's wars with Catholic France with a closeness resembling obsession. His reporting of the War of the League of the Augsburg (1688–97) and the War of the Spanish Succession (1702–13) was highly jingoistic as he characteristically bundled Catholicism, the French and despotism together as the chief enemies of the age.[32] His almanacs were packed full of accounts of the despicable deeds carried out under the umbrella of the Roman Catholic Church, and were counterpoised by stories of heroic English victories over the French and stories of Protestant resistance to Rome, whether during the reign of Mary I or the defeat of Guy Fawkes. These almanacs tapped into British neuroses about Roman Catholicism and arbitrary political power, at precisely the time when the threat from those powers, evinced in Britain by the persistence of the Jacobites, was most acute. Scaremongering of this sort had the desired effect of encouraging Welsh readers to take pride in the Protestant monarchy, the Church of England and the liberty that they had acquired.[33]

Secondly, for many the full implications of the threats being faced by international Protestantism were not brought home until they saw refuges from previously Protestant parts of Europe land on their doorsteps. French Huguenots had been forcibly ejected from France since the 1680s, and were a fairly common sight in some of the major cities of England by the early eighteenth century, but some also found their way to Wales. William III had established a fund to provide for their relief in 1685, and a number of prominent Welshmen served as its commissioners.[34] The fund was greatly expanded in 1718 to cope with the influx of refugees, and many in Wales applied for funds to offer practical assistance of various kinds. One of the first letters received by the fund emanated from a remote corner of Anglesey where a correspondent offered board and lodging to suitably needy candidates.[35] In South Wales one of the most generous individuals was the industrialist Sir Humphrey Mackworth of Neath. In 1720 he wrote: 'Poor Proselites may be boarded at Neath in Glamorganshire for half a crown a week, including fire and candle, if they'l be content with the Comon Roome.'[36]

But it was the expulsion of groups from provinces within the Holy Roman Empire in the early 1730s that caused greatest panic. Colin Haydon has pointed out that throughout the 1720s and 1730s the British press was full of lurid accounts of the persecution being experienced by European Protestants.[37] Their predicament was also championed by prominent and influential Dissenting evangelicals like Philip Doddridge who, as a result of his many continental contacts, became increasingly concerned at the suffering of his fellow Protestants.[38] However, nobody seemed prepared for the scale of the action taken against 25,000 Salzburg Protestants who were forcibly expelled from their city in 1731.[39] Many of these refugees headed initially for London, with hopes of eventually gaining passage to the American colonies. Awareness of this crisis reached Wales by means of circular letters sent through the correspondence networks of the SPCK; heavily influenced by Pietist ideals, many within the SPCK now saw it as their duty to come to the assistance and relief of their fellow Christians. Nobody was more committed to this activity than Sir John Phillipps of Picton Castle in Pembrokeshire. As a result of his correspondence and his circulation of accounts of the suffering being experienced by European Protestants, money began to pour in 'very fast' from SPCK subscribers in all parts of Wales.[40] At Oxford, Thomas Prado, the Kidwelly-born Principal of Jesus College, championed the cause of the Salzburgers in the university, once again through the circulation of accounts of their sufferings and the raising of substantial sums of money on their behalf.[41] But it was Phillipps's friendship with Griffith Jones that was to bear most fruit. In the course of 1732, Griffith Jones and his patron, Madam Bridget Bevan, collected over £120 from subscribers in Carmarthenshire and Pembrokeshire,[42] while at other times smaller, though far from inconsiderable sums, were collected by Jones from other supporters of his schools and even from some of the impoverished pupils themselves.[43]

Despite the rather precarious position of the Protestant enterprise, though, Protestants tended not to capitulate to fatalism. Rather, many within the international Protestant community harboured an optimistic view of the future. Taking a longer perspective, many Protestants bought into a post-millennial eschatology, which held that a worldwide revival would occur before the second coming of Christ in which the Protestant religion would spread to all corners of the globe.[44] In the immediate term, many Protestants expected God to intervene in a decisive way in order to turn around the present inauspicious circumstances. When news of religious revivals first at Herrnhut in 1727 and then at Northampton, Massachusetts, in 1735 began to circulate throughout the Protestant letter-writing networks, including the extensive networks of the SPCK and the SPG,[45] many felt that their deliverance was close at hand.[46]

These heightened expectations can also be detected in Wales. In the early 1730s, Griffith Jones had begun to establish a system of peripatetic schools, specially designed to teach people to read the Bible as quickly as possible. Established in communities all over Wales, they were looked upon by Jones as laying the foundation for the 'more glorious times than the present [that] are not very far off',[47] by which he clearly meant the more extensive spread of the gospel. In a letter published in *Welch Piety* in 1739 he gave even more clear expression to this expectation:

> As the gospel, in the beginning of it, was first preached to the poor, and from them went forth and spread over all the Earth, what if the Lord will think fit again to restore the gospel to its primitive force and lustre by the same method? Surely they must be happy and blessed men who assist in so glorious a work! . . . I would to God all good men did consider what is their interest to mind under fear of impending judgement, and the hope of future joy! If it should be but to prepare and preserve a seed and remnant to transmit the gospel light to a succeeding generation, it deserves to be esteemed a work worthy of the greatest zeal and expense to promote it in every place where God in his providence opens a way for it.[48]

By this stage there was also a network of evangelical ministers, Independents and Baptists mainly, but some Anglican clergy also who were hoping, even expectantly looking, for a religious awakening that would help reverse their declining fortunes.[49] Influenced by Phillip Doddridge and Isaac Watts, who were the authors of the foreword to the English edition of Jonathan Edwards's, *A Faithful Narrative of the Surprising Work of God . . . at Northampton* (1738),[50]

Dissenting ministers such as Edmund Jones at Pontypool and Phylip Pugh in Cardiganshire began preaching with a new urgency and taking a close interest in the activities of two individuals on their doorsteps, Howel Harris and Daniel Rowland, whose innovative evangelistic activities and lively preaching were beginning to stir up considerable interest in their local communities.

For others in Wales, identification with the international Protestant enterprise was still more tangible. Historians have until comparatively recently assumed that concerted missionary activity did not really begin until the later decades of the eighteenth century, a consequence of the confidence generated by the evangelical revival over the preceding fifty years.[51] There is now a greater appreciation of the missionary activities of groups like the Moravians, who were sending cross-cultural missionaries to Labrador, Greenland and the West Indies as early as the 1730s,[52] but the earliest co-ordinated missionary organisation was probably the Society for the Propagation of the Gospel in Foreign Parts (SPG). Established in 1701, originally to provide Anglican clergy for British subjects throughout the empire, the society also turned its attentions to pioneering missionary activity among previously unevangelised peoples.[53] In her study of the SPCK's activity in Wales, Mary Clement lists ninety-nine missionaries of Welsh origin who served overseas between 1675 and 1740, under the auspices initially of the Bishop of London, and then later of the SPG. The majority of these individuals served in New England and the plantations of Virginia and Pennsylvania, but representatives could also be found in the Caribbean, India, Syria and North Africa.[54] Some were genuine missionaries, working with previously unreached groups, but others, possibly the majority, served in a more conventional manner as parish priests or as schoolmasters. Very little detective work has been done to date to uncover the identity of many of these individuals, and how successful they were in their varied spheres of labour. However, the minutes and correspondence of the SPCK and the SPG show that there was considerable interest and support for their activities back home, giving some in Wales a tangible vested interest in the success and spread of the British Empire.

Supporters of the SPG in Wales tended to overlap very closely with those who had already been drawn into the ambit of the SPCK. Again no one was as keen as Sir John Philipps. A leading light within the SPG from the very beginning, Philipps was the most important link between the Society's London base and its Welsh supporters. He tirelessly publicised the activities of the SPG in Wales and by circulating letters and accounts of the missionary's activities he drummed up impressive levels of support. Initially, the easiest way for people in

Wales to express their commitment to the missionary task was by joining the SPG as a subscribing or corresponding member and sending in regular financial donations to its work. The £5 sent to the Society by a Mr Lewis of Margam in January 1706 was far from being untypical.[55]

At first, Welsh members of the SPG committee directed its resources to the support of Welsh religious communities in Pennsylvania. Between 1650 and 1700 somewhere in the region of 12,000 Welsh men, women and children had emigrated to the American colonies, most of whom had settled in Pennsylvania and Virginia.[56] The first package of books sent out by the SPG went to one of these Welsh communities in Pennsylvania, probably to Evans Evans who had been Rector of Christchurch, Philadelphia, for the use of St David's Welsh Church in Radnor County which had been established by him in 1700.[57] They were closely followed by the SPG's first resident missionary in America, Henry Nichols. A native of Cowbridge, Nichols served churches in Pennsylvania and Maryland, becoming an exemplar for many who would later follow him to America. But Nichols was merely one of many; of the 700 clergymen who went to America between 1695 and 1704, over 80 were of Welsh orgin.[58] Many of them served the small Welsh Anglican communities that had sprung up around Philadelphia itself, establishing schools and distributing godly literature. Letters home telling of their work and the difficulties they encountered were used for propaganda purposes, becoming a vital tool for soliciting funds and propping up interest levels in Wales.

However, the SPG was always much more than a missionary society. Boyd Schlenther has called the SPG missionaries 'storm-troppers, the ecclesiastical arm of eighteenth-century imperialism'.[59] They were at the forefront of the Anglican attempt to reinforce its superiority in the religious life of the colonies, at first through the dissemination of literature, but when the returns from that proved inadequate through the provision of personnel on the ground. It is difficult to tell how far many of the Welsh missionaries sent to the colonies by the SPG held on to their Welsh identity. Their determination not to use the Welsh language in the colonies would suggest that their Anglicanism overrode most other identities, but this meant that their efforts among Welsh émigrés in the colonies were hamstrung from the very beginning. Complaints about the lack of sermons in the Welsh language surfaced early from many of the Welsh Anglicans who had settled around Philadelphia, with the result that many were being driven into the more accommodating arms of the Independents, the Baptists or the Quakers.[60]

The energies of the Welsh members of the SPG committee did not point in a solely westward direction. The greatest flurry of missionary excitement for many in Wales surrounded the outpost established by the Danish East India mission at Tranquebar on the south-east coast of India. The Mission had been established by King Frederick of Denmark, but the prime mover behind it was August Hermann Francke, the influential Pietist leader from Halle, who had sent two missionaries there to establish the outpost in 1706. The mission had a difficult early life, finding it almost impossible to secure the support of other Europeans in India. One of its keenest defenders though was a Welshman, George Lewis of Fort St George, Madras, the chaplain to the East India Company. He kept the precarious position of the mission at the forefront of the minds of members of the SPCK through his regular correspondence with the committee in London. He presented the fortunes of the mission in genuinely apocalyptic terms, as being an essential tool in the continuing conflict with the Roman Catholic Church. In October 1712 he wrote to Henry Newman, secretary of the SPCK that 'The missionary's at Tranquebar ought and must be encouraged. It is the first attempt the Protestants have ever made of that kind. We must not put out the smoking flax. It would give our adversary's the Papists, who boast so much of their Congregation de Propaganda Fide too much cause to triumph over us.'[61]

Predictably it did not take long for Sir John Philipps to register his interest in the Indian missions. He was able to use his extensive contacts with members of the East India Company to secure protection and financial support for James Wendy's plans to establish a school for the training of missionaries at Fort St George in 1712.[62] But it was the Tranquebar mission that generated most interest and enthusiasm. Inspired by Francke's dedication to the mission, the two had met during Philipps's travels on the Continent[63] and had kept in fairly close touch through their shared commitment and interest in the work of the SPCK, Philipps using his powers of persuasion to raise funds for the mission from his friends in Wales.[64] For a few months at the end of 1712, Philipps even tried to persuade Griffith Jones to take up the position of schoolmaster at Tranquebar. Jones gave the proposal serious thought and at one point even began to learn Portuguese in preparation.[65] But after considerable soul-searching 'the extreamly miserable blindness of his own country'[66] exerted too heavy a pull on his loyalties and he turned down an offer which would effectively have made him Wales's first overseas missionary.

The network of communication and exchange that reached across the Atlantic, and in a more limited way as far east as the Indian subcontinent, through the agency of the SPG, had an enormous influence in the slightly longer term. It allowed many in Wales to claim a stake in the progress of Protestantism throughout Britain's colonial possessions, but it also became the conduit for news of new developments to circulate with dramatic speed. In 1735 exciting news of a religious awakening at Northampton, Massachusetts, was reported to the society's committee in London.[67] Five years later, as George Whitefield travelled up and down the eastern seaboard of the American colonies fanning the flames of the Great Awakening, some of the SPG's Welsh missionaries enthusiastically reported home about Whitefield's visits to their communities.[68] The networks that had been established by members of the Anglican religious societies were becoming more diversified, quickly being dwarfed by the web of communications that the mid-eighteenth-century evangelicals created for themselves as their local awakenings began to coalesce into a something resembling a movement with its own agenda and momentum.

In many regards the evangelical movement, as W. R. Ward has repeatedly pointed out, grew out of the international Pietist milieu. The overlap between those who took part in the revival and those who had been involved in the work of the SPCK or the SPG in England and Wales was often striking. In Wales, Sir John Phillipps, who was in regular contact with German Pietists like August Herman Francke at Halle, and had been George Whitefield's patron during his studies at Oxford,[69] was once again key. He had also supported Griffith Jones's ministry in Carmarthenshire and became one of the early patrons of his system of peripatetic schools; Jones himself went on to play a key role in the mentoring of both Howel Harris and Daniel Rowland through their first experiences of the highs and lows of heart religion. These conversions were really the catalyst for the evangelical movement in Wales. They mirrored the experiences which many others were passing through at the same time throughout Europe, the American colonies and beyond. Nothing was calculated to create a stronger sense of belonging among beleaguered Protestants than this shared experience of the new birth. When the incidences of the new birth began to increase, as Harris and Rowland, George Whitefield and John Wesley, and Jonathan Edwards and Gilbert Tennent in America began preaching for conversions with a new intensity, the incidence of conversions became more widespread and revival followed quick on their heels. Very soon there were evangelical awakenings in Wales, at Bristol and London in England, in Scotland and Ireland, and in the American colonies where the transatlantic itinerant ministry of George Whitefield galvanised the activities of scattered evangelicals, creating a Great Awakening.[70]

Initially these awakenings had begun under their own momentum, but they were quickly bound together in a variety of ways to create an international evangelical renewal movement. Key to this process was the English revivalist George Whitefield. Unlike any other Methodist leader, Whitefield had unlimited access to each of the evangelical awakenings. The self-styled 'Grand Itinerant',[71] Whitefield travelled incessantly throughout the British Isles, made thirteen transatlantic crossings between 1737 and his death in 1770, and became in effect the most visible face of the whole evangelical movement. He visited Wales for the first time in March 1739, having exchanged letters with Howel Harris a couple of months previously;[72] Whitefield toured Harris's Methodist societies, preached at Cardiff and Newport and brought the Welsh Methodists up-to-date with the progress of the international revival. Harris then travelled to London with Whitefield where he was immersed in the English Methodist movement, with its headquarters still at the Fetter Lane Society where Calvinists, Wesleyans and Moravians still just about managed to rub along together.[73]

These visits were the first of many as Whitefield became a common sight in Wales, and Harris likewise in London. The Welsh Methodists were integrated into the wider evangelical revival from this point onwards, and through the visits of Whitefield and other English revivalists to Wales, through a constant interchange of letters and the Calvinistic Methodist weekly religious magazine, they were able to keep abreast of the progress and fortunes of the international revival, and also ensure that news about the latest events in Wales received a consistently high profile. Close proximity to Whitefield and the receipt of regular updates on the progress of the revival around the world created a shared identity among the early Methodists; while still very much Welsh, the overriding loyalty of many was to the fortunes of the international revival movement in which they now found themselves.

Key to effective participation in this movement was a shared understanding of the nature of revival itself, the experience that lay at its heart. The main figure in this process, for Welsh Methodists as for evangelicals everywhere, was the New England theologian and revivalist Jonathan Edwards. Edwards had led a revival in his congregation at Northampton, Massachusetts, in 1734–35, and a year later he published his *A Faithful Narrative of the Surprising Work of God in the Conversion of Many Hundred Souls in Northampton* (1736). The work was an instant best seller and was avidly and enthusiastically read by evangelicals throughout the North Atlantic world. In Wales, Howel Harris read it in February 1738 and drew inevitable parallels between what was occurring in Wales and the events that Edwards described.[74] An in-depth description of the progress and effects of the Northampton revival, *A Faithful Narrative* charted in detail the conversion experiences of many of the Northampton converts and provided readers with a theological framework by means of which they could understand and explain their own revivals. Edwards's Northampton awakening soon became the archetypal evangelical awakening, against which all other claims to revival were assessed. While Edwards might have thought that the revival at Northampton was a 'surprising work of God', his account ensured that the element of surprise would often be in short supply in future awakenings.[75]

The transnational and transatlantic nature of the mid-eighteenth-century evangelical revival set a precedent for subsequent revivalism. Wales experienced periodic local and regional revivals throughout the later eighteenth and early nineteenth centuries, but the two further major outbreaks of revivalist fervour, in 1858–59 and 1904–5, were both similarly international in their scope and character. Richard Carwardine has shown how the strength of the transatlantic Welsh American community in the nineteenth century gave rise to what became know as Finney's Revival between 1839 and 1842,[76] but these links were to prove still more significant in 1858 when the revival that had begun in New York first crossed the Atlantic to Ulster, but then reached Wales following the return home to Cardiganshire of the Americanised revivalist Humphrey Jones.[77] Working in reverse, the 1904–5 Welsh revival acted as a major catalyst for the 1906 Azuza Street revival in Los Angeles, an awakening to which the modern Pentecostal movement traces its origins.[78]

The international dimensions of the early Welsh Methodist movement were far more multilayered than the generic affinity with similar movements in other countries and contexts outlined in the preceding paragraphs might suggest. As already mentioned, there were powerful forces binding the awakenings together, both in the form of access to revivalists like Whitefield, and shared experiences like the new birth and the excitement of religious revivalism. On these affinities and shared experiences was built an evangelical communications network which bound many of the awakenings together in more tangible ways; the sinews of this network were a series of different methods of communication which, according to Susan O'Brien, created a vibrant transnational print culture within early evangelicalism.[79] The focal point for these methods of communication was once more George Whitefield, who with a small band of dedicated printers, booksellers and publicists, took advantage of the new opportunities afforded by cheap print and the consumer revolution, to create a network consisting of letters, magazines and books which promoted both his own ministry and by extension the revivals themselves.

Recent scholarship has shown how Wales was gradually moving from being an oral to a print-based culture during the early eighteenth century.[80] The relative cheapness of popular print, a more reliable postal service and increasing levels of literacy in the wake of the success of Griffith Jones's circulating schools, enabled the Welsh Methodists to contribute fully to the evangelical print network and benefited enormously from that participation. In the first instance it was the close working relationship between Howel Harris and Whitefield that was key to its effective operation from the perspective of the wider community of Welsh Methodists. The primary method of communication was letter-writing. At first the revivalists themselves wrote to one another on a regular basis, more often than not making use of the same paths of communication that had been used by some of the Puritans in the seventeenth century and the early evangelicals in the more recent past.[81] But as the revival began to grow, these letters began to be circulated more widely, and it was not long before others, outside the orbit of the pioneer revivalists, were encouraged to take up their pens and contribute their own letters. While these letters tended to be written to one of the pioneer revivalists, most commonly either Harris or Whitefield in the first instance, the best of them were distributed more widely. Whitefield had a small group of printers and booksellers who acted like publicity agents, fanning letters out from London to all corners of the revival, while in Wales Harris ensured that letters were distributed to the leaders of societies throughout South and West Wales. It was not until 1741 that a more regularised system of monthly letter days was introduced at Whitefield's London Tabernacle headquarters at which the latest correspondence from throughout the revival was read aloud to the gathered throng.[82] Despite Whitefield's urging, Harris did not attempt to begin letter days in Wales, but he did ensure that letters from Wales were regularly sent up to the Tabernacle,[83] and Whitefield in turn ensured that reports of the letters read aloud at the monthly letter days were promptly sent back to Wales.[84]

It quickly became apparent to Harris and Whitefield that reliance on letter-writing alone was never going effectively to service the needs of widely scattered evangelicals. Whitefield, with the assistance of a London Welsh printer, John Lewis, therefore began publishing a weekly magazine; it remained in regular print for eight years, from 1740 until 1748, quickly establishing itself as the official mouthpiece of the English and Welsh Calvinistic Methodists.[85] *The Christian's Amusement* had been printed intermittently by Lewis himself, since September 1740, but it was not until April 1741, when Whitefield assumed control of the magazine, changing its name to *The Weekly*

History, that its contents became more lively and popular and its circulation figures began to take off.[86] The London-based magazine also spawned two other sister publications; the Scottish *Glasgow Weekly History* and the colonial *Christian History*, both of which relied heavily for material on the London edition; the three versions each contributed to the sense of solidarity that existed among Calvinistically-inclined evangelicals on both sides of the Atlantic.[87]

Howel Harris was an enthusiastic supporter of the magazine, and a regular contributor to its pages, providing a regular supply of both his own letters and the letters that were addressed to him by various members of the Welsh Methodist community. He ensured that the magazine received a decent circulation in Wales, even in areas where its exclusively English-language content was a potential barrier to monoglot Welsh-speakers. To get over this problem he encouraged society leaders who could understand English to read paraphrased ad hoc translations to their charges. Other society leaders and exhorters sold the magazines on their preaching itineraries; at the height of its popularity hundreds of copies were circulated among the Welsh Methodists every week.[88] It seems to have been particularly valued by many rank-and-file Welsh Methodists, such as Anne Thomas from Pembrokeshire who wrote to Harris in 1742: 'I receivd [. . .] the Weekly Histories which you was so kind as to send me [. . .] I think my soul has received some benefit in reading them. O how sweet is it to hear how the Lord brings in his work.'[89]

Welsh Methodists like Thomas used the magazine to follow closely the progress of the revival around the world. Some wrote accounts of their experience of revival in their own localities which they were able to see in print in a relatively short space of time; others contributed accounts of their conversion experiences and used the model conversion narratives that appeared in its pages to test the authenticity of their own experiences.[90] Many also discovered that the network could operate as a primitive self-help forum, in which many of the problems and difficulties associated with membership of the evangelical movement, particularly in these early pioneering days, could be regularly aired. For a while the magazine also facilitated a kind of primitive Christian communism in which some middling sort Methodists, particularly shopkeepers and tradespeople, advertised in its pages, at a discounted rate, services which they were prepared to place at the disposal of their fellow evangelicals.[91] Later in the 1740s, evangelicals were also able to use the magazine to keep track of some of the uses to which the generous and sacrificial financial contributions that they made to the orphanage Whitefield had established in the Georgia colony, were being put.[92]

If letters and magazines often enjoyed a wide circulation throughout the evangelical world, their weakness was that they could often also be ephemeral. Recognising this, the pioneer revivalists committed themselves to an ambitious publication programme which saw the printing of new material, sermons, theological treatises and polemical essays, and the reissuing of carefully chosen devotional and theological classics from the past. These books played a highly significant role in fostering a common identity between evangelicals from otherwise diverse cultural settings.[93] Howel Harris's reading of Jonathan Edwards's account of the 1735 Northampton revival during February 1738 has already been noted, but it was his immediate identification with Edwards and his work, and his ability to draw parallels between what was taking place in Wales and what had occurred in Massachusetts, that were the most remarkable and far-reaching consequences of Harris's reading of the text.[94] Unsurprisingly it was George Whitefield who once again demonstrated his entrepreneurial acumen by taking advantage of the opening up of the provincial book-trade that had occurred during the early decades of the eighteenth century.[95] In the early days of the revival Whitefield's journals seemed to be everywhere. Following the issuing of the initial instalment of his journal, outlining his first transatlantic journey,[96] Whitefield printed frequent updates of his autobiographical narrative, keeping his many readers closely in touch with the progress of the revival that he was leading.

However, it was perhaps Whitefield's sermons that became the most ubiquitous. Frank Lambert has written that Whitefield's sermons came to assume an 'important symbolic significance'[97] for the revival as a whole, distilling as they did all of its most important principles and emphases. During his first meeting with Howel Harris in Wales, Whitefield persuaded Harris to secure the translation of some of his best sermons into the Welsh language.[98] Within a few years four of them had been duly translated and published, including his sermon on the new birth[99] and his defence of the religious societies,[100] probably his two most effective and often-repeated sermons. Later, issues of *The Weekly History* publicised the latest books and pamphlets to roll from the evangelical presses in London, and contained advice on how interested individuals could get their hands on the newest publications, often at heavily discounted rates for bulk orders.[101]

Evidence for the enthusiasm with which some of the Welsh Methodists responded to these advertisements is not difficult to come by. In 1743, John Syms, one of Whitefield's London publicists and booksellers, offered Harris nine bound copies of Whitefield's entire journal at a special 16 per cent discount, and between 1744 and 1746 Syms regularly sent substantial packets of books to Harris for distribution in Wales. The 200 copies of Whitefield's *Letter to the Rev. Mr Thomas Church* (1744) and the 43 copies of a volume containing twenty-three of Whitefield's sermons[102] which he sent to Harris in June 1744 were unexceptional.[103] The commitment to translating some of the best evangelical literature persisted into the 1740s also; in 1743 the Welsh Methodist Association decided to fund the translation of Ralph Erskine's *Law-Death Gospel-Life* (1724)[104] and in July 1745 they decided to translate Elisha Coles' *A Practical Discourse on God's Sovereignty* (1673), although there does not seem to be any evidence that this ever actually appeared. What all of these publications represent is the commitment of many of the Welsh Methodists to the establishment and maintenance of a common print culture across the Calvinistic Methodist communities. While the early evangelicals' letters and magazines possessed an immediacy and rawness, publications such as these were considerably more far-reaching and contributed in a more permanent way to the defining of early evangelicalism.

Much of what has been said so far might give the impression that the mid-eighteenth-century evangelical movement was a single and relatively homogenous entity. This was far from being the case. While the Welsh Methodists always identified closely with the evangelical movement in its widest sense, their ability to make that identification was built on their transnational link with Whitefield and the English Calvinistic Methodist community. By 1741 the English Methodist awakening had splintered into three distinct groupings, some following John Wesley, others George Whitefield and still others the Moravians.[105] The strong personal bond existing between Whitefield and Harris ensured that as their revivals grew they also became inextricably intertwined; it was only natural, therefore, that a more formalised organisational structure should develop between the two awakenings.

Following the damaging splits in England, Whitefield was keen formally to unite with his fellow Calvinists in Wales. Both Harris and Whitefield had already begun to organise their revivals along similar lines; Harris formed his followers into small societies of between fifteen and twenty-five members, each society being put under the oversight of a steward. Societies in a given locality were grouped together and their leaders met monthly to discuss progress. Above the Monthly Association, the Quarterly Association met four times a year and drew in leaders from a slightly wider geographical area. At the apex of this structure was the Annual Association, the once-yearly gathering of all of the leaders of the movement.[106] Whitefield had developed a similar structure in England. The centres of English Calvinistic Methodist influence were conveniently concentrated in London, Bristol, Wiltshire,

Exeter and Plymouth, and each of the local leaders in these areas reported regularly back to headquarters at Whitefield's Tabernacle in London.[107] In 1743 these two structures were amalgamated at a summit meeting held at Watford near Caerphilly in South Wales which set up the Joint Association of English and Welsh Calvinistic Methodism. Whitefield was appointed the overall Moderator of the movement and Howel Harris was appointed General Superintendent of the Societies, a roving role which gave him *carte blanche* to go wherever he wanted, including spending over half of every year in London taking charge of the English Calvinistic Methodists during Whitefield's frequent and extended absences in the America colonies.

What was established was, in effect, a quasi-presbyterian system of administration, at this point still within the confines of the Church of England. This shared administrative structure initially worked very well, at least until Whitefield decided he no longer wished to head it and until Harris was turned out of the movement in 1750.[108] Responsibility for the working of this leadership structure in Wales was then taken on by Daniel Rowland, while in England the Countess of Huntingdon came to assume a greater degree of responsibility for Whitefield's converts. She was quickly forced to face up to the inconsistency of the Methodists' relationship with the Established Church, and from the mid-1760s began registering her own meeting houses.[109] But the link with the Welsh Methodist movement continued. In 1768 she established a college to train preachers for her new chapels which she based at Trevecka, the home of Howel Harris. During the twenty-five years of its existence the college trained 212 English and Welsh preachers for the Countess of Huntingdon's Connexion, establishing the priority and precedent of an educated ministry.[110] It was not until 1811 that the Welsh Methodists followed their English counterparts and took the inevitable step of seceding from the Church of England, ordaining their own ministers, and thereby establishing the Calvinistic Methodist church. Although not Presbyterian in name at this stage, the new denomination was Presbyterian in every other way.[111]

During the course of the nineteenth century the new denomination actually became more consciously Presbyterian. Densil Morgan writes that by the 1850s Lewis Edwards had transformed the Calvinistic Methodists from a revivalist sect into a fully fledged Presbyterian denomination, one that participated fully in the international network of Reformed churches.[112] Edwards himself had been educated in Edinburgh University during the 1830s; he had sat at the feet of Thomas Chalmers, the evangelical leader of the Disruption in the Church of Scotland, and had witnessed at first hand the value of an educated ministry, the necessity of a liberal education and a wide cultural perception.[113] Upon his return to Wales, Edwards established Bala College in 1837, for the education of candidates for the Calvinistic Methodist ministry, and close links were forged with the Calvinist Princeton Seminary in New Jersey, after it became the preferred place for the training of ministers for the American branch of the Calvinistic Methodist denomination.[114] Once they were firmly connected to the Presbyterian Church in the United States, this part of the Calvinistic Methodist diaspora drew the Welsh Methodists still deeper into the international Reformed world.

An organisational structure that had been established on the hoof in the heat of the revival during the 1740s, had initially wedded the fortunes of Welsh and English Calvinistic Methodism together. But the adoption of elements of Presbyterian church order meant that in subsequent generations the Calvinistic Methodists would share a close affinity with Reformed churches throughout Britain and America, particularly in the nineteenth century. Wedded to revivalism, the heirs of the pioneer Welsh Methodists continued to see themselves as part of a more extensive religious community than that prescribed by the physical borders of Wales itself.

The international dimensions of the Welsh Methodists' world-view conditioned their responses to the hostility that came their way from those in ecclesiastical and political authority. Initially, Methodism was regarded with deep suspicion; its tendency to enthusiasm and its network of small cell-groups appeared to many to be a throwback to the chaotic days of the mid-seventeenth century when enthusiastic and millenarian religious beliefs had engulfed the country in civil war and resulted in the execution of the King. The heightened political atmosphere of the mid-1740s, which saw the Methodists in England and Wales become the targets of mob violence,[115] forced them repeatedly to protest their loyalty to both the Hanoverians and the Protestant faith as enshrined in the established Church of England. Between 1744 and 1745, when the political situation looked particularly precarious as a result of the threat posed by the Jacobite Pretender, Howel Harris was among the first to urge the Methodists to set aside special seasons for prayer and fasting to invoke God's help and the deliverance of the nation. To James Beaumont he wrote in February 1744:

> We are like to be called to the Field of Blood soon [. . .] the French fleet now lay at anchor in one of our Ports being come over with a firm Resolution to dethrone his Majesty & set the Pretenders Son on the Throne of England & consequently not only take away all Toleration & liberty of Protestants but establish Popery again [. . .] Next Monday we have

> settled for fasting and prayer for the Kg & Nation. We all hold it our Duty to preach loyalty to the King set over us by the Ld & as he is a Protestant & tolerates the true Religion & as he is laid deeply on our hearts too.[116]

It was the guarantee of the continuance of religious toleration that led the Methodists, like all other Nonconformist groups, enthusiastically to support George II. Led by Harris, Methodists in Wales fasted and interceded for their King and his armies, and avidly followed the course of military campaigns in Europe and further afield. From being suspected of subversion, Jacobitism and even clandestine Popery, and at times facing the full brunt of mob violence, the Methodists reinvented themselves as model and loyal subjects of the British state. When the Jacobite armies were finally defeated, they enthusiastically celebrated their national deliverance and Harris rejoiced that 'our national trials have been [. . .] instrumental in turning the hearts of many to the King'.[117] The extent of Harris's own identification with British Protestant nationalism was evident at the height of the Seven Years' War; in 1759 Harris enlisted as an ensign in the Breconshire militia, along with twenty-five members of his Trevecka Family, a few of whom fought under General Wolfe at the Battle of Quebec.[118] Harris regarded the war as a conflict between Protestant England and Catholic France; stationed at Great Yarmouth in East Anglia, he used his considerable oratorical powers to preach virulently anti-Catholic sermons in an effort to recruit soldiers to fight in the British army on the Continent.[119]

If political realities forced the Methodists into adopting British loyalism with all that that entailed, it was often intermingled with optimistic millenarian expectations, bred in part by the realities of the international dimensions of the evangelical movement. By the later 1740s some of the initial enthusiasm surrounding the revivals had begun to wane, and the tense political situation had led some Methodists to view the future with a degree of trepidation. It was in this less than fortuitous context that the Calvinistic Methodists bought into the Concert for Prayer that had been established by a select group of Scottish and American evangelicals in 1746.[120] In 1748 Jonathan Edwards published *A Humble Attempt to Promote Explicit Agreement and Visible Union of God's People in Extraordinary Prayer*, in which he argued that specially organised seasons of prayer throughout the international evangelical community would enable the revival to recapture its original intensity and, perhaps more importantly, usher in the dawn of the millennium, Christ's thousand-year reign on earth.[121]

Howel Harris responded to this upbeat eschatological vision with characteristic enthusiasm, recommending to his fellow Welsh

Methodists that a regular day for prayer should be set aside once every three months and that every Sunday morning should be set aside to intercede for 'ye late work in England, Scotland, Wales and America, both to praise God for it and intercede and pray for its furtherance'.[122] The Methodists had a carefully articulated view of history that was both simultaneously linear and cyclical; periods of declension would be followed by periods of revival, all of which were merely precursors to the final worldwide revival that would inaugurate the thousand-year earthly reign of Christ. This necessitated a global vision; they were, first and foremost, citizens of the worldwide kingdom of God, and fully expected all national and denominational divisions to be subsumed once the millennial age had dawned, an age that many of them firmly suspected was just around the corner. It was this consideration more than any other that led many of them to seek contact and fellowship with those from other countries throughout the North Atlantic world who were also standing on tiptoes as it were, expecting to be caught up in the next chapter of this cosmic divine drama at any moment.

What all this suggests is that despite significant cultural and linguistic differences, the mid-eighteenth-century evangelical awakenings brought about a significant meeting of minds across national and cultural boundaries. By exchanging letters with one another, subscribing to the same weekly magazines, listening to the same sermons, reading the same books and praying similar prayers, evangelicals, whether they happened to be American Congregationalists, Scottish Presbyterians or Welsh Calvinistic Methodists, spoke the same religious language and thought in broadly familiar ways.

Protestantism in Wales had enjoyed a chequered history ever since the sixteenth-century Reformation. It had first to get over the perception that it was the *ffydd saeson* (faith of the English), and it was only after the dedicated labours of scholarly churchmen who sought to ensure that the Bible, the Prayer Book and other Protestant literature was widely available in the Welsh language, that the Welsh were won over to a grudging acceptance of the Church of England. In the decades following the death of Elizabeth I the religious fortunes of the Welsh became subject to a degree of what Michael Hechter has called internal colonialism.[123] Although the Anglican church had soon abandoned any notions of enforcing linguistic conformity in Wales, it tended largely to be English-orientated movements such as Puritanism and Anglican institutions like the Welsh Trust and the SPCK who attempted to address the perceived religious deficit in Wales. Charles Edwards's depiction of the English as 'embracing shepherds' in his *Y Ffydd Ddi-ffvant* (1677), was indicative of the conviction of many of Wales's religious leaders that only through the careful cultivation of the relationship with England could the resources necessary for the successful evangelisation of Wales be mobilised.[124]

Ever since the Acts of Union and the Elizabethan religious settlement the Welsh had been thoroughly integrated into national British institutions, the most ubiquitous being the Church of England.[125] In this sense Linda Colley's assertion that British identity was built on Protestant election has some resonance for the Welsh,[126] but the influence of European Pietism and the identification with the general Protestant enterprise in the latter half of the seventeenth century and the opening decades of the eighteenth century indicates the extent to which other identities, both European and transatlantic, often weighed more heavily in the minds of many Welsh evangelicals.[127] It was not until the evangelical revival, though, that Protestantism bedded down more deeply in the Welsh psyche. But by this stage the Protestant world had shrunk; the movement of peoples and ideas around the Atlantic basin had enabled the creation of an international evangelical community. From this point on, Welsh evangelical religion would be resolutely outward-looking.

Notes

1 John Lewis (ed.), *The Weekly History*, no. 13 [no date], 1.
2 W. R. Ward, *The Protestant Evangelical Awakening* (Cambridge, 1992).
3 Jeremy Gregory, 'The long eighteenth century', in Randy L. Maddox and Jason E. Vickers (eds), *The Cambridge Companion to John Wesley* (Cambridge, 2010), pp. 14–15.
4 Eifion Evans, *Daniel Rowland and the Great Evangelical Awakening in Wales* (Edinburgh, 1985), pp. 47ff; Geraint Tudur, *Howell Harris: From Conversion to Separation, 1735–1750* (Cardiff, 2000), ch. 2.
5 Susan O'Brien, 'A transatlantic community of saints: the Great Awakening and the first evangelical network, 1735–1755', *American Historical Review*, 91 (1986), 811–32.
6 David Ceri Jones, *'A Glorious Work in the World': Welsh Methodism and the International Evangelical Revival, 1735–1750* (Cardiff, 2004).
7 David Hempton, *Methodism: Empire of the Spirit* (New Haven, 2005).
8 Some of the best of this recent work is showcased in Bill Jones and Aled Jones, 'The Welsh world and the British Empire, c.1851–1939: an exploration', in Carl Bridge and Kent Fedorowich (eds), *The British World: Diaspora, Culture and Identity* (London, 2003), pp. 57–81.
9 See Chris Williams, 'Problematizing Wales: an exploration in historiography and postcoloniality', in Jane Aaron and Chris Williams (eds), *Postcolonial Wales* (Cardiff, 2005), pp. 4–6.
10 See Elwyn T. Ashton, *The Welsh in the United States* (Hove, 1984), especially chs. 5 and 6; Richard C. Allen, *Quaker Communities in Early Modern Wales: From Resistance to Respectability* (Cardiff, 2007), pp. 182–5.
11 For introductions to Atlantic history, see Bernard Bailyn, 'The idea of Atlantic history', *Itinerario*, 20 (1996), 19–44; Nicholas Canny, 'Writing Atlantic history; or, reconfiguring the history of colonial British America', *Journal of American History*, 86 (1999), 1093–114.

12 P. J. Marshall, 'Introduction', in P. J. Marshall (ed.), *The Oxford History of the British Empire*, vol. 2: *The Eighteenth Century* (Oxford, 1998), p. 7.
13 D. W. Meinig, *The Shaping of America: A Geographical Perspective on 500 Years of History*, vol. 1: *Atlantic America, 1492–1800* (New Haven, 1986), p. 3.
14 J. H. Elliot, 'Atlantic history: a circumnavigation', in David Armitage and Michael J. Braddick (eds), *The British Atlantic World, 1500–1800* (Basingstoke, 2002), p. 239.
15 Douglas R. Egerton, Alison Games, Jane G. Landers, Kris Lane and Donald R. Wright, *The Atlantic World: A History, 1400–1888* (Wheeling, 2007), pp. 1–2.
16 David Armitage, 'Three concepts of Atlantic history', in Armitage and Braddick (eds), *The British Atlantic World*, p. 16.
17 Gwyn A. Williams, *When was Wales? A History of the Welsh* (Harmondsworth, 1985), p. 141.
18 See, for example, Gwyn A. Williams, *The Search for Beulah Land: The Welsh and the Atlantic Revolution* (London, 1980).
19 Stefan Berger, 'Comparative history', in Stefan Berger, Heiko Feldner and Kevin Passmore (eds), *Writing History: Theory and Practice* (London, 2003), pp. 169–71.
20 Benedict Anderson, *Imagined Communities: Reflections on the Origins and Spread of Nationalism* (London, 1983). For the idea of Protestantism as an imagined identity, see Tony Claydon and Ian McBride, 'The trials of chosen peoples: recent interpretations of Protestantism and national identity in Britain and Ireland', in Tony Claydon and Ian McBride (eds), *Protestantism and National Identity: Britain and Ireland, c.1650–c.1850* (Cambridge, 1998), pp. 3–29.
21 To some extent this essay engages with the debate on the contribution of Protestantism to Welsh national identity recently revisited in E. Wyn James, '"The new birth of a people": Welsh language and identity and the Welsh Methodists, c.1740–c.1820', in Robert Pope (ed.), *Religion and National Identity: Wales and Scotland c.1700–c.2000* (Cardiff, 2001), pp. 14–42; and Eryn M. White, '"The people called Methodists": early Welsh Methodism and the question of identity', *Journal of Welsh Religious History*, 1 (2001), 1–14.
22 W. R. Ward, *Christianity Under the Ancien Régime, 1648–1789* (Cambridge, 1999), pp. 14, 17.
23 Tony Claydon, *Europe and the Making of England, 1660–1760* (Cambridge, 2007), pp. 61ff.
24 Thomas Kidd, *The Protestant Interest: New England after Puritanism* (New Haven, 2005), pp. 12–13.
25 Boyd Stanley Schlenther, 'Religious faith and commercial empire', in Marshall (ed.), *The Eighteenth Century*, pp. 12–50.
26 Kidd, *The Protestant Interest*, pp. 12–13.
27 Bernard Capp, *Astrology and the Popular Press: English Almanacs, 1500–1800* (London, 1979), pp. 251–3.
28 Eryn M. White, 'Popular schooling and the Welsh language 1650–1800', in Geraint H. Jenkins (ed.), *A History of the Welsh Language Before the Industrial Revolution* (Cardiff, 1997), pp. 319, 321–2.
29 Geraint H. Jenkins, *The Foundations of Modern Wales, 1642–1780* (Oxford, 1987), p. 199.
30 W. R. Ward, *Early Evangelicalism: A Global Intellectual History, 1670–1789* (Cambridge, 2006).
31 Geraint H. Jenkins, *Literature, Religion and Society in Wales, 1660–1730* (Cardiff, 1978), p. 36.
32 Geraint H. Jenkins, '"The sweating astrologer": Thomas Jones, the Almanacer', in R. R. Davies, Ralph A. Griffiths, Ieuan Gwynedd Jones and Kenneth O. Morgan (eds), *Welsh Society and Nationhood: Historical Essays Presented to Glanmor Williams* (Cardiff, 1984), pp. 168–9.
33 Linda Colley, *Britons: Forging the Nation, 1707–1837* (New Haven and London, 1992), especially ch. 1.
34 Mary Clement, *The S. P. C. K. and Wales, 1699–1740* (London, 1954), pp. 87–8.

35 *Ibid.*
36 Mary Clement (ed.), *Correspondence and Minutes of the S. P. C. K. relating to Wales, 1699–1740* (Cardiff, 1952), p. 108.
37 Colin Haydon, *Anti-Catholicism in Eighteenth-Century England: A Political and Social Study* (Manchester, 1993), pp. 28–30.
38 Geoffrey F. Nuttall, *Calendar of the Correspondence of Philip Doddridge, D. D. (1702–1751)* (London, 1979), pp. xxxiii–xxxiv, 76.
39 Ward, *The Protestant Evangelical Awakening*, pp. 103–7.
40 Clement (ed.), *Correspondence and Minutes of the S. P. C. K.*, p. 167.
41 *Ibid.*, p. 171.
42 Clement, *The S. P. C. K. and Wales, 1699–1740*, p. 88.
43 Clement (ed.), *Correspondence and Minutes of the S. P. C. K.*, p. 307.
44 Kidd, *The Protestant Interest*, pp. 54–5, 157–66.
45 Mary Clement (ed.), *Correspondence and Records of the S. P. G. relating to Wales, 1701–1750* (Cardiff, 1973), p. 72.
46 Michael J. Crawford, *Seasons of Grace: Colonial New England's Revival Tradition in its British Context* (New York, 1991), pp. 130–2.
47 Moses Williams (ed.), *Selections from Welch Piety* (Cardiff, 1938), p. 23.
48 *Welch Piety: or a Succinct Account of the Rise and Progress of the Circulating Welch Charity School, from the year 1737, to the Year 1761* (London, 1761), pp. 8–9.
49 T. M. Bassett, *The Welsh Baptists* (Swansea, 1977), pp. 67, 95; Roger Lee Brown, *Evangelicals in the Church in Wales* (Welshpool, 2007), pp. 44ff.; Tudur, *Howell Harris*, pp. 23ff; R. Tudur Jones, *Congregationalism in Wales* (Cardiff, 2004), p. 110.
50 D. Bruce Hindmarsh, 'The reception of Jonathan Edwards by early evangelicals in England', in David W. Kling and Douglas A. Sweeney (eds), *Jonathan Edwards at Home and Abroad: Historical Memories, Cultural Movements, Global Horizons* (Columbia, SC, 2003), pp. 203–4.
51 See, for example, Andrew Porter, *Religion versus Empire? British Protestant Missionaries and Overseas Expansion, 1700–1914* (Manchester, 2004), pp. 32–3.
52 J. C. S. Mason, *The Moravian Church and the Missionary Awakening in England, 1760–1800* (London, 2001), p. 5.
53 Brian Stanley, *The Bible and the Flag: Protestant Missions and British Imperialism in the Nineteenth and Twentieth Centuries* (Leicester, 1990), p. 55. The primacy of the SPG in the history of British Protestant missions is reinforced strongly by Rowan Strong, *Anglicanism and the British Empire, c.1700–c.1850* (Oxford, 2007), pp. 11ff.
54 Clement, *The S. P. C. K. and Wales*, pp. 178–95.
55 Clement (ed.), *Correspondence and Records of the S. P. G.*, p. 29.
56 Edward George Hartmann, *Americans from Wales* (New York, 1978), pp. 44ff.
57 Clement, *The S. P. C. K. and Wales*, p. 67.
58 *Ibid.*
59 Schlenther, 'Religious faith and commercial empire', p. 131.
60 Clement, *The S. P. C. K. and Wales*, p. 70.
61 Clement (ed.), *Correspondence and Minutes of the S. P. G.*, p. 52.
62 Clement (ed.), *Correspondence and Minutes of the S. P. C. K.*, p. 49.
63 NLW, Picton Castle Collection, MS 1469: Sir John Philipps to Lady Mary Philipps, 12 August 1719.
64 Clement (ed.), *Correspondence and Minutes of the S. P. C. K.*, p. 88.
65 *Ibid.*, p. 52.
66 *Ibid.*, p. 57.
67 Clement (ed.), *Correspondence and Records of the S. P. G.*, p. 72.
68 *Ibid.*, p. 74.
69 George Whitefield, *A Short Account of God's Dealings with the Reverend Mr George Whitefield, . . . from his infancy, to the time of his entring holy orders* (London, 1740), pp. 65, 68, 70–1.

70 For introductions to the evangelical revival on both sides of the Atlantic, see Henry D. Rack, *Reasonable Enthusiast: John Wesley and the Rise of Methodism in England* (London, 1989); Hempton, *Methodism: Empire of the Spirit*; Thomas S. Kidd, *The Great Awakening: The Roots of Evangelical Christianity in Colonial America* (New Haven, 2007).

71 Harry S. Stout, *The Divine Dramatist: George Whitefield and the Rise of Modern Evangelicalism* (Grand Rapids, 1991), p. xiii.

72 NLW, Calvinistic Methodist Archive [CMA], Trevecka Group, Trevecka Letters 133: George Whitefield to Howel Harris, 20 December 1738; Trevecka 137: Howel Harris to George Whitefield, 8 January 1739.

73 Colin J. Podmore, *The Moravian Church in England, 1728–1760* (Oxford, 1998), pp. 29–71.

74 NLW, CMA, Howel Harris' Diary 25, 27 November 1738. See also David Ceri Jones, '"Sure the time here now is like New England": what happened when the Welsh Calvinistic Methodists read Jonathan Edwards?' in Kenneth P. Minkema, Adriaan C. Neele and Kelly Van Andel (eds), *Jonathan Edwards and Scotland* (Edinburgh, 2011), pp. 50–2.

75 Hindmarsh, 'The reception of Jonathan Edwards', p. 204.

76 Richard Carwardine, 'The Welsh evangelical community and Finney's Revival', *Journal of Ecclesiastical History*, 29 (1978), 472–3.

77 Eifion Evans, 'Humphrey Jones: "the youngster who lit the fuse"', in Eifion Evans, *Fire in the Thatch: The True Nature of Religious Revival* (Bridgend, 1996), pp. 186–205.

78 Allan Anderson, *An Introduction to Pentecostalism* (Cambridge, 2004), p. 36.

79 See Susan O'Brien, 'Eighteenth-century publishing networks in the first years of transatlantic evangelicalism', in Mark A. Noll, David W. Bebbington and George A. Rawlyk (eds), *Evangelicalism: Comparative Studies of Popular Protestantism in North America, the British Isles, and Beyond* (New York, 1992), pp. 38–57.

80 Richard Suggett and Eryn M. White, 'Language, literacy and aspects of identity in early modern Wales', in Adam Fox and Daniel Woolf (eds), *The Spoken Word: Oral Culture in Britain, 1500–1850* (Manchester, 2002), pp. 152–3.

81 David Cressy, *Coming Over: Migration and Communication between England and New England in the Seventeenth Century* (Cambridge, 1987), especially ch. 9; Charles E. Hambrick-Stowe, 'The spirit of the old writers: the Great Awakening and the persistence of Puritan piety', in Francis J. Bremer (ed.), *Puritanism: Transatlantic Perspectives on a Seventeenth-Century Anglo-American Faith* (Boston, 1993), pp. 277–91.

82 Susan O'Brien, 'A transatlantic community of saints', *American Historical Review*, 91 (1986), 826–7.

83 NLW, CMA, Trevecka 644, Howel Harris to Daniel Rowland, 14 September 1742; Trevecka 697, Howel Harris to Howell Davies, 15 October 1742.

84 NLW, CMA, Trevecka 626, Howel Harris to Thomas James, 7 September 1742; Trevecka 723, Howel Harris to Thomas James, 2 November 1742; Trevecka 1088, Howel Harris to James Beaumont, 21 January 1744.

85 Jennifer Snead, 'Print, predestination, and the public sphere: transatlantic evangelical periodicals, 1740–1745', *Early American Literature*, 45 (2010), 93–110.

86 Susan Durden, 'A study of the first evangelical magazines, 1740–1748', *Journal of Ecclesiastical History*, 27 (1976), 260–2.

87 Jones, *'A Glorious Work in the World'*, pp. 31, 83–4.

88 NLW, CMA, Trevecka Group 2946; Records of Associations, volume 2, part 2, 6 July 1747, pp. 38–9; Frank Lambert, *'Pedlar in Divinity': George Whitefield and the Transatlantic Revivals, 1737–1770* (Princeton, 1994), p. 70.

89 'The copy of a letter from Mrs Anne T__s of Pembrokeshire in Wales to Mr Howel Harris in London (Longhouse, 3 September 1742)', in John Lewis (ed.), *The Weekly History*, no. 80 (Saturday, 16 October 1742).

90 See David Ceri Jones, 'Narratives of conversion in English Calvinistic Methodism', in Kate Cooper and Jeremy Gregory (eds), *Revival and Resurgence in Christian History*, Studies in Church History, 44 (Woodbridge, 2008), pp. 128–41.

91 'Editorial comments', in John Lewis (ed.), *The Christian's Amusement*, issue 12.
92 Jones, *'A Glorious Work in the World'*, pp. 294–302.
93 O'Brien, 'Eighteenth-century publishing networks', pp. 41–2.
94 NLW, CMA, Howel Harris's Diary no. 25, 27 November 1738.
95 See John Feather, *A History of British Publishing* (London, 1988), pp. 93–105.
96 George Whitefield, *A Journal of a Voyage from London to Savannah in Georgia (December 1737–May 1738)* (London, 1738).
97 Lambert, *'Pedlar in Divinity'*, p. 76.
98 See George Whitefield to Daniel Abbot, 10 March 1739, in Graham C. G. Thomas, 'George Whitefield and friends: the correspondence of some early Methodists', *National Library of Wales Journal*, 27 (1991), 176.
99 George Whitefield, *Nodau'r Enedigaeth Newydd. Sef Pregeth a Bregethwyd yn Eglwys Plwyf St. Mary, Whitechapel* (Bristol, 1739).
100 George Whitefield, *Llythyr Oddiwrth y Parchedig Mr G. W. at Societies neu Gymdeithasau Crefyddol a Osodwyd yn Ddiweddar ar Droed Mewn Amriw Leodd yng Nghymru a Lloegr* (Bristol, 1740).
101 See John Lewis (ed.), *The Weekly History*, no. 30 (Saturday 31 October 1741), 4; no. 62 (Saturday 12 June 1742), 1.
102 George Whitefield, *Twenty-Three Sermons on Various Subjects* (London, 1745).
103 NLW, CMA, Trevecka 1188, John Syms to Howel Harris, 9 June 1744.
104 Ralph Erskine, *Traethawd am Farw i'r Ddeddf, a Byw i Dduw* (Bristol, 1743).
105 These divisions are examined in considerable detail in Arnold A. Dallimore, *George Whitefield: The Life and Times of the Great Evangelist of the Eighteenth-Century Revival* (Edinburgh, 1980), chs. 1–4; Herbert Boyd McGonigle, *Sufficient Saving Grace: John Wesley's Evangelical Arminianism* (Carlisle, 2001); Jones, *'A Glorious Work in the World'*, pp. 173–87; James L. Schwenk, *Catholic Spirit: Wesley, Whitefield, and the Quest for Evangelical Unity in Eighteenth-Century British Methodism*, Pietist and Wesleyan Studies, 26 (Lanham, 2008).
106 Jones, *'A Glorious Work in the World'*, ch. 5.
107 Edwin Welch (ed.), *Two Calvinistic Methodist Chapels, 1743–1811: The London Tabernacle and Spa Fields Chapel* (London, 1975), pp. 19ff.
108 This division is best dealt with in Tudur, *Howell Harris*, chs. 7 and 8.
109 See Boyd Stanley Schlenther, *Queen of the Methodists: The Countess of Huntingdon and the Eighteenth-Century Crisis of Faith and Society* (Durham, 1997), ch. 11.
110 *Ibid.*, pp. 76–9; Edwin Welch, *Spiritual Pilgrim: A Reassessment of the Life of the Countess of Huntingdon* (Cardiff, 1995), ch. 7.
111 See Glanmor Williams, William Jacob, Nigel Yates and Frances Knight, *The Welsh Church: From Reformation to Disestablishment, 1603–1920* (Cardiff, 2007), pp. 209–22.
112 D. Densil Morgan, 'Lewis Edwards (1808–87)', *Welsh Journal of Religious History*, 3 (2008), 19.
113 For Chalmers, see Stewart J. Brown, *Thomas Chalmers and the Godly Commonwealth in Scotland* (Oxford, 1982).
114 D. Densil Morgan, 'Wales, the Princeton theology and a nineteenth-century battle for the Bible', *Journal of Welsh Religious History*, 2 (2002), 53–5. For Princeton seminary itself, the best introduction is probably Mark A. Noll (ed.), *The Princeton Theology, 1812–1921: Scripture, Science, and Theological Method from Archibald Alexander to Benjamin Warfield* (Grand Rapids, 2001).
115 John Walsh, 'Methodism and the mob in the eighteenth century', in G. J. Cuming and D. Baker (eds), *Popular Belief and Practice*, Studies in Church in History, 8 (Cambridge, 1972), pp. 213–28.
116 NLW, CMA, Trevecka 1118, Howel Harris to James Beaumont, 18 February 1744.
117 See 'From Mr Howel Harris at Trevecca, near the Hay in Breconshire, south Wales to Mr Thomas Adams, at the Tabernacle House near Moorfields, London', John Lewis (ed.), *The Christian History* (London, 1747), 21–3.
118 Quoted in Eifion Evans, *Howell Harris, Evangelist, 1714–1773* (Cardiff, 1974), p. 60.

119 Edward Morgan, *The Life and Times of Howel Harris, Esq.* (Holywell, 1852), pp. 220–1.
120 Harold P. Simonson, 'Jonathan Edwards and his Scottish connections', *Journal of American Studies*, 21 (1987), 372–3.
121 See, for example, John F. Wilson (ed.), *The Works of Jonathan Edwards*, vol. 9: *A History of the Work of Redemption* (London and New Haven, 1989), p. 353.
122 NLW, CMA, Trevecka Group 2945, 'At an Association held at Trevecka, 29 March 1745' p. 145.
123 See Michael Hechter, *Internal Colonialism: The Celtic Fringe in British National Development, 1536–1966* (London, 1975).
124 Quoted in Jenkins, *Literature, Religion and Society*, p. 42.
125 Philip Jenkins, 'The Anglican Church and the unity of Britain: the Welsh experience, 1560–1714', in Steven G. Ellis and Sarah Barber (eds), *Conquest and Union: Fashioning a British State, 1485–1725* (London, 1995), pp. 115–38.
126 Linda Colley, *Britons*, especially ch. 1.
127 Some of these European identities are explored further in Claydon, *Europe and the Making of England.*

CHAPTER 5

From periphery to periphery: the Pennants's Jamaican plantations and industrialisation in North Wales, 1771–1812

Trevor Burnard

Little work has been done about Wales and the Americas before 1776 and virtually none on Wales and the Caribbean.[1] The reason is pretty clear. Welsh migration to British America was relatively insignificant and Welsh impact on its culture was insignificant, except in limited cases such as in areas of Pennsylvania where the Welsh presence is marked by a series of Welsh place names, the most famous being the town of Bryn Mawr, home to a leading private women's college. Perhaps 2,000 Welsh Quakers left for America between 1682 and 1700, arriving mostly in Pennsylvania where they purchased 40,000 acres in south-eastern Pennsylvania. Some of the Welsh migrants may have sought to establish a Welsh barony in the area but they soon merged into the general Quaker population. James Horn estimates that only 1 to 2 per cent of indentured servants moving from London to British America between 1689 and 1754 came from Wales and free migration was not especially pronounced. Indeed, it is difficult to know how many Welsh people went to America before the nineteenth century as Welsh migration tended to be indistinguishable from English migration. As Horn argues, 'from similar backgrounds and leaving for similar reasons, Welsh migrants who moved to London, Bristol, Liverpool, and the lesser outports went to America alongside thousands of their English contemporaries and, apart from (in some cases) distinctive surnames, are largely indistinguishable from them'.[2] It was only in the 1790s when harvest failures in Wales encouraged out-migration that there was any sizeable movement of Welsh people to America. Most wanted nothing more than economic opportunity but a few Welsh men and women dreamed utopian dreams and tried to set up a separatist Welsh-speaking homeland in Beulah, Pennsylvania. This settlement quickly failed, meaning that any distinctive Welsh presence in North America was lost.[3]

Welsh migration to the British West Indies was similarly insignificant. Certainly, few Welsh people went to the major island, Jamaica, before 1780. An examination of servant indentures and wills shows that the numbers of people moving to Jamaica from Wales was tiny. The Welsh made up fewer than 2 per cent of European migrants to Jamaica in the late seventeenth century and just over 1 per cent of migrants arriving in the 1750s and 1760s.[4] The low levels of Welsh migration meant that the Welsh did not have the networks that Scots and Londoners, who came in large numbers to the island, used to adapt to new environments.[5] Having said that, letters exchanged between three brothers, Miles, John and Thomas Williams, who had moved to St Catherine Parish between 1779 and 1786 to work as artisans, show how help from countrymen aided adaptation.[6] In a letter written soon after arrival, on 15 February 1779, Miles and John gave word of their safe arrival and rejoiced that they had 'got out of their indentures when we came to the Island which was very lucky for us'. They told their father that they 'have met with a gentleman one David Thomas who has been a great friend to us since we have bin out Employ'd'.[7] David Thomas was a Welshman.

It was different for their brother, Thomas, when he arrived in the island six years later. He had no friends to smooth his way. He hated Jamaica. To his brother in Wales, he wrote:

> The best information I can give you of the nature of this wretched Country is that my health nor spirits will not admit to write more than quarter of an hour at a time. The contry in no way agrees with my Constitution . . . Jamaica is like all other places, pour'd with gold till known then found to be poor nourishment for the body. Me and my brothers work as hard as at Home [with] only this ideal advantage of being plaug'd with ignorant Blackeds that they call [their] stranger Slaves. But in my opinion we are in great Measure Slaves to them. Power and Oppression only are rules here.[8]

Thomas quickly declined into despair, and John wrote in 1795 that 'Brother Thomas has behaved here more like a lunatic than a brother.'[9] Thomas died in 1803 but his brothers persevered, becoming sugar planters and the owners of 240 slaves.

In quantitative terms, therefore, the impact of Welsh people on the Americas and especially upon the British West Indies, the subject of this essay, was not great. Of course, individual Welshmen and women played important roles in West Indian history. One of the most interesting was Teresia Constantia Phillips (1709–65), a beautiful courtesan and 'scandalous woman', born into a well-connected Welsh family and related on the distaff side to the Phillips family, Lords Milton, of Picton

Castle, near Haverfordwest, Pembrokeshire. She eloped with a Jamaican planter to Spanish Town, Jamaica, where she lived between 1738 and 1741 and 1752 and 1765. She earned the reputation as a 'black widow', in honour of the men she seduced and whose fortunes she spent before their convenient deaths. An actress and great beauty, her life highlighted, so Kathleen Wilson tells us, both the advantages and dangers that lay in the way of unconventional female sexuality.[10] Just as scandalous was Sir Thomas Picton (1758–1815), also from Haverfordwest. Picton was a war hero killed at Waterloo and is buried (seemingly the only Welshman to have had this honour) in St Paul's Cathedral. He served as Governor of Trinidad but this office was beset with controversy, leading to his prosecution in December 1803 for the supposed torture of a free mulatto girl.[11]

Most famous of all Welshmen in the Caribbean was the buccaneer and Governor of Jamaica, Sir Henry Morgan (c.1635–88). Richard Dunn, rather dismissively, comments that to have Morgan as the most famous seventeenth-century Englishman (*sic*) in Jamaica 'is rather like having Al Capone as the most famous American of the twentieth century'.[12] The dismissive note is unnecessary. Morgan's exploits caught the imagination of his fellow countrymen and not only made him a fortune but also made him the only recognisable seventeenth-century colonial American besides Captain John Smith and William Penn. He was probably from a minor gentry family (at best) near Cardiff. A protégé of Governor Sir Thomas Modyford, he became Spain's mortal enemy after he sacked various Spanish possessions, most notably Panama in 1671. He became Governor of Jamaica in the mid-1680s before dying of dropsy, aggravated by excessive drinking.[13]

More important than the impact of Wales on the West Indies was the impact of the West Indies on Wales. To an extent, this influence merely shows the extent to which all parts of Britain and all kinds of Britons were implicated in the slave trade and in slavery. Much of Wales lay in the hinterlands of the two provincial towns – Bristol and Liverpool – most involved in the slave-trade. Unsurprisingly, Welsh entrepreneurs participated in the industries that fed into these trades. As an excellent BBC website on slavery and Wales states, during the late eighteenth century the African with his hand stuck in the sugar rollers might have been caught in rollers made out of iron from the Dowlais ironworks in Merthyr Tydfil, and the machete he was about to use to cut off his arm might also have been made from Welsh iron. There was Welsh involvement in every aspect of British slavery.[14] Indeed, some of the most distinguished Britons who lived in Wales, men who do not at first glance seem to be connected with slavery, were beneficiaries of the system. Sir Foster Cunliffe (1755–1834) of

Wrexham, for example, was grandson of the major slave-trader in Liverpool in the first half of the eighteenth century. Even more egregiously, William Ewart Gladstone (1809–98), the British Prime Minister, who lived at Hawarden, Flintshire, derived his family fortune from his father's extensive plantations in Jamaica and Demerara.[15]

What is particularly interesting, however, about the impact of the West Indies on Welsh life is that it is connected more directly than elsewhere in Britain with the process of industrialisation in late eighteenth- and early nineteenth-century Wales. As the BBC website on slavery and Wales points out, men with significant West Indian links were heavily involved in the development of three of the most important nineteenth-century industries in Wales – slate, copper and iron. Two slave-traders – Anthony Bacon and Thomas Coster – pioneered iron and copper production in Wales, with Bacon investing his profits from slave-trading into the Cyfarthfa ironworks in Merthyr, which became the most important centre for gun-founding in Britain. Coster developed the White Rock copper works near Swansea. But the most direct link between the West Indies and Welsh industrialisation came in the massive industrial slate quarry at Port Penhryn, near Bangor in North Wales, developed by Richard Pennant (1737–1808), an extremely wealthy Jamaican slave-owner who came into a large estate in North Wales after his marriage to the heiress Anne Susannah Warburton, the daughter of General Hugh Warburton.

Richard Pennant and the Pennant family of North Wales seem to fit perfectly the thesis put forward by Eric Williams in 1944 in which he argued, inter alia, that the profits of slavery were used to underwrite British industrialisation. Williams argued that slave-trade profits 'provided one of the main streams of accumulation of capital in England which financed the Industrial Revolution'. Indeed, he went so far as to argue that 'the profits from this trade fertilized the entire productive system of the country'.[16] Recent scholars have been sceptical of such sweeping claims, questioning estimates that see slave-trading profits and the inflow of wealth from the Caribbean as especially large. Kenneth Morgan, for example, doubts both whether profits from slavery were particularly large and also questions whether slavery, the slave-trade and sugar produced important multiplier effects. He does believe, however, that slavery and the slave-trade were important in expanding industrial production so as to meet the desire for exports in Africa and the West Indies. While West Indian wealth was not that important in financing industrialisation it did, through the encouragement of exports, help stimulate the British economy.[17]

Nevertheless, if Williams's argument does not work in the generality of cases (money from slavery and the slave-trade, either earned in Britain or brought back to Britain from the West Indies, tended to be spent in conspicuous consumption and in gaining political influence rather than in industry),[18] it might work for specific examples. One such example was the Pennant family's development of the slate industry in North Wales. Richard Pennant, the first Pennant to own the vast Penrhyn estates of North Wales, fits Williams's idea of a slave-owner turned industrialist. He and his kinsman, George Hay Dawkins-Pennant (1763–1840), who inherited the Penrhyn estate after Richard's death, parlayed the wealth from 'valuable Jamaican estates' into a transformation of the large slate holdings and mineral deposits of North Wales into productive industrial wealth. Richard Pennant was especially visionary in transforming his estates into an integrated industrial slate quarry through building road and rail links that connected the quarry to Port Penhryn, built at the mouth of the River Cegin in 1790. From this port, the Pennants shipped slate throughout the world.[19]

The remainder of this essay examines the contribution that Jamaican wealth made to the realisation of the Pennant dreams. The Pennant experience in Jamaica and North Wales tells two stories. First, it shows how wealth could be made in the colonies through a combination of hard work, luck and demographic fortune. Second, it illustrates the contributions that colonial money made to British economic development, especially in the peripheries. The Pennants made money in one periphery of empire – eighteenth-century Jamaica – and spent it in another periphery – North Wales. Fortunately, the Pennants kept abundant records of both processes. These records, not yet fully catalogued, reside at Bangor University Archives.[20] They form a particularly fine example of how a great Jamaican estate was formed and how it was managed during the eighteenth century. These records are the most informative records about life in Jamaica kept in Wales, with the possible exception of the papers of Nathaniel Phillips, a Jamaican merchant and planter who from 1793 was proprietor of Slebech estate, Pembrokeshire. This essay focuses on the Pennants rather than the Phillips, partly because the history of the Phillips family have been well covered by Clare Taylor in a series of articles,[21] and more particularly because the development of the Penryhn properties into large-scale industrial enterprises has greater resonance to larger issues of the relationship between the economic development of industrial Wales and the exploitation of resources and people in the British Empire.[22]

The first Pennant to arrive in Jamaica was Giffard Pennant (d. 1676), the son of Henry Pennant from Holywell, Flintshire. Giffard arrived very early in the English history of Jamaica, within ten years of the conquest from the Spanish. He must have come as a free settler and with some wealth as he was able to begin buying land as early as 1665. Between 1665 and his death in 1676 he patented and bought 7,327 acres in central Jamaica, 5,800 acres in Clarendon Parish, and 1,500 acres in the south-western parish of St Elizabeth. This land formed the basis of the Pennant holdings. Little is known about Giffard, except that his economic success was matched by political achievements. He died as an assemblyman, leaving an undeveloped but potentially very valuable estate to his sole surviving son, Edward. His personal estate was valued at a healthy £2,048 sterling, of which £1,082 was made up of slaves. He owned fifty-nine slaves – twenty-seven men, twenty-six women and six children – making him one of the larger slave-holders whose estate was inventoried in the 1670s.[23]

Edward Pennant (1672–1736) was a native-born Jamaican who combined the advantages of a good inheritance and easy access to advantageous political offices with a longevity remarkable in a country notorious for the brevity of white lives.[24] He consolidated Giffard's successes and transformed the Pennant properties into large-scale integrated plantations producing great quantities of sugar and other crops through the exploitation of a very sizeable labour force of enslaved Africans. Only a small number of records of Edward's activities survive but they give us a good glimpse into how a major Jamaican estate was built in the period after initial English settlement.[25] Chief Justice of Jamaica from 1707 until his death and, like his father, an assemblyman and island councillor, Edward was one of the most powerful and wealthy men in the island during a phase of aggressive expansion. His lands at death amounted to 8,365 acres in the contiguous southern and central parishes of Clarendon, St Elizabeth and Westmoreland. Most of his land came from inheritance from his father but Edward also participated in the Jamaican land market, buying Kupius estate in 1719, Coates estate in 1721, and 1,400 acres in Westmoreland and Clarendon in 1724–26. By his death, Edward was a very wealthy man. As well as his extensive landed estate, he had personal property of £29,048 sterling.[26]

Crucial to this wealth were slaves. Edward became one of the most substantial slave-owners in British America, owning at his death 610 slaves, which placed him among the ten largest slave-holders in the second quarter of the eighteenth century. Of these enslaved people, 271 were adult men, 252 were women, 38 were boys, 19 were girls, while 30 were listed as being children. The total value of his enslaved property was £15,538 or 52 per cent of his non-landed wealth. Slaves were the single biggest element of Edward's wealth, outstripping considerably the £6,093 that he was owed in debts. These enslaved people worked mostly in sugar. Some worked on the cattle-pens that provided livestock for sugar mills while others were probably tradesmen or domestics. Edward's otherwise detailed inventory unfortunately does not list occupations or ethnicity or family groupings so it is difficult to ascertain precisely what his slaves did. It does, however, show the prices of slaves carefully attached to the name of each enslaved person.[27]

The wealth that Edward accumulated enabled his three sons, Samuel (1709–50), John (c.1711–81) and Henry (1713–82) to be educated in England and, after each briefly returned to Jamaica in the 1730s, to settle in England and set up successful mercantile careers in the West Indian consignment trade. The eldest, Samuel, did best, becoming Lord Mayor of London in 1749 and receiving a knighthood. The second son, John, father of Richard, also became prosperous. He established himself as a merchant in Liverpool from around 1739 and did not, it seems, return to Jamaica again. To his large inheritance was added an advantageous marriage. In 1734 he married Bonella, the fourteen-year-old heiress of Joseph Hodges, a planter of Westmoreland Parish who had died in 1721. Bonella brought with her land in Westmoreland and a dowry reputed to be £10,000 Jamaica currency (£7,143 sterling). The dowry was useful; the land less immediately valuable. With abundant land elsewhere to cultivate, the Hodges' land in Westmoreland was not developed into a sugar plantation for over fifty years, laying ruinate (or uncultivated). It was a common complaint among Jamaicans that absentee planters left land fallow, to the detriment of the development of the island, either to benefit from rising land prices or to enable them to produce low-cost sugar through concentrating production in a small area, or even to limit the number of planters and their output of sugar, thus raising prices in Britain.[28]

Sir Samuel Pennant and Henry Pennant died without heirs, leaving the Pennant properties to be once again consolidated under a single heir, John's son, Richard, born in Jamaica in 1737 but brought up from 1739 in England. It does not appear that Richard spent any time in Jamaica as an adult. Unlike his even wealthier contemporary, William Beckford II (1760–1844), the dissolute author of *Vathek*, and heir to the vast Beckford estates of his father William Beckford (1709–70), Lord Mayor of London, Richard was more than just a recipient of Jamaican monies. He kept a close eye on the management of his Jamaican estates, which may be one reason why, unlike the properties of William Beckford II, they produced large profits over a considerable period of time that were then ploughed into the slate industry in North Wales.[29] As part of the 'Jamaican cousinage', a group of loosely allied well-born absentees who became parliamentarians, Richard became, aged twenty-four, MP for the Beckford sinecure of

Petersfield in Hampshire. He was MP for Liverpool from 1767 to 1780 and again from 1784 to 1790, during which time he was a prominent anti-abolitionist. In recognition of his political prominence and great wealth he was made an Irish peer in 1783 as Lord Penrhyn. In 1785, he bought from Sir George Yonge (1731–1812) the moiety of the Penryhn estates that he had not inherited in 1771 through his wife, thus reuniting a property that had been split into several hands following the death without male heirs of Sir Griffith Williams in 1684.[30]

Richard Pennant was a fortunate heir. He inherited the bulk of the Jamaican properties from his uncle, Samuel, while an adolescent, giving him a substantial income from the early 1750s. In his marriage settlement, it was noted that his Jamaican properties had been producing on average £6,400 per annum 'or upwards' for the previous ten years.[31] These were good times to own unencumbered Jamaican sugar properties, and Pennant's West Indian debts were small. Following the peace of Aix-la-Chapelle in 1748, Jamaica had entered into a prolonged period of growth and prosperity that Richard Pares has termed 'the silver age' of sugar (differentiating it from the 'golden age' of plantation expansion in Barbados in the mid-seventeenth century). Settlement proceeded apace in the frontier regions of Jamaica as sugar prices recovered from decades of depression. The numbers of Africans shipped to Jamaica increased dramatically, with 270,150 Africans arriving in the island between 1750 and 1775 compared with 186,500 arriving in the previous quarter century, while the proportion of Africans transshipped to Spanish America declined dramatically, from 42.7 per cent in the 1720s to 13.8 per cent in the 1760s. Slave prices and real estate values rocketed, making both forms of property valuable forms of investment as well as necessary for production. Estates tripled in value in this period. Their value was underpinned by rapid expansion in both slave numbers and commodity production. The number of slaves in Jamaica increased from approximately 113,416 in 1739 to 228,571 in 1775. Sugar production leaped from 205,000 cwt in 1745 to 953,800 cwt in 1775, reaching a peak for the period before the American Revolution at 1,017,100 cwt in 1773. The West Indies became a prime area for British mercantile investment, as merchants sought quick profits both in Jamaica and also in the rapidly developing areas of the Ceded Islands (Islands in the Lesser Antilles handed over to Britain by France as a result of the Seven Years' War). Commercial optimism was aided by transformations in West Indian trading operations as the consignment system, in which large planters shipped their crops direct to London commission houses offering attractive credit facilities, rather than selling locally to Jamaican merchants, took increasing hold from mid-century. The profits from sugar made Jamaica very wealthy. As early as 1748, it was Britain's wealthiest American colony, with annual produce and foreign trade worth £1,700,000, second only in its value to the British Crown, in the view of an experienced observer, Robert Dinwiddie, to the New England and Nova Scotian region, which had trade worth £1,850,000. The physical wealth of the island was in the region of £28,000,000, approximately ten per cent of the wealth of England and Wales and over a quarter the wealth of the thirteen colonies that rebelled in 1776. To get some perspective on what this wealth means, it was probably equivalent to the wealth of Yorkshire and probably a good deal more than the wealth of Wales. It was almost exactly equal to one quarter of the national income of England in 1779.[32]

Richard Pennant owned four major sugar properties – Denbigh, which was divided into an 'Old' and a 'New' plantation (it reverted to one plantation in 1807), Thomas River and Kupius estate. In addition, he ran two pens,[33] Coates Pen and Bullards' Pen. These properties were in Clarendon Parish, bordering on the upper reaches of the Rio Minho River. The river's interior basin was a centre of sugar planting from the seventeenth century, outposts of slave communities in a relatively thinly populated area. After the death of his father in 1781, he came into possession of King's Valley estate in Westmoreland Parish. Large sugar plantations in the Jamaican interior impressed contemporary writers as being lonely and isolated places. Labour on these estates may have been particularly onerous, as these estates were 'planting' estates rather than 'ratooning' or 'dry-weather' estates. On 'planting' estates, new canes had to be planted every year, a very intensive task requiring slaves to dig cane holes. 'Planting' estates often required large inputs of additional labour, which may explain the sums expended by Pennant's attorney, John Shickle, on hiring slave labour in the 1780s.

The profits made from these properties were substantial, and in 1788 Richard cleared over £30,000 from rum and sugar. After the deduction of expenses (which were considerable that year, as Richard needed to restock the plantation and make necessary repairs after years of poor profits), this left him with £18,502 in clear profit. Profits in 1792 were even greater. Gross profit from sugar and rum were £27,555 but expenses were small and net profit was an impressive £23,382. Richard's income was over double the average annual income of a peer and close to the average income in the upper reaches of the aristocracy. As a supplement to an aristocratic English estate the Pennant Jamaican fortune was substantial. As late as 1775, for example, the Bloomsbury estate in London of the Russells, Dukes of Bedford, was bringing in just £9,000 per annum.[34]

Table 5.1 *Production of sugar and rum at Denbigh estates, 1741–1812*

Year	Sugar hogsheads	Sugar tierces	Sugar pounds	Rum puncheons	Rum gallons	Total value £ sterling
1741	183	37	327,318	42	4,452	6,991
1753	137	36	267,725	71	7,171	6,757
1781	258	22	442,081	86	9,890	10,573
1784	82	127	286,198	71	8,165	5,608
1785	154	144	422,756	82	9,430	8,448
1788	326	170	731,240	146	16,790	14,747
1812	347	0	688,101	137	15,755	10,872

Note: The measurement of hogsheads, tierces and puncheons – the standard measures used for describing the weights of sugar and rum – was complex. A hogshead was meant to weigh 16 cwt but managers commonly consigned hogsheads lower than this in order to mask the true size of the crop. London grocers normally discounted for this as well as making allowance for 'tare' (sugar gaining weight during the passage to Britain because of moisture seeping into the casks) and 'wastage' (leakage during the passage to Britain). Rum was usually shipped in puncheons and was weighed in gallons. Sugar went in hogsheads and tierces and was measured in pounds. For estimating gallons and pounds, I have used the figures derived by David Ryden from careful observations in Jamaican archives. For prices current in London for sugar and rum, I have used Ryden and estimates by Richard B. Sheridan. See David Ryden, 'Producing a peculiar commodity: Jamaican sugar production, slave life, and planter profits on the eve of abolition, 1750–1807' (unpublished PhD thesis, University of Minnesota, 1999), pp. 279–82, 299–302; and Richard B. Sheridan, *Sugar and Slavery: An Economic History of the British West Indies, 1623–1775* (Bridgetown, 1974), pp. 496–7. For general issues of measurement, see John J. McCusker, 'Weights and measures in the colonial sugar trade: the gallon and the pound and their international equivalents', *William and Mary Quarterly*, 3rd ser., 30 (1973), 599–624, and S. D. Smith, *Slavery, Family and Gentry Capitalism in the British Atlantic: The World of the Lascelles, 1648–1834* (Cambridge, 2006), p. 249.
Source: Bangor University Archives, Penrhyn MSS.

If the profits were substantial, they were also variable. Table 5.1 shows the amount of production and profits gained at Richard's principal estate, Denbigh. When he took over in the early 1750s, profits were relatively low. They increased gradually until by 1788, Richard was clearing nearly £15,000 from Denbigh. Yet gradual upward growth hides several sharp decreases in plantation profitability. For example, 1784 was a bad year, with the number of hogsheads produced going under 100 and annual gross profits reaching levels even lower better than in 1741 and 1753. Profits from the crop made in 1784 were 53 per cent of the profits made four years earlier and 38 per cent of what they were three years later.

Table 5.2 *Sugar and rum production on Richard Pennant's Jamaican estates, 1781–92*

	1781	1782	1783	1784	1785	1786	1787	1788	1789	1790	1791	1792
Sugar (hogsheads)	645	663	493	424	454	270	298	784	592	571	394	582
Sugar (tierces)	146	198	103	367	188	154	280	188	189	88	161	207
Sugar (lbs × 1000)	1,216	1,308	919	1,128	959	783	981	1,490	1,183	1,107	874	1,257
Rum (puncheons)	268	334	174	220	238	206	262	349	278	240	202	206
Rum (gallons × 1000)	31	83	20	25	27	24	30	40	22	28	23	24

Source: Bangor University Archives, Penrhyn MSS.

Table 5.3 *Gross profits from sugar and rum on Richard Pennant's Jamaican estates, 1781–91 (£s)*

	1781	1782	1783	1784	1785	1786	1787	1788	1789	1790	1791
Sugar	26,113	25,865	15,215	19,450	17,371	15,395	17,692	27,320	19,997	19,116	17,820
Rum	3,344	4,244	1,691	2,087	2,299	1,860	2,199	3,211	2,590	2,172	2,132
Total	29,547	29,929	16,906	21,537	19,761	17,255	19,891	30,531	22,587	21,289	19,952

Source: Bangor University Archives, Penrhyn MSS.

If the general trend was upwards, variations from year to year could be considerable, as can be seen in Tables 5.2 and 5.3, which detail production and profitability over a concentrated period in the 1780s and early 1790s. Production varied from year to year, with the high-producing 1781 and 1782 crops being followed by a series of very poor harvests from 1783 to 1787. Production was especially poor in 1783 and 1786, with annual receipts being 55–57 per cent of the peak year of production, 1788, and 69–71 per cent of the averaged receipts for five years between 1788 and 1792. Sugar production was always an uncertain business. But even during the worst years of the mid-1780s, receipts probably matched those of the more prosperous 1770s, reflecting the expanded size of the estate after 1781 and the growing efficiency of sugar and rum cultivation during and after the American Revolution.[35] Lord Penrhyn was as notable an agricultural innovator in Jamaica as he was an industrial pioneer in North Wales. He was one of the first proprietors to introduce steam, initially to pump water for irrigation and by 1806 to crush canes.[36] Moreover, during a dread decade where Jamaica was buffeted by the collapse of trade between Jamaica and British North America and by a series of destructive hurricanes, what is noteworthy is that there were several years of boom production on the Pennant estates, most notably in 1788 but also in 1781 and 1782.[37] By the 1790s, the profitability of the Pennant estates was very strong, with annual net profits reaching over £20,000 per annum, as Table 5.4 shows. That profitability was sustained until after Richard's death in 1808. The accounts for 1811 and 1812, listed in Tables 5.5 and 5.6, indicate that the abolition of the slave-trade in the year before Richard's death did not dent profitability. Indeed, gross profits of £33,977 in 1811 and £32,576 in 1812 were higher than any gross profits achieved between 1781 and 1792. By then production was concentrated on three large estates: the consolidated Denbigh estate, which had 350 enslaved persons in 1808, Thomas River, with 234 enslaved people, and Kupius, with 180 slaves.

These profits were ample. A proportion was reinvested into improving Richard's Jamaica estates, as the transition to steam showed. Nevertheless, the Pennants were content to maintain the sustainability and profitability of the Jamaican plantations rather than to increase their investment and involvement in the Jamaican economy. There were no major new acquisitions of land in Jamaica after the purchase of 1,100 acres in Clarendon in 1726. Instead, money was spent on building slate quarries in Wales. It is significant that on gaining his inheritance from his father after his father's death in 1781, Richard immediately forced individual slate producers off his Caernarvonshire land and took over himself the working of slates, doing so on an

Table 5.4 *Net profits from Richard Pennant's Jamaican estates, 1771–92 (£s)*

Year	Profit	Year	Profit
1771	9,886	1779	21,141
1772	15,740	1781	18,797
1773	14,645	1788	18,502
1774	12,705	1789	19,080
1775	13,679	1790	19,292
1776	10,292	1791	19,344
1777	10,213	1792	23,382

Source: Bangor University Archives, Penrhyn MSS.

Table 5.5 *Produce and gross profits from George Hay Dawkins Pennant's Jamaican estates, 1811*

Property	Sugar (hogsheads)	Sugar (profit in £s)	Rum (puncheons)	Rum (profit in £s)	Total profit (£s)
Denbigh	309	12,039	140	3,419	15,458
Thomas River	228	9,261	101	2,336	11,597
Kupius	141	5,467	64	1,455	6,922
Total	678	26,767	305	7,210	33,977

Source: Bangor University Archives, Penrhyn MSS.

Table 5.6 *Produce and gross profits from George Hay Dawkins Pennant's Jamaican estates, 1812*

Property	Sugar (hogsheads)	Sugar (profit in £s)	Rum (puncheons)	Rum (profit in £s)	Total profit (£s)
Denbigh	347	11,979	137	3,671	15,650
Thomas River	135	6,429	70	1,878	8,307
Kupius	164	6,910	64	1,709	8,619
Total	646	25,318	271	7,258	32,576

Source: Bangor University Archives, Penrhyn MSS.

industrial scale. In 1782, he opened a new quarry at Caebrachycafn near Bethesda. Within ten years it had grown to resemble in its size, its labour force and its managerial organisation and deployment of labour the agricultural 'factories in the field' that were large integrated sugar plantations. By 1792, the Penrhyn quarry employed 500 men, living in abject conditions and bunking down in quarry barracks that were similar in form to slave housing. These men produced 15,000 tons of slate per annum.[38]

Both the slate industry and sugar production relied upon the efficient deployment of labour and upon effective management techniques. Labour on plantations took two forms. First, it required a small cadre of experienced and long-serving white employees, the most important, in the case of estates with owners resident in Britain, being the attorney. Second, it required a labour force of enslaved Africans. On a large integrated sugar plantation, the numbers of slaves required for greatest efficiency was between 150 and 250.[39]

White labour was not numerous but very important in ensuring the smooth running of an estate. The quality of white managers on sugar estates has had a mixed press over the years. Contemporaries were contemptuous of the whole range of white managers – attorneys, overseers, bookkeepers – who worked for non-resident planters, convinced that they were lazy, avaricious and incompetent. Much of this argument can be dismissed as the typical complaints of an owner class not as involved in the management of their properties as they might have been.

Yet if there was any group of whites involved in Jamaican plantation agriculture which tended to short-termism and incompetence, it was that of non-resident owners. The contemporary historian Edward Long, a careful observer of Jamaican affairs, even if he has to be read with due attention to his prejudices, was convinced that resident planters were necessary to run an estate properly: 'The residence of the planter necessarily occasioned a better attention to the management of his estate, the cultivation of more land, the increase of produce, and greater security of property in general.'[40] Early twentieth-century historians, who thought absentee landlordism to be 'the curse of the Caribbean' and a management form that was inherently conservative and short-termist, followed Long's critique. Lowell Ragatz, for example, thought that on non-resident estates 'all change was scoffed at while time-hallowed custom was obdurately followed'.[41]

But recent work has challenged such views – views, moreover, which are rooted in assumptions drawn not just from Caribbean but also from Irish history in which it is axiomatic 'that absenteeism implies improvidence and neglect'.[42] The developing consensus is, first, that absenteeism was not as extensive before the early nineteenth century as usually considered; second, that its effects were not as deleterious as Long and other eighteenth-century commentators opined; and, third, that the people chosen to run estates in the absence of the owner were often highly skilled, practically experienced, well-regarded and remarkably modern in their management techniques. As Barry Higman concludes about absenteeism, in a book that includes a compelling analysis of the role of attorneys on plantations 'Rather than millstones around the necks of proprietors, the attorneys were in large part their saviours. It was the management practised by the attorneys that squeezed the maximum possible product from the system and the people it oppressed.'[43] Whites further down the occupational scale may have been better prepared for the demands of slave supervision and sugar cultivation than is usually presented in the literature, where historians often take at face value derogatory and class-inflected descriptions of poorer whites made by nineteenth-century observers. Managing slaves was hard work and took a hard man to do it. If that man proved to be effective in keeping slaves under control and the estate functioning, then he would be well rewarded and able to pick whatever job he chose.[44]

Richard's principal contact in Jamaica was his attorney. From 1754 until his death from fever, the attorney was John Shickle (1713–82), a very wealthy Clarendon proprietor who at his death was worth nearly £40,000 sterling and was the owner of a slave force of 502. Shickle was one of the largest slave-owners in Jamaica and a respected and skilled manager.[45] Shickle also worked for Richard's father, John, who, in 1781, as Shickle lay ill, appointed Alexander Falconer and William Atherton jointly to act for his Clarendon properties in the event of Shickle dying. When Shickle did die, a few months after the death of John Pennant, Alexander Falconer took over all of Shickle's Pennant responsibilities. Falconer served as attorney for the next twenty years. Richard Pennant was fortunate to have continuity in management, with two attorneys in half a century of ownership, and fortunate in the men he appointed to the job. Both Shickle and Falconer kept excellent accounts, had good knowledge of local conditions and communicated regularly with an owner who kept a careful watch on his Jamaican interests.[46] The salaries they received were very large, making it a desirable avocation for a resident planter. In 1785, for example, Alexander Falconer received £969 in a year of low profits. In 1812, the attorney claimed £1,738. These were gross rather than net sums, as an attorney needed to pay for a variety of plantation expenses, but they meant that an attorney could become, if not already wealthy, rich himself.[47]

The principal problem that the Pennants faced in Jamaica was finding sufficient labour, both white and black. White mortality was so high that it was only through considerable migration that population numbers were maintained. The white population barely increased in number during the eighteenth century, reaching no more than around 15,000 and perhaps 16,750 by the end of slavery.[48] Black mortality was not as pronounced but it was still dire, with deaths greatly exceeding births before 1834, and mortality rates were especially high and fertility rates especially low before the abolitionist onslaught against the slave-trade in the 1780s. It was only massive importation of Africans through the slave-trade that allowed overall numbers to grow. Such forced migration was not possible with whites. Jamaican leaders fretted about the low levels of white population increase and tried to promote schemes for white settlement.[49] But these schemes did not lead to more than a few hundred migrants from Britain moving to Jamaica each year. The Pennants tried to encourage white migration. In 1774, for example, they sponsored the voyages of three husbandmen to Clarendon, agreeing to pay them salaries for three years' indenture of between £20 and £25 per annum.[50]

The result was that the white workforce on the Pennant estates was always small. In 1783, the Pennant accounts note nineteen white employees on five properties (no records exist for newly acquired King's Valley). Each estate had four employees (except for Kupuis, which had three) headed by an overseer and accompanied by one or two bookkeepers, a tradesman or a pen-keeper. It meant that slaves heavily outnumbered white managers: ratios ranged from one employee to sixty-six slaves on Kupuis estate to one to forty-nine slaves on Coates Pen. The small number of whites meant that management was in part delegated to slave-drivers, the hinge of the plantation system, responsible for work and discipline within slave forces. There were sixteen drivers on Richard's estates in 1781. Whites were well compensated for their troubles. John Bell, overseer on Denbigh received £200 currency while Joseph Carruthers, overseer on Thomas River, made £160 currency. Six men were given salaries, not including room and board, of over £100 each. In 1783, salaries amounted to £1,117 sterling. With the addition of King's Valley to the Pennant property portfolio, plantation salaries increased to £1,455 in 1785. Fees paid to doctors and tradesmen need to be added to this figure, making expenditure in 1785 on white labour £1,878.[51]

White managers had two tasks. First, they had to maximise production while preserving the viability of the estate for the future. Sugar and rum production was a complex business requiring skill and close attention to details. The reason attorneys and overseers received such good wages was in part because results varied considerably on plantations, depending on the abilities of managers. An analysis of the productivity of sugar estates in St Andrew Parish in 1753 indicates that the amount of sugar produced per slave varied wildly from estate to estate.[52] Second, they had to manage a large, traumatised enslaved population, working on isolated estates, ripped from their families and familiar environment in Africa and forced, usually reluctantly, to work in back-breaking labour making sugar and rum.[53]

Table 5.7 *Richard Pennant's slave force, 1775–85*

Property	1775	1776	1780	1781	1782	1783	1784	1785
Denbigh (Old)	212	210	207	226	228	234	237	231
Denbigh (New)	196	191	186	183	202	205	207	212
Thomas River	225	253	254	251	254	249	244	247
Coates	185	178	180	187	197	195	197	202
King's Valley[a]	–	–	–	–	161	161	176	176
Kupuis	198	190	190	189	189	197	191	189
Total	1,016	1,022	1,017	1,036	1,231	1,241	1,252	1,257

Note: [a] The Pennants did not acquire King's Valley until 1781, explaining the absence of data before then.
Source: Bangor University Archives, Penrhyn MSS.

Richard Pennant and his kinsman George Hay Dawkins Pennant were among the most substantial slave-owners in Jamaica, as Table 5.7 reveals. Richard had increased the slave force inherited from his grandfather in 1736 and his uncle in 1750 from 610 slaves to 1,036 in 1775. After his father's death in 1781, his slave force increased again, amounting to 1,231 enslaved persons in 1782 and peaked at 1,264 slaves in 1788 (see Table 5.8). In short, the Pennant slave force doubled in fifty years. This doubling took place in extremely adverse circumstances, as what little evidence we have of slave demography from the second and third quarters of the eighteenth century suggests that natural reproduction rates were especially poor in this period.[54]

How Richard acquired additional slaves to increase substantially his slave force is not noted in the records. It must have involved, however, large outlays in the internal slave-trade or in the transatlantic slave-trade. The result would have been a slave force that was largely African. Even on long-established plantations, death rates meant that the slave force had to be constantly replenished from Africa. On Mesopotamia plantation in Westmoreland and on Golden Grove plantation in St Thomas in the east, large plantations slightly smaller in size than the two Denbigh plantations, attorneys were constantly purchasing 'new Negroes'. On Mesopotamia, 159 slaves were purchased between 1763 and 1789 (or 5.9 per annum) to maintain a population of 278 slaves. On Golden Grove, 251 slaves were bought between 1765 and 1794 (or 8.4 per annum) to maintain a population of 378 slaves.[55] The importation of large numbers of Africans kept up numbers but also aggravated problems of fertility and mortality. The trauma of the Middle Passage and slaves' experience during the 'seasoning' period – the first three or four months after arrival – as well as the intensity of the plantation regime exposed Africans to great risk of disease, infertility and death.[56]

Table 5.8 *Richard Pennant's slave force, 1786–1808*

Property	1786	1787	1788	1789	1790	1791	1792	1793	1800	1808
Denbigh (Old)	223	227	221	217	217	207	203	200	190	350
Denbigh (New)	214	214	210	211	203	208	206	206	201	–
Thomas River	245	242	241	239	234	222	238	236	253	234
Coates	202	197	201	208	212	209	205	207	191	222
King's Valley	169	165	210	198	198	172	202	207	204	–
Kupius	186	187	181	176	182	198	172	168	130	180
Pennants	–	–	–	–	–	–	–	–	–	225
Total	1,239	1,232	1,264	1,249	1,246	1,216	1,226	1,224	1,169	1,211

Note: By 1808 the two Denbigh plantations had been combined into one plantation. Pennants has no information recorded for it before 1808 because it did not replace King's Valley until that date.
Source: Bangor University Archives, Penrhyn MSS.

Given that the Pennant properties had between three and four times as many slaves in total as either of these plantations, and given that it appears that numbers increased considerably over time, slave purchases must have been at least twenty per annum, perhaps double that. Certainly, Richard bought heavily in the Jamaican slave market in the 1770s and 1780s. In 1772, John Shickle advised Richard that despite there being 'No such thing as Credit for Negroes' (meaning he had to pay cash or agree to pay back credit very quickly) he had bought 'six men for Kupius and six for Denbigh and 10 boys and girls for Kupius and 10 for Denbigh and I must buy six more for each and six for Thomas River'. In short, he had bought thirty-two Africans and intended to buy twelve more in a single year, at £65 for men and £58 for boys and girls, making an outlay of £1,943 sterling. More slaves than usual were bought in 1772 than was possible during the years of the American Revolution and the tough times of the hurricane-affected mid-1780s. But by the late 1780s, Richard was expending large sums in the purchase of 'new Negroes' with forty-seven bought in 1788 and thirty-eight in 1793.

These purchases maintained slave numbers but were not sufficient to meet labour needs entirely. In the mid-1780s, Alexander Falconer hired many slaves from neighbouring slave-owners to make up for a slave force that was deficient in the numbers of healthy slaves. Between 1782 and 1790, he spent an average of £342 sterling per annum on hired slave labour. On 27 January 1783, he concluded a letter advising Richard to settle a new cattle-pen, using hired slaves from a 'jobber' to 'plant Guiney grass and fence in some of the Savannah land', with a plea that Richard needed to buy 'twenty Negroes'. Labour was a continual problem. Falconer explained to his employer in the same 1783 letter that Richard's hope of putting more land into sugar production was hampered by a declining slave force because 'nothing can be done without Negroes', even though he had sufficient land to employ a further '300 Negroes'. But, Falconer advised, 'we cannot think of finding any Negroes there while we can Imploy them as Well or better at or near us'.[57]

The difficulty for planters was that the sugar regime was so arduous that slave life expectancy was very low, morbidity was chronic and fertility was too low for natural reproductive growth. Table 5.9 shows the gap between fertility and mortality in 1776. From a slave force of 1,022, 24 children were produced, making a birth rate of 23 per 1,000. At the same time, 43 slaves died, making a death rate of 42 per 1,000. Morbidity was also very high: in 1781 336 of 1,017 enslaved persons were sickly, 'indifferent' or superannuated. There is no data on ages that enables fertility rates for women of childbearing age to

Table 5.9 *Natural increase and decrease on Richard Pennant's estates, 1776*

Plantation	Births	Deaths
Denbigh Old	9	11
Denbigh New	4	9
Thomas River	7	8
Kupuis	3	10
Coates	1	5
Total	24	43

Source: Bangor University Archives, Penrhyn MSS.

be worked out, but the birth and death rates for the general population are so close to those recorded for York estate in the north-west of Jamaica between 1776 and 1783 (26 per 1,000 birth rate and 44 per 1,000 death rate) that it is possible to speculate that the fertility rate of 108 births per 1,000 women aged between 15 and 44 was replicated on the Pennant estates.[58] As on other Jamaican estates in the mid- to late eighteenth century, the Pennant properties fell well short of sustaining themselves demographically.[59]

Nevertheless, while the Atlantic slave-trade flourished the inevitable tendency of slave forces to decline and for workers in sugar to suffer extraordinary rates of sickness and accident was not a major problem for proprietors. Preferring to buy rather than breed, they relied on having a slave force heavily oriented towards young adults in their twenties and thirties who could be worked very hard and then discarded when they sickened and died. Population pyramids of slave forces on eighteenth-century Jamaican estates, such as York estate and Mesopotamia, show that over two-thirds of slaves were aged between fourteen and forty-five, with a concentration in the mid-twenties.[60] The occupational distribution on the Pennant properties in 1781 set out in Table 5.10 shows a slave population that had a large concentration of slaves in working occupations, suggesting a population heavily oriented towards prime-age adults. The abolition of the slave-trade in 1807 forced Richard to rethink. He started to press his attorneys to develop pro-natalist policies in order to increase the proportion of children in the population. A new attorney, Rowland William Fearon, appointed in 1805, drew Richard's attention to the shameful neglect of the condition of pregnant women by white managers and 'adopted My Lord the same mode of management on your Estates as I have on my own, which is, as soon as I see a woman slave Pregnant, she ceases from the hardest labour of the Field and [is] put to light work'. He also gave women monetary rewards for children

Table 5.10 *Occupational distribution of slave forces on Richard Pennant's Jamaican estates, 1781 and 1808*

Occupation	No. 1781	% 1781	No. 1808	% 1808
Drivers	16	1.7	14	1.4
Field men	192	20.1	144	14.8
Field women	230	24.1	269	27.6
Livestock	83	8.7	141	14.5
Tradesmen	95	9.9	107	11.0
Domestics	45	4.7	23	2.4
Invalids	98	10.3	63	6.5
Grass gang	93	9.7	95	9.7
Children	104	10.9	117	12.0
Agriculture	614	64.2	663	68.1
All working	754	78.9	793	81.5

NB Not all slaves were assigned an occupation: thus these figures do not tally with those given in Tables 5.7 and 5.8.
Source: Bangor University Archives, Penrhyn MSS.

surviving to one month old. His successor as attorneys, Samuel Jefferies, David Ewart and John Shand, all wrote about how they were 'giving great encouragement to Breeding' and holding out 'several rewards to the Women, which few others do'.

It did not work. Numbers were declining by 1814, as John Shand lamented. He argued that he had kept the decrease small, 'Your people are worked moderately, have abundance of food and are treated with care and kindness. I think they ought to keep up their numbers.' But at the moment 'the balance does not turn the other way and we cannot boast of a regular increase, however small'. Managers wanting to aid reproduction competed against a stronger imperative: maintaining production. Women may have been given small treats when falling pregnant but that was not enough to compensate for a work regime that was getting harder rather than easier. In the interests of efficiency, more and more men were moved out of field-work into caring after livestock and into trades. Women took their place. By 1808, 84 per cent of working females worked in the field as opposed to 46 per cent of working males. Women comprised 62 per cent of the agricultural workforce. Ultimately, the demands of sugar and rum limited female fertility.[61]

John Shand may have thought that the Pennant slaves were 'treated with care and kindness' in 1814. 'Care and kindness' was not noticeable prior to 1800 in the sparse records that refer to slave treatment. Hints of slavery's brutality can be seen in notations of how slaves died in 1776. In addition to nine infant deaths, eleven deaths from old age and eight deaths from dropsy, Quaw died 'from a kick from a young steer' while Cambridge and an unnamed slave were both killed by neighbouring whites when caught thieving from nearby estates. Most chillingly, Marlborough was 'burnt for obia'. Mid-eighteenth-century Jamaican slavery was spectacularly violent, leading to a slave population that was traumatised and brutalised into submission.[62] Perhaps unsurprisingly many slaves chose to kill themselves rather than suffer further. For instance, suicide was a leading cause of death among Thomas Thistlewood's enslaved charges.[63]

The above analysis of the ways in which the Pennant fortune in North Wales was sustained by Jamaican money seems to confirm the Williams thesis for a small corner of North Wales. But seen from another perspective, the Pennants resemble more gentry capitalists concerned about shoring up their social position, gaining respectability and indulging in conspicuous consumption practices through which they attempted to acquire a false patina of ancient lineage.[64] For families who felt that their nouveaux riches origins and the taint of colonial wealth made them not proper gentry, it was necessary to mask the source of their wealth by pretending through architectural fancies that they were families of ancient heritage and ancient traditions. For the Pennants, this was done through the building of a mock-Norman spectacular, Penrhyn Castle. This strange yet beautiful building, built between 1820 and 1845, when the Jamaican properties were declining and when the wealth of the Pennants had been largely transferred to North Wales, is a neo-Norman castle which hides the slave-derived and industrial origins of the Penrhyn fortune. But Penrhyn Castle is curiously similar in function, if not in form, to the sugar canes and slate quarry that provided the money to build it. It is a disturbing intrusion into a settled landscape of an alien form falsely trying to signify that it was not modern but ancient. By fashioning their house as a neo-Norman fantasy, the Pennants tried to suggest their permanence in a landscape that was being profoundly reshaped by their recent arrival. That they chose a medieval form to express their intentions was common among their particular group. William Beckford chose to use the form of Gothic revival in creating his folly, Fonthill Abbey, in Wiltshire, between 1795 and 1813. He did so in order to suggest that his nouveau riche family had links into the medieval past.[65] If we focus on Penrhyn Castle, then what is revealed is how *arriviste* colonials became British gentlemen. It tells us as much about invented traditions as it does about transitions to industrial capitalism. It also occludes Wales. To build a neo-Norman Castle in a landscape where real castles built by the regal descendants of Norman conquerors of England flourished, and where such castles signified the colonial conquest of Wales by Edward I, had meanings for Welsh miners employed in harsh conditions at the Penrhyn quarry different from those intended by the Pennants in creating their country mansion. Neo-Norman was neo-colonial in Caernarvonshire.

Crucial to Eric Williams's thesis in *Capitalism and Slavery* is that profits from plantation agriculture were invested into the early stages of British industrialisation. Some links can be found. Rose and Stephen Fuller, scions of gentry in Sussex, parlayed some of their Jamaican profits into gun foundries in the Sussex Weald. But usually planter profits went into conspicuous consumption and into agricultural estates. William Beckford, John Tharp of Hanover and the Kingston merchant George Hibbert all invested their money in becoming landed gentlemen in Wiltshire, Cambridgeshire and Buckinghamshire respectively. As Richard Pares acidly noted, 'there seem to have been more Fonthills than factories among them, and more overdrafts and protested bills than either'. Although slavery was important in stimulating demand for manufactures it was relatively unimportant in financing industrialisation. In Patrick O'Brien's words, 'for the economic growth of the core, the periphery was peripheral'.[66]

Such a finding might be disputable for the Penrhyn-controlled corner of North Wales. What needs emphasising is that it was not only Jamaican money that was important in fashioning Pennant industrialisation. Even though Richard Pennant never managed his Jamaican properties directly and probably never met any of his enslaved property, he was an active, committed and involved participant in the management of his large sugar- and rum-producing properties. What he learned from his fifty-year ownership of estates with over 1,000 slaves was how to integrate production efficiently and how to maximise labour productivity. Slave-holders were often denounced as reactionary conservatives in the early nineteenth century, wasteful managers, in Adam Smith's reading, of an economically deficient system.[67] Richard Pennant himself, as MP for Liverpool, was involved in rebutting these assumptions. His most convincing rebuttal was in the transfer of managerial techniques and organisational skills learned from managing a large, complex and labour-intensive agricultural holding into an industrial form that in its harsh treatment of labourers, in its insistence on vertical integration of production and in the paternalistic distance cultivated by owners with workers resembled 'factories in the field'. Richard Pennant brought not just money but also ideas and values from the West Indies to North Wales.

Notes

1 But see A. H. Dodd, *The Character of the Early Welsh Emigration to the United States* (Cardiff, 2nd edn, 1957).

2 James Horn, 'British diaspora: emigration from Britain, 1680–1815', in P. J. Marshall (ed.), *The Oxford History of the British Empire*, vol. 2: *The Eighteenth Century* (Oxford, 1998), pp. 38–9.

3 James T. Lemon, *The Best Poor Man's Country: A Geographical Study of Early Southeastern Pennsylvania* (Baltimore, 1972); H. M. Davies, ' "Very different springs of uneasiness": emigration from Wales to the United States of America', *WHR*, 15 (1991); Gwyn A. Williams, *The Search for Beulah Land: The Welsh and the Atlantic Revolution* (London, 1980).

4 Trevor Burnard, 'European migration to Jamaica, 1655–1780', *William and Mary Quarterly*, 3rd series, 53 (1996), 782.

5 For Scottish and English networks, see Douglas Hamilton, *Scotland, the Caribbean and the Atlantic World, 1750–1820* (Manchester, 2005); David Hancock, *Citizens of the World: London Merchants and the Integration of the British Atlantic Community, 1735–1785* (New York, 1995); and S. D. Smith, *Slavery, Family and Gentry Capitalism in the British Atlantic: The World of the Lascelles, 1648–1834* (Cambridge, 2006). See also Alan Lester, *Imperial Networks: Creating Identities in Nineteenth Century South Africa and Britain* (London and New York, 2001).

6 These were the brothers of Iolo Morganwg (born Edward Williams), the radical Welsh nationalist and anti-slavery advocate, who found what his brothers were doing in Jamaica abhorrent, declaring in 1803: 'May the vast Atlantic ocean swallow up Jamaica and all the other slave trading and slave holding countries before a boy or girl of mine eats a single morsel that would prevent him or her of perishing from hunger, if it is the produce of slavery', Geraint H. Jenkins, Ffion Mair Jones and David Ceri Jones (eds), *The Correspondence of Iolo Morganwg* (3 vols, Cardiff, 2007), vol. 2, p. 537.

7 NLW, Iolo Morganwg MSS 96/8, 120/4.

8 *Ibid.*

9 *Ibid.*

10 Kathleen Wilson, *The Island Race: Englishness, Empire and Gender in the Eighteenth Century* (London and New York, 2003), pp. 129–68.

11 Picton was exonerated in 1806. James Epstein, 'Politics of colonial sensation: the trial of Thomas Picton and the cause of Louisa Calderon', *American Historical Review*, 112 (2007), 712–41.

12 Richard S. Dunn, *Sugar and Slaves: The Rise of the Planter Class in the English West Indies 1624–1713* (Chapel Hill, 1972), p. xv.

13 Nuala Zahedieh, 'Morgan, Sir Henry (c.1635–1688)', *Oxford Dictionary of National Biography* (Oxford, 2004).

14 www.bbc.co.uk/wales/history/sites/slavery/pages/slavery_and_wales.shtml; Chris Evans, *Slave Wales: The Welsh and Atlantic Slavery, 1660–1850* (Cardiff, 2010).

15 Lorena S. Walsh, 'Liverpool's slave trade to the colonial Chesapeake: slaving on the periphery', in David Richardson, Suzanne Schwarz and Anthony Tibbles (eds), *Liverpool and Transatlantic Slavery* (Liverpool, 2007), pp. 102–12; S. G. Checkland, *The Gladstones: A Family Biography, 1764–1851* (Cambridge, 1971).

16 Eric Williams, *Capitalism and Slavery* (Chapel Hill, 1944), pp. 52, 105.

17 For a cogent analysis of the Williams debate, see Kenneth Morgan, *Slavery, Atlantic Trade and the British Economy, 1660–1800* (Cambridge, 2000), and *Slavery and the British Empire: From Africa to America* (Oxford, 2007), pp. 82–3; and Barbara L. Solow, 'Caribbean slavery and British growth: the Eric Williams hypothesis', *Journal of Development Economics*, 17 (1985), 99–115. For an account broadly sympathetic to Williams, see Joseph E. Inikori, *Africans and the Industrial Revolution: A Study in International Trade and Economic Development* (Cambridge, 2002).

18 Hancock, *Citizens of the World.*

19 The Penrhyn properties reached their industrial peak in the late nineteenth century. Despite or perhaps because of the paternalistic management style of George Sholto Gordon Douglas, 2nd Lord Penrhyn, the properties were at the centre of one of the most bitter and prolonged industrial disputes in early twentieth-century Britain from 1900 to 1903. See R. Merfyn Jones, *The North Wales Quarrymen 1874–1922* (Cardiff, 1981); E. H. Douglas-Pennant, 'The second Lord Penrhyn (1836–1907): a study of the political career of the Rt. Hon. George Sholto Gordon Douglas-Pennant, second Baron Penrhyn of Llandegai' (unpublished MPhil thesis, University of Wales (Bangor), 1994).

20 Bangor University Archives, 'The Papers of the Pennant Family and Wicken and Penryhn Estates'.

21 For the Slebech MSS, see B. G. Charles, 'The records of Slebech', *National Library of Wales Journal*, 5 (1947–48), 188–9. For Nathaniel Phillips (d. 1813), see Clare Taylor, 'Aspects of planter society in the British West Indies', *National Library of Wales Journal*, 20 (1977–78), 361–72, and 'The journal of an absentee proprietor: Nathaniel Phillips of Slebech', *Journal of Caribbean History* 18 (1984), 67–82.

22 For articles on the Pennants, see Jean Lindsay, 'The Pennants and Jamaica, 1665–1808. Part I: the growth and organisation of the Pennant estates', *Caernarvonshire Historical Society Transactions*, 43 (1982), 37–82, and 'The Pennants and Jamaica, 1665–1808. Part II: the economic and social development of the Pennant estates in Jamaica', *ibid.*, 44 (1983), 59–93; E. H. Douglas-Pennant, *The Pennants of Penrhyn: A Genealogical History of the Pennant Family of Clarendon, Jamaica, and Penrhyn Castle* (Bethesda, 1982), and 'The Penryhn estate, 1760–1997: the Pennants and the Douglas-Pennants', *Caernarvonshire Historical Society Transactions*, 59 (1998), 35–54; Alistair Hennessy, 'Penrhyn Castle', *History Today*, 45 (1995), 40–5.

23 Jamaica Archives, Spanish Town, IB/1/11/1, Inventories.

24 Trevor Burnard, '"The countrie continues sicklie": white mortality in Jamaica, 1655–1780', *Social History of Medicine*, 12 (1999), 45–72.

25 The best description of this process is Michael Craton and James Walvin, *A Jamaican Plantation: A History of Worthy Park, 1670–1970* (London, 1970), which describes how Francis Price and his son and grandson set up a grand sugar estate, producing £10,000 annually in rum and sugar by the mid-eighteenth century. See also an account of the rise of the Dawkins family (with whom the Pennants intermarried) in Richard B. Sheridan, *Sugar and Slavery: An Economic History of the British West Indies, 1623–1775* (Bridgetown, 1974), pp. 224–7; and an account of the ascent of the Ellis family in B. W. Higman, *Montpelier, Jamaica: A Plantation Community in Slavery and Freedom 1739–1912* (Kingston, 1998), pp. 18–28. In each case, the key figure in land aggrandisement and the transformation of frontier properties into large integrated sugar plantations was a second- or third-generation planter active in the 1720s and 1730s: Edward Pennant (1672–1736); Charles Price (d. 1730); Henry Dawkins (1698–1744); and George Ellis (1704–40). Each died with very large personal estates: Dawkins's, £78,342 sterling, including 1,315 slaves; Price's, £15,910, including 499 slaves; and Ellis's, £88,443, including 158 slaves.

26 TNA, CO 142/31, 'List of Landholders and holdings in Jamaica [1754]'.

27 Jamaica Archives, Spanish Town, IB/1/11/18, Inventories. For the principles of how enslaved people were listed in inventories, see Trevor Burnard, 'Collecting and accounting: representing slaves as commodities in Jamaica, 1674–1784', in Peter C. Mancall and Daniella Bleichmar, *Collecting Across Cultures in the Early Modern World* (Philadelphia, 2010).

28 Sheridan, *Sugar and Slavery*, pp. 218–21. The genealogy of the Pennants can be followed in Lindsay, 'The Pennants and Jamaica. Part I'.

29 Boyd Alexander, *England's Wealthiest Son: A Study of William Beckford* (London, 1962).

30 *Welsh Biography Online*, http://yba.llgc.org.uk/en/s1-WILL-COC-1389.html; http://yba.llgc.org.uk/en/s-PENN-ANT-1734.html.

31 Bangor University Archives, Pehrhyn MSS 455–56, 'Marriage settlement, 1765'. Only some of the Penrhyn MSS have been catalogued. Recent additions – which form the majority of the sources used in this essay – are available for consultation but have not to date been fully catalogued. It should be assumed that when reference is made to correspondence and accounts of the Pennants and no reference is given in the text that the material used is part of the uncatalogued Penrhyn manuscripts.

32 BL, Additional MS 18273, Long Papers, fols. 93–4; Noel Deerr, *The History of Sugar* (2 vols, London, 1949–50), vol. 1, pp. 193–204; K. G. Davies, 'The origins of the commission system in the West India trade', *Transactions of the Royal Historical Society*, 5th ser., 2 (1952), 89–107; Richard Pares, *Merchants and planters, Economic History Review*, Supplement 4 (Cambridge, 1960); Sheridan, *Sugar and Slavery*, pp. 222–31, 488–9, 502–3; Michael Craton, *Searching for the Invisible Man: Slaves and Plantation Life in Jamaica* (Cambridge, Mass., 1978); Patrick K. O'Brien and Philip A. Hunt, 'The rise of a fiscal state in England, 1485–1815', *Historical Research*, 66 (1993), 175; David Ryden, '"One of the fertilest plesentest spotts": an analysis of the slave economy in Jamaica's St Andrew parish, 1753', *Slavery and Abolition*, 21 (2000), 32–55; David Eltis, 'The volume and structure of the transatlantic slave trade: a reassessment', *William and Mary Quarterly*, 3rd series, 58 (2001), 44; Trevor Burnard, '"Prodigious riches": the wealth of Jamaica before the American Revolution', *Economic History Review*, 2nd series, 54 (2001), 516–20; S. D. Smith, '*Merchants and Planters* revisited' *Economic History Review*, 2nd series, 55 (2002), 457–8; Smith, *Slavery, Family and Gentry Capitalism*, pp. 142, 169, 196; Kenneth Morgan, 'Robert Dinwiddie's reports on the British American colonies', *William and Mary Quarterly*, 3rd series, 65 (2008), 341–2.

33 A pen was an estate that raised livestock, usually cattle or horses.

34 Patrick Colquhoun, *A Treatise on Indigence* (London, 1806), p. 23; Paul Langford, *A Polite and Commercial People: England 1727–1783* (Oxford, 1989), p. 594.

35 For improvements in West Indian agriculture after 1790, see B. W. Higman, *Plantation Jamaica 1750–1850: Capital and Control in a Colonial Economy* (Kingston, 2005), and Heather Cateau, 'Conservatism and change implementation in the British West Indian sugar industry 1750–1810', *Journal of Caribbean History*, 29 (1995), 1–36.

36 Higman, *Plantation Jamaica*, p. 288; Veront M. Satchell, 'Early use of steam power in the Jamaican sugar industry, 1768–1810', *Transactions of the Newcomen Society*, 6 (1995–96), 221–31.

37 For hurricanes in Jamaica in the 1780s see Matthew Mulcahy, *Hurricanes and Society in the British Greater Caribbean, 1624–1783* (Baltimore, 2006), pp. 107–15. For views that the American Revolution initiated a fatal and irreversible decline in West Indian sugar production, see Lowell J. Ragatz, *The Fall of the Planter Class in the British Caribbean, 1763–1833: A Study of Social and Economic History* (New York, 1928), and Selwyn Carrington, *The Sugar Industry and the Abolition of the Slave Trade, 1775–1810* (Gainesville, 2002). For an interpretation that sees the 1780s as difficult but not terminal see John J. McCusker, 'The economy of the British West Indies, 1763–1790: growth, stagnation, or decline?' in John J. McCusker, *Essays in the Economic History of the Atlantic World* (London, 1997), p. 330. Historical opinion suggests that decline did not fully set in until the 1820s. See J. R. Ward, 'The British West Indies in the age of abolition, 1748–1815', in Marshall (ed.), *The Eighteenth Century*, pp. 415–39. The strongest statement is Seymour Drescher, *Econocide: British Slavery in the Era of Abolition* (Pittsburgh, 1977). David Ryden, however, argues for short-term problems in the economy around 1805–7, which may help account for abolition. See David Ryden, 'Does decline make sense? The West Indian economy and the abolition of the British slave trade', *Journal of Interdisciplinary History*, 31 (2001), 347–74. Studies of lending suggest that British financiers continued to think that Jamaican plantations were good investments until the 1820s but also show that planters were increasingly labouring under unsustainable levels of indebtedness, especially after 1815. See S. G. Checkland, 'Finance for the West Indies, 1780–1815',

Economic History Review, 2nd ser., 10 (1958), 461–9; Smith, *Slavery, Family and Gentry Capitalism*, pp. 226–59.

38 Jean Lindsay, *A History of the North Wales Slate Industry* (Newton Abbot, 1974), 45; Alun John Richards, *Slate Quarrying in Wales* (Llanrwst, 1995), pp. 21–2.

39 Edward Long calculated that the value of a medium-sized sugar plantation in 1774 was £19,027 sterling. Long based his estimates on the average cost and output of a sugar estate in 1768 on a slave force of 200. Using that measurement (one slave on a sugar estate being worth £95), then the Pennant properties would have been worth £98,560 sterling in 1775 and well over £100,000 after 1782. See Edward Long, *The History of Jamaica, or a General Survey of the Antient and Modern State of the Island* (3 vols, London, 1774, reprinted 1970), vol. 1, pp. 456–63. Similarly, Sheridan established that the average slave force on a sugar estate, 1771–75, was 204 (Sheridan, *Sugar and Slavery*, p. 230). The average slave force on seventy-three sugar estates enumerated in a census for St James in 1774 was 199; BL, Add. MS 12435, Long Papers, 'Census of St James, Sept. 1774'.

40 Long, *History of Jamaica*, vol. 1, pp. 386–7.

41 Lowell J. Ragatz, 'Absentee Landlordism in the British Caribbean, 1750–1833', *Agricultural History*, 5 (1931), 7, 18–19; Williams, *Capitalism and Slavery*, pp. 55–6; Pares, *Merchants and Planters*, pp. 42–3. For a recent recapitulation, see Selwyn Carrington, 'Management of sugar estates in the British West Indies at the end of the eighteenth century', *Journal of Caribbean History*, 33 (1999), 27–53.

42 A. P. W. Malcolmson, 'Absenteeism in eighteenth-century Ireland', *Irish Economic and Social History*, 1 (1974), 15–35. In Jamaica, laments about absenteeism are also rooted in distaste for the harsh effectiveness of the plantation system and in nostalgia for the vanishing of a settler society. See Higman, *Plantation Jamaica*, pp. 292–3; Trevor Burnard, 'A failed settler society: marriage and demographic failure in early Jamaica', *Journal of Social History*, 28 (1994), 63–82.

43 Higman, *Plantation Jamaica*, pp. 22–8, 91–2, 293; Douglas Hall, 'Absentee-proprietorship in the British West Indies, to about 1850', *Jamaican Historical Review*, 4 (1964), 15–35; Trevor Burnard, 'Passengers only: the extent and significance of absenteeism in eighteenth-century Jamaica', *Atlantic Studies*, 1 (2004), 178–95.

44 For the career of a mid-eighteenth overseer in south-west Jamaica, see Trevor Burnard, *Mastery, Tyranny, and Desire: Thomas Thistlewood and His Slaves in the Anglo-Jamaican World* (Chapel Hill, 2004). For a nuanced account of poor whites' social and ideological position, see David Lambert, *White Creole Culture, Politics and Identity during the Age of Abolition* (Cambridge, 2005), pp. 73–104.

45 For a touching tribute to Shickle, see a deathbed letter from Robert Helbye of Lucky Valley (Edward Long's estate) in 1746 in which Helbye hoped that Shickle would 'continue to persevere in doing what is laudable and praiseworthy'; Island Record Office, Twickenham, Jamaica, Wills 26/177, Will of Robert Helbye, 10 October 1746. Indirectly, Shickle had a lasting presence in Jamaica through the descendants of Sampson Facey, a Londoner apprenticed to Shickle on arrival in Jamaica in 1744. Sampson's illegitimate free coloured children were the ancestors of the prominent Kingston commercial family, the Faceys. Maurice Facey (b. 1925) has been prominent in the redevelopment of downtown Kingston. Shickle was Custos (chief magistrate) of Clarendon and Brigadier-General of the militia, dying on 17 June 1782, after a residence in Kingston and Clarendon of fifty-five years (Personal communications, Valerie Facey, June 2003).

46 Relations between the Shickles and the Pennants soured after John Shickle's death. Richard took Shickle's heirs to court in 1785, alleging that Shickle 'did not act with propriety' in 1764 in patenting 200 acres which before 1764 Shickle had allowed the Pennants to develop as part of the Denbigh estate.

47 Simon Taylor, the richest resident Jamaican in the early nineteenth century, derived much wealth from acting as an attorney for estates in the 1780s and 1790s. See Higman, *Plantation Jamaica*; Betty Wood, *Travel, Trade and Power, 1765–1884* (Cambridge, 2002).

48 Burnard, 'European migration'; Burnard, ' "The countrie continues sicklie" '; Higman, *Slave Population and Economy*, p. 144.

49 Burnard, 'Not a place for whites? Demographic failure and settlement in comparative context, Jamaica, 1655–1780', in Kathleen Morteith and Glen Richards (eds), *A History of Jamaica, from Indigenous Settlement to the Present* (Kingston, 2002).

50 Indentures noted in the Pennant records: 14 August 1755 – Isaac Robertson, Carlisle, carpenter; 24 January 1763 – Andrew Inglis, Lanarkshire, carpenter; 3 February 1767 – James Anderson, Glasgow, blacksmith; 22 September 1774 – William Lamb, Truro, Cornwall, husbandman, and Robert McComb, Chelsea, Middlesex, husbandman; 23 September 1774 – Edward Hayes, Winchester, husbandman. It does not appear that the Pennants sponsored any Welsh migrants to Jamaica.

51 Overseers' salaries would have placed them in the lower half of the middling sort (farmers with 100 acres) or in the top quarter of household heads, according to Patrick Colquhoun's survey of 1801. Miners in the Penrhyn Quarry would have been lucky to get as much as £40 per annum. See Colquhoun, *Treatise on Indigence*, p. 35.

52 Ryden, ' "One of the fertilest, plesentest spotts" ', 48; J. R. Ward, 'The profitability of sugar planting in the British West Indies, 1650–1834', *Economic History Review*, 2nd ser., 31 (1978), 206.

53 The demographic consequences of working on sugar in the Americas is assessed in Michael Tadman, 'The demographic cost of sugar: debates on slave societies and natural increase in the Americas', *American Historical Review*, 105 (2000), 1534–75. That slaves on sugar plantations in the British West Indies suffered from malnutrition and disease is best made clear from palaeo-demographic studies based on the excavation of eighteenth century bodies from the Newton plantation in Barbados. See Robert S. Corruccini, Jerome S., Handler, and Frederick W. Lange, 'Osteology of a slave burial population from Barbados, West Indies', *American Journal of Physical Anthropology*, 59 (1982), 443–59.

54 Betty Wood and T. R. Clayton, 'Slave birth, death and disease on Golden Grove plantation, Jamaica, 1765–1810', *Slavery and Abolition*, 6 (1985), 99–110.

55 *Ibid.*, 103; Richard S. Dunn, 'A tale of two plantations: slave life at Mesopotamia in Jamaica and Mount Airy in Virginia, 1799 to 1828', *William and Mary Quarterly*, 3rd series, 34 (1977).

56 Craton, *Searching for the Invisible Man*, p. 103; Kenneth F. Kiple and Virginia Himmelsteib King, 'Deficiency Diseases in the Caribbean', *Journal of Interdisciplinary History*, 11 (1980), 197–215.

57 Bangor University Archives, Penrhyn MS 1211.

58 J. R. Ward, *British West Indian slavery, 1750–1834: the process of amelioration* (Oxford, 1988), pp. 134, 138–9.

59 Michael Craton, 'Death, disease and medicine on Jamaican slave plantations: the example of Worthy Park, 1767–1838', *Histoire Sociale – Social History* 18 (1976), 237–55; S. D. Smith, 'Life and labor on a Jamaican sugar plantation: Prospect Estate, 1784–1832', *Wadabagei*, 9 (2006), 82–104.

60 Figures for York in 1778 are 67.8 per cent aged between 14 and 45; for Mesopotamia in 1789, 61 per cent. See Richard B. Sheridan, *Doctors and Slaves: A Medical and Demographic History of Slavery in the British West Indies, 1680–1834* (Cambridge, 1985), p. 197; Dunn, 'Tale of Two Plantations'.

61 Bangor University Library, Penrhyn MSS 1361, 1467, 1477, 1527; letters of 26 January 1805, 20 April 1807, 6 August 1807 and 26 October 1814. For the relationship between work and demography, see Kenneth Morgan, 'Slave women and reproduction in Jamaica, c.1776–1834', *History*, 91 (2006), 231–53.

62 It did not lead, however, to slaves running away. In 1808 four slaves were listed as runaways (0.4 per cent of 977 slaves).

63 Burnard, *Mastery, Tyranny, and Desire*, pp. 263–4. Obeah was a customary form of traditional African religion and obeahmen were powerful figures in the slave community. Planters feared its power and passed a law in 1760 making the practice of obeah punishable by death. For a general overview of obeah, see Kenneth Bilby

and Jerome S. Handler, 'Obeah: healing and protection in West Indian slave life', *Journal of Caribbean History*, 38 (2004), 153–83.

64 For gentry capitalism see Smith, *Slavery, Family and Gentry Capitalism*.

65 Hennessey, 'Penrhyn Castle'. Another great house built with West Indian money is the Palladian Harewood House in Yorkshire. Until recently, the West Indian origins of the wealth that built both houses was seldom discussed but is now addressed in exhibitions attached to the houses. See Marian Gwyn, 'Interpreting the slave trade: the Penrhyn Castle exhibition', *entertext*, 7 (2007), http://arts.brunel.ac.uk/gate/entertext/issue_7_1.htm; Harewood exhibition leaflet of 2007, www.harewood.org/files/events381-1.pdf.

66 Richard Pares, 'The economic factors in the history of the empire', *Economic History Review*, 7 (1936–37), 130; Patrick K. O'Brien, 'European economic development: the contribution of the periphery', *Economic History Review*, 2nd series, 35 (1982), 18; R. C. Nash, 'The balance of payments and foreign capital flows in eighteenth-century England: a comment', *Economic History Review*, 2nd series, 50 (1997), 110–28.

67 The major antagonists on the slave labour versus free labour issue were Adam Smith and Jean-Baptist Say. See Seymour Drescher, *The Mighty Experiment: Free Labor Versus Slavery in British Emancipation* (New York, 2002), pp. 19–33, 62–70.

CHAPTER 6

A 'reticent' people? The Welsh in Asia, c.1700–1815[1]

Andrew Mackillop

In the introduction to a volume of essays on the 'New British History' and its relationship to Irish and Scottish historical studies, the editors allude to Wales in a way that might equally be applied to the Principality's place within British imperial history. Explaining how 'four-nation' approaches have developed strongly in certain chronological and geographic areas and not in others, they note that 'Wales, notwithstanding distinguished work on its history, seems to be the dog that seldom barks within the New British History.'[2] If the Welsh 'dog' has rarely barked in the context of insular British history, it is surely saying nothing contentious to add that this also holds true for British imperial studies. Books and articles on Ireland and Scotland's place in the empire are now commonplace and range from surveys of a supposed 'Scottish empire' to the contentious suggestion that eighteenth-century Ireland's intellectual and cultural development rendered that kingdom an innately anti-imperial society.[3]

As noted in the introduction to this volume and by several other contributions, the position of Wales in the historiography of the British Empire is far more understated when set against the high profile of Ireland and Scotland. This situation is thankfully beginning to change. Scholarly surveys that routinely incorporate evidence of Welsh involvement in imperial affairs during the eighteenth century include Stephen Conway's *The British Isles and the War of American Independence* and Huw Bowen's *The Business of Empire: The East India Company and Imperial Britain*. Both books emphasise that Welsh society felt the full political and economic effects of the empire.[4] The importance of such works notwithstanding, there are many areas of British imperial history where next to nothing is known about Wales and the Welsh. An intriguing aspect of the *lacuna* is its capricious variability, with some periods and geographical sectors of the empire receiving far more attention than others. If Wales did indeed experience an imperial age it is assumed to have occurred in the second half of the nineteenth century and in the first decade of the twentieth century.[5] Gwyn Alf Williams has argued that imperialism played a fundamental role in the emergence of modern Wales. The development of large-scale coal and metallurgical industries meant that by the 1790s South Wales played an integral part in the Atlantic economy. The influence of colonial markets helped to drive substantial migration within and immigration to Wales, inducing a spate of linguistic, social and cultural changes that continue to define the country to the present day.[6] With its conscious effort to bring the empire centre-stage, Williams's thesis is striking in a number of ways; sensitivity to regional distinctiveness is matched by a willingness to expand the parameters of Welsh history and look beyond national and even European boundaries for the origin of developments that might otherwise be considered particular to Wales. The potential hinted at by the idea of 'imperial South Wales' underlines the value of applying Welsh evidence to British Empire studies and of exploring the country's domestic history in the context of overseas expansion.

Recognition of Wales's prominence in imperial affairs after c.1850 has not been matched by scholarly investigation of Welsh involvement in the empire of the long eighteenth century. Wales lacked the multifaceted participation that characterised post-Jacobite Scotland, and never experienced the mass mobilisation of manpower for imperial service which swept across Ireland after the 1750s.[7] In the century or so before Waterloo, the political, economic, social and cultural factors shaping Wales seem to have been born largely of the country's political and economic position within the British Union. Wales underwent crucial processes of evolutionary agrarian, manufacturing and commercial development.[8] Equally significant were patterns of religious change, Anglicisation and the 'cultural renaissance' in Welsh language and culture which constituted both a manifestation of, and reaction to, the new political, social and economic forces at work in Welsh society.[9] Whereas eighteenth-century overseas connections have attracted comment the focus is invariably upon the ephemeral and even declining nature of Welsh emigration to the Atlantic colonies. The apparently marginal role of Welsh mobility within the empire has in turn resulted in a correspondingly greater emphasis upon developments within Wales itself.[10] The economic, social and cultural dominance of England and the slow but fundamental changes reshaping the Principality help to explain why eighteenth-century Wales is so often viewed within the framework of domestic British, rather than imperial, history.[11]

Yet the apparent consensus that Wales was the 'least restive' or most 'reticent' part of the British–Irish Isles in relation to overseas expansion remains an unproven contention, and even if true does not mean that Welsh history should be decoupled from that of the empire.[12] The country's distinctive experience begs an intriguing set of questions about the relationship between empire and political, socio-economic and cultural conditions within Wales. Indeed Wales is so worthy of exploration precisely because its unique condition and historical position within the United Kingdom has yet to be fully related to recent trends in eighteenth-century British imperial studies.

Few areas of Welsh involvement in the pre-1815 empire have been quite as neglected as the Asian hemisphere of expansion. With the exception of one or two conspicuous individuals like Elihu Yale, governor of Madras from 1687 to 1699 or the Anglo-Welsh 'orientalist' scholar, Sir William Jones, founder of the Bengal Asiatic Society in 1784, Welsh sojourners in India have attracted remarkably little interest.[13] As with so many other aspects of Welsh interaction with the empire, links with India are not taken on their own terms but usually measured against the much larger Irish and Scottish sojourning presence in Asia.[14] Rather more is known about the impact of the eastern empire upon Wales, the subject of detailed consideration in Huw Bowen's chapter in this volume. In the main, however, eighteenth-century Britain's territories and commerce in Asia can seem all but irrelevant to Welsh history. The assumption that only very small numbers of individuals from Wales were involved in the East India Company's service has left little incentive to chart the nature of any Welsh profile in Asia.[15]

Any effort to explore Wales's connections with the East Indies must therefore first attempt to chart when, how and in what numbers Welsh personnel infiltrated the London-based East India Company. Compared with Scotland and Ireland, Wales had in fact a number of key advantages in the intense competition for Company employment. The historic nature of the country's links with English society by the early eighteenth century meant that Wales's entrepreneurial and professional classes were in pole position to gain access to the corporation's financial, administrative, shipping and mercantile activities. The Welsh were, after all, very well established in the metropole by the second half of the seventeenth century at the latest, with an expatriate community in the 1690s numbering at least 5,000. If new migrants and first generation 'Anglo-Welsh' are counted together, the Welsh presence in London may have been as high as 20,000 by the middle of the eighteenth century.[16] This substantial demographic bridgehead enabled the development of connections that linked Welsh shires and towns to the civic, educational, professional, financial and mercantile world of London. The requirements of legal training, for example, witnessed approximately 1,000 Welsh gentry and other middling elites enrol in the Inns of Court between 1600 and 1700.[17] While the political, social and cultural dominance of London has ensured that this migration is seen as emblematic of the corrosive Anglicisation of Wales, the city did constitute the key entry-point into the wider empire.

As Welsh migrants acculturated to the metropole's civic and professional norms they began to acquire the social contacts and business acquaintances that opened up a range of employment options. Only through such webs of patronage and influence could Welsh gentry and merchants hope to access the East India Company's lucrative civil service. The Company's directors usually accepted bonds of security for the good behaviour of appointees from a limited pool of respected and well-known London associates, while after 1714 all nominees for posts in the mercantile and marine services required formal nomination at East India House.[18] Reliable London contacts were therefore a vital prerequisite for obtaining any post of significance in the Company. This reality made the historically established Welsh expatriate community in the metropolis a potentially powerful resource for facilitating emigration to the Asian half of the empire.

The surviving evidence of Welsh participation in the East India Company during the early part of the eighteenth century not only reveals the importance of social and patronage contacts in the capital but also the problem of definitively identifying Welshmen. On 28 January 1698 William Kyffin was appointed as a writer to Surat on the west coast of India.[19] Nowhere does the Company's record explicitly state that Kyffin was Welsh: but he or his family undoubtedly had links to Cerrigydrudion in Denbighshire. This can be said with certainty when Kyffin's London connections are traced in detail. Two months after his appointment a Mr Roderick Lloyd and Robert Price, both of Lincoln's Inn, provided the bond of £500 security that would underwrite William's good behaviour in India and his adherence to the directors' instructions. Price was none other that Robert Price from Cerrigydrudion, a former attorney general of South Wales and a prominent MP. Lloyd, who hailed from Hafodwryd in Caernarvonshire, was a clerk at the Court of Commons Pleas and an legal associate of Price.[20] Both men typify Welsh professional migration to London, and their willingness to support Kyffin provides compelling evidence of the neglected role played by metropolitan expatriates in determining the pattern of Wales's participation in imperial affairs.

The clinching evidence of Kyffin's Welshness is the fact that on 15 November 1710, twelve years after first supporting his entry into the East India Company, Price wrote again to the directors asking that they advance the career of his 'relative'. Following his promotion and a posting to the Company's factory at Anjengo near the south west tip of India, Kyffin died in 1718. His will, proven at the Probate Court of Canterbury on 13 August 1719, appointed his 'uncle', Robert Price Esq. of London as his executor.[21] The associative behaviour of Kyffin, Price and Lloyd reveals the considerable obstacles that historians face when they attempt to understand the extent and nature of Welsh infiltration of the Company. These men may well have been acutely conscious of their Welsh origins; indeed, Price's career in Parliament during the 1690s was such that he earned the reputation as a Welsh patriot.[22] Yet at no point in their dealings with the Company did any of these men allude to their Welshness; their nationality was largely irrelevant in the context in which they operated. The patronage and networking activity required to secure a career in the East Indies occurred almost exclusively in London or at one of the presidency settlements at Calcutta, Madras and Bombay.[23] While Welshmen may have been motivated by Welsh loyalties and local identities, logic required them to emphasise their status as established and respectable men of the metropole or their position and experience within the Company.

These contemporary political and cultural realities have ensured that many Welshmen remain hidden within the official Company record. The problem of uncovering this submerged Welsh presence is especially acute for the first five decades of the eighteenth century, the period before the corporation began to keep detailed muster lists of its mercantile, maritime and military personnel. More often than not, the origin of an individual becomes apparent only if a laborious and circuitous process of research is undertaken to unearth the social and patronage networks that initiated and supported a career in the east. Without such background research, the full scale of Welsh involvement can be easily underestimated.

Sometimes, however, the Company's records make the connection with Wales easy to ascertain. When on 21 January 1702 Arran Jones was appointed as a writer, Thomas Mansell of Briton Ferry in Glamorgan agreed to supply one half of his £500 bond of security.[24] Similarly, when Thomas Lloyd was made a factor in Benkulen in south-east Asia in 1709, those willing to act as collateral for his probity included Messrs John and Holwell Lloyd of Wickfair in St Asaph parish, Denbighshire.[25] These are not merely parochial examples; such shire-to-metropole connections show that Company's directors were willing to countenance financial assurances from Welshmen at a time when it was highly unusual for the corporation to accept collateral from outside the elite circles of London's East India interests.

Given the historic and entrenched position of the Welsh in London, what is surprising is not that such networking occurred but that the volume of Welshmen entering the East India Company's elite civil service remained so small. Between 1754 and 1790 only three Welshmen sat as directors of the Company, including Sir William James, who returned in the 1760s from a career in the Bombay Marine and served on the directorate throughout the 1770s. In the case of Robert James, a director in the mid-1750s and again from 1765 to 1768, it was his earlier experience as a Portugal merchant which led to his gradual involvement in the financial and political world of the East Indies trade. The ways in which the established Welsh commercial presence in the metropole combined with kinship links to facilitate imperial careers is clearly evident in the case of Thomas Rous, originally from Piercefield in Monmouthshire. His uncle's activities as a major purchaser of tea provided the initial link with the Company; and once Thomas established himself as director in the 1750s and 1760s he acted as patron in turn for his sons, Robert and Thomas, who both went on to command East India merchant ships.[26]

But drawing attention to one or two high-profile examples like Rous cannot form the basis of a wider interpretation of Welsh links with the eastern empire. Welsh and imperial history can only be related to each other in mutually productive ways if there is a move away from anecdotal case studies towards a systematic examination of the social, regional and professional backgrounds of those entering the Company's service. Table 6.1 profiles the known Welsh presence among the civil service and provides evidence of general patterns of participation in the East Indies. The most obvious feature is the small number of people involved. Between the 1690s and early 1810s the Company directors appointed, at a conservative estimate, just over 3,060 civil servants, either as writers, factors or merchants. Even allowing for an unknown number of Welshmen that cannot be identified as a result of the Company's metrocentric recruitment process, Table 6.1 confirms a pattern of conspicuous non-participation.

There seems little doubt that when set against the total number of civil service appointments, the Welsh gained no more than 2 or 3 per cent of the Company's prestigious mercantile and administrative offices. This ratio is best understood in comparison with Wales's weight of population within the United Kingdom as a whole. It is estimated that by around the 1750s Wales had a population of approximately 489,000, rising to c.587,000 by the 1801 census – roughly 5 to 6 per cent of the UK total.[27] By this reckoning Welshmen gained well under half – and possibly as little as a third – of the amount of civil service posts that might reasonably be expected.

Besides this pattern of under-representation, a range of geographic and social features characterised the drift of Welshmen into the

Table 6.1 *Welsh East India Company civil servants, 1690–1813*

Appointments	Region	Social background	Education	Presidency
1690–1730 = 6	South Wales = 16	Landed gentry = 11	London = 6	Bengal = 15
1731–70 = 15	East Wales = 13	Clergy = 4	Liverpool = 3	Bombay = 9
1771–1813 = 18	London = 5	Merchant/Artisan = 2	Wales = 2	Madras = 7
	North Wales/West Wales = 3	Military = 1	Essex = 2	Benkulen = 2
	Wales = 1	Medical = 1	English	Unknown = 6
	England = 1	Mariner = 1	Town/Uni. = 6	
		EIC = 2	Unknown = 20	
		Unknown = 17		

Source: The information for this and all subsequent tables is drawn from an AHRC-funded database, 'The Scots, Irish and Welsh in British Asia, 1695–1813'. The records used to compile the findings for this table are BL, IOR, B/40-B/70 and J/1/1-26.

Company's civil elite. The prominence of the southern and eastern counties, which between them accounted for nearly three-quarters of the total, no doubt reflects the political and socio-economic dominance of these regions within Welsh society.[28] The surviving data for social origins is, unfortunately, far less comprehensive but does provide some evidence that Welsh political and patronage networks catered to more than just the established landed class. A substantial minority of Company writerships were acquired by non-landed elites, especially the clerical estate. Thomas Morris Heate, son of the Prebendary of St David's Cathedral in Pembrokeshire, and Henry Hall, son of the Reverend Benjamin Hall of the parish of Llandaff in Glamorgan, obtained posts in Bombay and Madras respectively in 1797. Heate's exalted position in the Welsh Anglican church, allied to Thomas's education at Cambridge, was enough to win influence in London, while the Halls relied on the patronage of the director, John Roberts.[29] These Wales-to-London connections cast new light on the responsive nature of the pre-reformed Welsh political culture and confirm the benefits of integrating imperial and domestic perspectives. The profile of social origins in Table 6.1 shows that Welsh politics were far from stagnant or geared only towards the shire and town oligarchs. Indeed, the emphasis by historians of the period on the increasing importance of new professional and servitor classes finds a clear resonance in the social backgrounds of some of the Welshmen taking up employment in Asia.[30] Moreover, the suggestion that the country maintained only a 'ghostly presence at Westminster' underestimates the diverse ways in which Welsh political culture in the metropolis developed informal patronage networks beyond Parliament that linked into the major institutions of the state and the empire.[31]

The central role of London comes across in other ways, with 13 per cent of all known Welsh East India Company civil servants clearly linked with the city, if not already domiciled in the capital. A substantial minority among the known Welsh civil servants received their education in the metropolis. They also frequently relied on schools in Liverpool, Chester, Shrewsbury and Bristol.[32] Regional economic and social links between North Wales and the port of Liverpool, for example, explain why Samuel Peake from Denbigh and Charles Lloyd from Wrexham were educated in the English city prior to applying for the civil service in 1758 and 1762 respectively.[33] What is not clear is how far this pattern of Welsh educational mobility facilitated or hindered involvement in the overseas empire. The Company directors demanded high standards of literacy, numeracy and familiarity with conventional business and accountancy practices.[34] Training in English schools or merchant houses inculcated accepted styles of learning, business customs and social etiquette, and would have earned crucial cultural kudos at East India House. Equally, however, such educational experience might just have easily generated social and economic networks which opened up opportunities within the domestic English economy and so reduced the need to look further afield. What is not in doubt is that any understanding of eighteenth-century Wales's place within the empire must entail a critical re-examination of the education and training of the country's middling classes and the social, economic and migratory links with England created by such intellectual mobility.

Intense competition for the corporation's mercantile and administrative offices constitutes another reason why the Welsh presence in the civil service was so much smaller proportionally than Wales's share of Britain's population. The disappointed mother of an individual rejected for such a post in 1775 noted: 'It requires the greatest interest to send out a young man in a civil employment to the East Indies, as the nomination of a writer is now commonly valued at £1,500, it is even very difficult to get leave to go out if they have friends there to provide them'.[35] Although in this case the family hailed from Scotland, Welshmen faced exactly the same sort financial and political constraints.

Other avenues existed by which the wealth and opportunities afforded by the growing empire in Asia could be exploited. Until the later 1740s the East India Company's military offered only a limited number of posts, although the example of Captain John Lloyd from Cardiganshire who served in Fort William's 2nd infantry company and who made his will in Calcutta in November 1741 shows that a small number of Welshmen had already drifted into the Company's army.[36] By the early 1750s the Company had begun a prolonged build up of its military machine. Few other areas of the British Empire offered such a rapidly expanding source of socially honourable and materially secure offices.[37] Attrition rates ensured that the Company's presidency armies of Bengal, Madras and Bombay required an annual replenishment of officers and rank and file. Military migration to the East Indies, while never large in any given year, has been sorely neglected in comparison with the greater levels of transatlantic mobility.[38] Yet the movement of ordinary soldiers, sailors and officers generated an accumulative volume of British and Irish emigration that amounted to tens of thousands between 1750 and the 1810s. A parliamentary investigation in 1770 revealed that in the previous seven years the Company had raised 13,885 men in Britain and Ireland and embarked them for Asia.[39] Competition for the post of cadet, the junior military rank that led to an officer's commission in one of the European or sepoy regiments at Bombay, Madras or Bengal, was far less than the pressure for civil service places. By the early 1800s the Company appointed between 320 to 500 cadets annually, an impressive rate of recruitment that offered a realistic chance of success for those Welsh families that maintained even a semblance of political connections in the capital.[40]

Another attractive aspect of the Company's military machine was that prospective officers or their families did not have to purchase a commission, as was the case with the British Army.[41] A military career in the east offered a relatively cheap entrée to the status of officer and gentleman. This fact alone helps to explain why so many Irish, Scots and English middling and lower gentry took up the option of a Company commission.[42] Given these substantial financial and social incentives, the evidence of Welsh involvement in the Company's army is intriguing. The detailed military records for the period from c.1750 to 1815 lead to no other conclusion than that Welshmen did not enter the Company's military in anything like the numbers that the country's population would warrant.

Table 6.2 shows that patterns of under-representation hold true for the ordinary rank and file and for commissioned officers alike. In light of these figures it is difficult to avoid the conclusion that Wales seems to have experienced a distinctive set of political, economic, social and cultural conditions which acted to curtail the country's involvement in military migration to Asia. If not conclusive proof of Welsh 'reticence' in relation to the empire, the percentage of commissioned officers and enlisted men certainly shows that Wales's participation in a major sector of eighteenth-century British imperial expansion was muted, to say the least. An especially telling aspect of Welsh interaction with the Company's military is that, like the Scots but in sharp contrast to the Irish, the social classes who comprised the officer corps consistently made up a higher percentage of the country's profile within

Table 6.2 *Welsh participation in the East India Company military, c.1755–1800*

Years	Military force	Total	Total Welsh
1753–63	Rank & file embarkations	7,268	170 (2.3%)
1753–63	Cadet embarkations	377	13 (3.4%)
1765	Madras army officers	133	2 (1.5%)
1775–81	Rank & file embarkations	5,121	66 (1.2%)
1775–81	Cadet embarkations	928	14 (1.5%)
1800	Cadet appointments	479	14 (2.9%)

Sources: Figures drawn from BL, IOR, L/MIL/9/85, 'Military Embarkations, 1753–63'; L/MIL/9/90, 'Military Embarkations, 1775–81'; L/MIL/11/109, 'A Roll of the Officers in the Honourable Company's Service on the Coromandel Coast [Madras], 1764–5'.

the Company than did the labouring poor who constituted the enlisted European manpower.[43] The mass of Wales's poor rural and urban populations considered many migratory destinations within Britain and its Atlantic possessions, but Asia was never a remotely popular option. The sons of gentry, clergy and the other professional orders were, ironically, far more mobile and prepared to take the high-risk option of sojourning in the East Indies. The value of linking Welsh evidence to the empire comes across clearly in the case of the Company's military: far from conforming to the stereotype that the domestic provinces or 'Celtic margins' of Great Britain and Ireland relied excessively on military service to access the benefits of empire, Wales experienced a diametrically opposite dynamic.[44] Contrary to the theory of a 'Celtic fringe' uniformly subordinated to England's political and economic centralism, Wales provides salutary proof that the reaction of such regions to imperial expansion was invariably subtle, multifaceted and diverse.[45]

More Welshmen served as commissioned officers of the Company's three presidency armies than gained posts in the mercantile and administrative civil service. This is hardly surprising; with significantly less competition and a much larger annual volume of cadet appointments, the Welsh landed, professional and middling orders stood a far better chance of obtaining employment in the military. Yet the underlying pattern in Table 6. 2 is broadly similar to that of the civil service ratios in as much as Welshmen persistently made up a lower percentage of soldiers and military officers than the country's share of population.

The largest sector of the East India Company's burgeoning military complex was the army of Bengal. Drawing on that institution's muster rolls, Table 6.3 profiles the known geographic and social origins of

Table 6.3 *Welsh officers in the army of Bengal, 1757–1813*

Appointments	Regional origins	Social origins	Rank
1757–70 = 17	South Wales = 37	Landed gentry = 15	Cadet = 5
1771–90 = 14	East Wales = 17	Clergy = 7	Ens. = 8
1791–1813 = 44	Wales = 12	Medical = 3	Lt = 37
	North Wales/ West Wales = 6	EIC = 3	Capt. = 18
	Anglo-Welsh = 3	Finance/Legal = 3	Major = 2
		Education = 2	Lt-Col. = 3
		Merchant/ Manufacturer = 2	Lt-Gen. = 2
		Unknown = 40	

Source: V. C. P. Hodson, *List of the Officers of the Bengal Army, 1758–1834* (4 vols, London, 1927), *passim*.

the seventy-five Welshmen who can definitely be identified as having served as commissioned officers between 1757 and 1813, the year the Company lost its monopoly of trade with India. The Welsh presence in the Bengal army shares a number of general characteristics with patterns of participation in the civil service. The eastern and southern shires supplied the vast majority of commissioned personnel, providing further proof of the way in which Wales's internal political, economic and social make-up directly shaped the nature of Welsh interaction with the empire. Not surprisingly, the landed elites did well, but the country's mercantile, manufacturing and other 'middling sort' also gained a sizeable minority of commissioned posts.

The small volume of army officers and civil servants was not the result of an innate inability on the part of Welsh society to infiltrate the East India Company. By the end of the century a number of Welsh families had developed a tradition of service in the corporation, as one generation followed another out to Asia. A fine example of this process was the Lloyd family from Wrexham: John joined the Company as a writer on the Bengal civil establishment in December 1771, and his sons, Thomas and Charles, were born shortly afterwards in Calcutta in 1776 and 1778 respectively. By the time Thomas obtained one of the coveted writerships in 1796, his father had already retired back to Wales; Charles followed his elder brother into the same service a year later.[46]

A similar service ethic characterised the Scott family from Eyton, near Wrexham. John joined the Bengal army as a twenty-one-year-old cadet in 1794, with his younger sibling, Jonathan, following him to South Asia six years later.[47] This professional chain migration was a common practice designed to provide mutual financial, professional and social support once in Asia's challenging environment. In this respect at least, Welsh officers differed little if at all from their English, Irish or Scottish counterparts.[48] But given Wales's historic political, economic, social and cultural links with England and London, what is fascinating about the Welsh example is that such integration did not produce a high level of involvement in the East Indies.

Another key sector of the Company was the merchant marine. This branch of the service offered lucrative trading privileges that enabled the commanders and ship's officers of East Indiamen to carry goods between Britain and Asia on their own private accounts.[49] Catering to the Company's shipping needs was a capital-intensive business that necessitated a close overlap between the command of credit in the City, trustworthy partners and influence among the shareholders and directors. Centred almost exclusively upon London this 'shipping interest' was one of the most powerful cartels anywhere in the empire.[50]

Table 6.4 *Welsh East India Company merchant marine officers, 1765–1813*

Origins	Previous experience	Rank
Pembroke = 5	Coasting trade = 5	Commander = 7
Denbigh = 1	RN = 4	1st Mate = 5
Glamorgan = 6	West Indies trade = 5	2nd Mate = 9
Cardigan = 1	Africa trade = 1	3rd Mate = 7
Carmarthen = 4	Mediterranean trades = 1	4th Mate = 4
Anglesey = 1		5th Mate = 2
Monmouth = 2		Midshipman = 2
Radnor = 2		Ship's surgeon = 3
Montgomery = 2		
Flint = 1		
Brecon = 4		
Wales = 10		

Source: Anthony Farrington, *A Biographical Index of East India Company Maritime Service Officers, 1600–1834* (London, 1999).

Table 6.4 profiles those Welshmen known to have served in the merchant marine between the 1760s and 1810s. Given the volume of maritime officers that passed through the Company's service in this period – there were at least 580 commanders of East Indiamen between 1737 and 1832 – the Welsh profile is strikingly low.[51] However the origins and careers of these individuals are significant. From the surviving evidence it is clear that Wales contributed, albeit in a small way, to the emergence of a class of highly mobile mariners who moved easily between the Royal Navy, maritime trade in the Atlantic, Western Europe and the East Indies. As a result, these men experienced truly global careers.

The patterns of professional migration exhibited by these Welsh mariners underline the importance of the coasting trade and the movement of coal, iron and non-industrial produce into London in defining the nation's links with the wider empire. Once a reputation was established in the metropolis it became easier to secure a foothold in the charmed circles of the shipping interest. As was the case with the educational backgrounds of the civil servants, a key aspect of charting involvement in imperialism involves recognising that migration from Wales to the rest of Britain was often the first crucial stage in a process of emigration to destinations much further afield.

The overall quantitative evidence is remarkably consistent. Across a diverse range of civil, mercantile and military occupations it is clear that Wales was conspicuous for its lack of engagement with the empire in Asia. This is the case even among the private 'country traders' who increasingly garnered financial and economic influence at Bombay, Madras and Calcutta from the 1770s and 1780s onwards.[52] As in other areas of the Company's empire, there were individual Welshmen who carved out successful careers for themselves as private entrepreneurs. Among the most prominent was Thomas Parry from Leighton Hall in Montgomeryshire, who arrived in Madras in 1788. Within a decade he had emerged as one of the port's major free merchants, creating a shipping and financial organisation that would go from strength to strength during the early 1800s.[53] Another successful Welsh private merchant was Joseph Price, who controlled one of the largest shipping concerns operating out of Calcutta in the 1770s. A prominent contractor for the Bengal presidency's merchant-marine and naval needs, Price shipped grain and salt in such quantities that he owned or held shares in a fleet of twenty-four 'country ships' by the end of the 1770s.[54] But these isolated examples disguise the prosaic reality that the Welsh presence in the country trade was all but negligible. A list of private British traders in Calcutta in 1812 that includes nationality reveals only six Welshmen from a total of 683 individuals. A similarly low proportion of 3 out of 160 characterised the Welsh profile in the private trading community of Madras in 1786.[55]

There are a number of important caveats to the conclusion that the Welsh were seriously under-represented in the British East Indies. Although the totals shown for civil servants, free merchants, military and marine officers seem insignificant, they should be taken as indicative rather than strictly comprehensive. Indeed the overall sum of Welsh involvement was undoubtedly greater than the figures in Tables 6.1 to 6.4 would suggest. The dubiety arises from the nature of the East India Company's records, which are something of a double-edged sword if viewed from the perspective of historians charting the Welsh presence in the empire. On the one hand, the quality of the surviving archive is remarkable in some respects and offers, alongside army and navy records, the best resource for studying human mobility within the pre-1815 British Empire. Company army muster lists and ship rolls, which begin to survive in quantity and quality after c.1750, provide indisputable evidence for the presence of Welsh personnel in the lower rungs of the Company's overseas workforce. The certainty arises from the fact that the corporation did not register the nationality of its employees as 'British' or 'Irish' but instead recorded individuals as 'English', 'Irish', 'Scots' or 'Welsh'.[56] This method of compiling of the Company's workforce directly addresses one of the key problems facing historians of Wales attempting to uncover Welsh emigration overseas. The 'statistical indignity of being lumped in with the English' has long been recognised as one of the major barriers to securely identifying Welsh men and women and evaluating their role in British expansion.[57]

Given that the East India Company explicitly listed Welshmen rather than incorporating personnel under more general definitions, this problem is far less evident when studying the empire in Asia, a fact that makes the neglect of Welsh involvement in the East Indies all the more surprising. It is possible to ascertain the patterns and percentage of Welsh participation in some sectors of the East India Company with a degree of certainty that simply is not possible in the Atlantic empire, where British and Irish subjects could move about in relative freedom. Indeed, historians of Wales would do well to note that the Asian hemisphere of the empire is one where Welsh individuals can be consistently and definitively extrapolated out from the mass of other Britons. The number of rank and file soldiers shown in Table 6.2, for example, can be taken as an accurate snapshot of Welsh immigration of the lower social classes into the eastern hemisphere of the empire.

But definitive findings are not always possible. One of the ironies of the East India Company's archive is that, unlike almost all other areas of British activity overseas, the nationality of personnel at the lower levels of the workforce can in some instances be more easily ascertained than the identities of the mercantile and military elites. For the first half of the eighteenth century the Company directors stressed the social and professional background of individuals applying for writerships, military and maritime commissions rather than their nationality. The surviving information for these men invariably focused on their status as 'gentlemen', the name of the director who nominated them, and the date of their appointment.[58] Much like the case of William Kyffin noted earlier, the contemporary assumptions that shaped the listing of new employees to the middling and elite offices serves to downplay the Welsh presence in the Company. Only from the late 1740s, once the paperwork supporting applications for writerships survive, and from 1789, the first year of extant cadet applications, is it possible to identify elites from Wales with any degree of certainty.[59] Prior to this date, it is often only surname evidence that provides clues to the origin of individuals joining the commissioned level of the civil, military and maritime services.

However relying on surnames is a deeply problematic methodology and almost certainly results in distortion and vagueness. The records of the army of Bengal, for example, list two 'John Lloyds', one serving as an ensign and the other as a lieutenant in the 1760s and 1770s. But there is no concrete evidence that either of these men came from Wales, and so they and others like them are not included in Table 6.3.[60]

In the case of maritime officers the disguising effect is probably even greater. A total of eighteen 'Lloyds' without any indication of nationality are listed as having served as senior officers on East Indiamen between 1720 and 1813, including one commander, two surgeons and three pursers. If the examples of 'Griffiths' and 'Price' – both typical Welsh surnames – are included the number of possible officers rises to forty.[61] Not all these men were Welsh, but it is highly likely that some at least hailed from Wales. If a balance is struck between acknowledging the indeterminate number of men who cannot be definitely identified while avoiding the excessive use of surname evidence, there is a strong case for arguing that at least 250 Welshmen served in the elite of the Company during the second half of the eighteenth and first decade of the nineteenth centuries.

The tiny numbers involved explains why the subject of the Welsh in the East India Company has received scant attention. The Welsh do seem especially 'reticent' if contrasted against the much higher volume of Scots and Irish evident throughout Asia in this period.[62] By such national comparisons are only partially helpful. For a start, Wales had a much smaller population. By 1800 it was probably not much more than a third of the size of Scotland in a demographic sense, and less than one fifth that of Ireland. In these circumstances it was inevitable that Wales's human profile within British imperialism would be significantly less than that of the other two 'Celtic' societies. One of the significant insights to be gained from the Welsh example is that it is not always appropriate to overly rely on numerically based methods of assessing a society's participation in British expansion. There is no reason whatsoever for historians of Wales to adopt uncritically the quantitative emphasis that characterises studies of the Scots and Irish in the empire. Scholars beginning the task of recovering Welsh perspectives on British imperialism are surely correct when noting that simply categorising and counting people is not especially enlightening in the case of Wales. There is instead a growing recognition that attention should focus on the ways in which 'Welshness' might have played a part in the development of the empire and helped to shape the experience and identities of those participating in British activities.[63] In this context the volume of people is less important. Indeed, far from constituting a disincentive to research into Wales in the empire, the fact that the country experienced such limited emigration overseas provides an excitingly different challenge from the better-known Scottish and Irish examples, and points towards the need for qualitative as opposed to quantitative approaches.

How might Welsh historical studies begin to answer the question: did Welshness matter in an imperial context? The existing lines of inquiry mirror the current emphasis on Wales's place within the mid- to later nineteenth-century empire. It has been postulated, for example, that one useful methodology would be an examination of Welsh-language literature and newspapers, especially the voluminous output of the missionary societies. The influence of enhanced Welsh educational infrastructure after the 1870s, especially with the emergence of university provision, is rightly seen as another probable explanation for Wales's growing profile within the empire's administrative, diplomatic and technical sectors.[64]

However apposite these ideas might be for the post-1850 period, they are of little or no utility in relation to the pre-1815 empire. When dealing with the very different political, economic, social and cultural conditions of the long eighteenth century other research perspectives are required. One obvious way forward is to apply the recent emphasis on local, regional and kin networks which has characterised British imperial studies in general and in particular reassessments of the Scottish and Irish role within the empire.[65] Viewed in this way there is evidence that Welshmen in the East Indies did retain a clear sense of themselves as Welsh; in some respects it could not be otherwise given that annual muster rolls and the census of private traders listed individuals in such terms. The Company's enumerating policy for the British populations at its settlements in India ensured that, for ordinary soldiers and free merchants at least, Welshness was an annually reaffirmed label.[66] Higher up the Company's intricate occupational hierarchy notions of nationality gave way to definitions that stressed status and length of service. However, it is significant that when they embarked on East Indiamen to make the psychological as well as geographic transit to Asia cadets were asked to state their identity for the official record.[67] For many Welshmen, Englishmen, Scots and Irish, one of their last acts before departing from Europe was to reflect upon and respond to the question: where within the British–Irish Isles did they hail from?

It was not just the East India Company's official labelling that sustained notions of Welshness among individuals thousands of miles from Wales. Informal Welsh identities constituted a small but nevertheless discernible part of the political and social milieu of the main presidency settlements. Recalling how he had been nicknamed 'Taffy' upon first arriving in the East Indies, Joseph Price portrayed himself as an honest no-nonsense entrepreneur from 'Taffyland'. In his case Welshness was a rhetorical tool in the highly polemical world of Company politics. It enabled Price to establish an oppositional identity to the perceived corruption and cronyism, as he saw it, afflicting the Company as a direct result of the growing presence in the East

Indies of Scots and ministerial placemen.[68] There is other evidence of kin, local and regional Welsh networks among sojourners in Asia. Although few in number, the registered wills submitted by Welsh individuals to the Bombay, Madras and Calcutta courts are a key source which reveal how connections were maintained between Wales and the far reaches of the empire. Welshmen certainly acted as legal trustees for each other. On 20 March 1782 the will of Thomas Evans from Glamorgan, then a surgeon on the East Indiaman *Essex*, was recorded at Madras. One of his executors was a fellow Welshman, John Lloyd from Brecon, then chief mate on the East Indiaman *Fortitude*. Similar legalistic bonds of association occurred in the same year when a surgeon from Pembroke, John Evans, used a Welsh merchant at Madras, John Jones, as the administrator of his estate.[69] In the case of Daniel Kempthon, a clear sense of Welshness and professional identity played a major role in defining the conditions of his will, which he completed in 1704 while on board HMS *Severn* off Bombay. After noting that he hailed from 'the Dominion of Wales', Kempthon went on to leave all his property to his 'loving shipman, William Lewis of the Dominion of aforesaid'.[70]

These links between Welshmen in the East Indies were in all likelihood based on practical concerns rather than a direct expression of national sentiment. For almost all sojourners in the eastern empire the ultimately objective was to secure a fortune and remit it back to Britain. In this context using executors with information on remittance networks that could move property from Asia, through London back to Wales was imminently sensible. Welshness, in other words, had a practical meaning and utility in the East Indies and was not simply a romantic gesture. When John Williams, a merchant in Calcutta who originated from Haverfordwest in Pembrokeshire, died in 1784 he entrusted his £6,000 fortune to Robert Wigram, a prominent Irishman in the shipping interest, and William Money, another East Indiaman owner whose nationality is unclear, but who held substantial estates in Carmarthenshire. Holding property in Wales meant that Money understood the best means of remitting from London the £1,000 which Williams wished to send back to his mother.[71]

Nothing better illustrates what could be defined as 'working Welshness' than the business tactics of the free merchant Thomas Parry. Once he established his own enterprise at Madras, Thomas naturally sought secure and reliable partners. He invited his nephews, David and Joseph Pugh, to join the firm in 1808 and 1815 respectively. Parry, Pugh & Co. continued to expand as one of the largest private merchant houses in Madras, with a fleet of several 'country ships' and the holders of government contracts worth nearly £10,000.[72] While strong kin networks are invariably associated with Scots operating within the empire, they were not alone in appreciating the intrinsic value of family loyalties overseas.

Welsh identities could be expressed in a number of ways, not all of them obvious. The complexity of 'working Welshness' comes across clearly in the 1695 will of Anthony Williams, a merchant in Madras. The document typifies the problems of defining individuals as unambiguously Welsh: his last testament makes no allusion to his nationality but does reveal the subtle political, economic, social and cultural ties that could bind individuals to Wales. Williams conceded that 'by my long absence from my native country and family I am become wholly a stranger to their state': despite (or perhaps because of) the loss of such connections he left 100 Pagodas (approximately £40) to the poor of his 'native parish'. On top of this he left a further £583 to his brothers and sisters. It is Williams's choice of executors that point to his Welsh origins. He entrusted the administration of his affairs to 'his dear friend' Thomas Yale, brother of Elihu, and Dr Reverend John Evans from Caernarvonshire who had served as an East India Company chaplain at Madras through the 1680s to 1690s.[73] Too much interpretation should not be built upon the basis of a few limited examples. However, given the small presence of the Welsh in the East Indies it is significant that the surviving evidence reveals Welshmen readily associating together, conducting important business on the basis of mutual reliance while retaining a strong sense of place and origin, often after decades abroad.

What does the Asian half of the eighteenth-century empire offer to historians of Wales undertaking a re-evaluation of the country's involvement in British imperialism? On the one hand, there is no doubt that Wales did not engage directly in the mercantile and military opportunities afforded by the Company on a scale proportionate to its population. Although not entirely invisible or 'reticent', Welsh personnel were noticeably and persistently under-represented in Asia. However, this 'numeric' conclusion should in no way detract from the value of charting Wales's place within the eastern empire. The theme of a substantially reduced level of presence in the East Indies makes the Welsh a useful comparator to the better-known examples of the Scots and Irish. The upsurge in Scottish and Irish studies of the empire has uncovered much of the political, economic, social and cultural factors which shaped Scotland and Ireland's disproportionate commitment in many areas of imperial activity. This pre-existing template can be used to explore why the Welsh were not driven in large numbers to the high-risk, high-return economies of Asia. The renewed emphasis upon the importance of pre-reformed patronage politics in determining the success or otherwise of Irish and Scottish infiltration of imperial institutions offers one area of potentially productive comparison.[74] Could it be that Welsh political networks, firmly established in London since at least the mid-sixteenth century, reduced the need to compete for the new forms of imperial patronage which became available in the eighteenth century?[75] Whatever the answer to that question might be, it is clear that Welsh history will have to undertake a major reinterpretation of its political culture and investigate thoroughly the extent to which the country's political leaders did or did not forge durable connections with the major institutions of the empire. The critical part of this reassessment must involve charting anew the importance of the Welsh community in London in defining Wales's place and profile within the British Empire.

It is important, too, that the small number of individuals in places like India is not associated with a 'failure' on the part of Welsh society to engage actively with imperialism. A strong emphasis on human mobility is only right and proper in the case of Ireland and Scotland, but Welsh historical studies must develop avenues of investigation that best suit the historical distinctiveness of Wales. Indeed, one of the real benefits of reflecting on the Welsh experience is that it chimes with the new emphasis on the need to be wary of breaking British expansion into overly defined sections such as 'home' and 'overseas'.[76] Rather than assuming that the insignificant number of Welshmen in the East Indies is atypical, Welsh history can make a real contribution to British imperial history by highlighting the political, economic, social and cultural forces that kept populations at home rather than moving abroad in large numbers. One of the defining developments in the country's eighteenth-century experience was the demographic crisis of its landed gentry, as the number of male heirs born to the propertied elite fell away dramatically. A substantial percentage of old and established Welsh families failed, with the result that the estates passed by marriage to newcomers from across Britain and Ireland.[77] Although usually associated with a change of economic, social and cultural leadership in Wales, this demographic extinction may also have had severe consequences for the Welsh presence in the elite and professional echelons of the empire. The contrast with Scotland in the same period could not be more obvious. It is now recognised that a major social spur to the disproportionate presence of Scotland's aristocratic and landed families in places like Asia was the rapid growth from the later seventeenth century onwards in the number of surviving male children.[78] Welsh society faced far less pressure in this respect, as traditional English clerical, administrative, legal and medical employment careers helped to soak up the country's reduced pool of middling elites.

Such a process could have ensured that it was not necessary for many Welsh gentry to contemplate a physically dangerous and financially unpredictable imperial career in India.

Similar forces may have been at work further down the social hierarchy. Could the lack of Welsh manpower in the mass of the East India Company's European regiments be attributable to the centripetal influence of the urban manufacturing economies in Manchester, Liverpool, Chester, Shrewsbury, Birmingham and Bristol? Supplying labour to the manufacturing and maritime economies of regional England meant that the Welsh did indeed participate in the empire in large numbers; however the geography and indirect nature of this involvement has conspired to mask the process. Wales is in fact an ideal case study of the neglected role of insular migration, as opposed to high profile patterns of emigration and sojourning to the colonies of settlement and conquest, in shaping imperial Britain. This perspective enables an entirely different construction to be placed on the supposed 'reticence' and historiographical silence of the Welsh within British imperialism. Returning one last time to the 'barking dog' metaphor with which this chapter began: perhaps Wales has made so little 'noise' within British imperial studies because Welsh society did not experience the sort of intense political, economic or social imperatives that forced populations elsewhere out into the empire. Maybe the 'Welsh dog' was able to remain close to home, and so has had little or no obvious reason to 'bark' as loudly as its Irish and Scottish equivalents.

Notes

1 For the striking description of a 'reticent' Wales within the British Union and Empire that supplies the title of this article see Andrew Thompson, 'Empire and the British state', in Sarah Stockwell (ed.), *The British Empire: Themes and Perspectives* (Oxford, 2008), p. 51.

2 Terry Brotherstone, Anna Clark and Kevin Whelan (eds.), *These Fissured Isles: Ireland, Scotland and British History, 1798–1848* (Edinburgh, 2005), p. 12, n. 30. The failure to include Wales consistently in the 'New British History' has also been noted by Welsh historians. See Philip Jenkins, *A History of Modern Wales, 1536–1990* (London, 1992), p. 57.

3 These are too extensive to list exhaustively. For general surveys see M. Fry, *The Scottish Empire* (East Linton, 2001); T. M. Devine, *Scotland's Empire, 1600–1815* (London, 2003); Kevin Kenny (ed.), *Ireland and the British Empire* (Oxford, 2004). For the apparent anti-imperialism of the Enlightenment in Ireland, see Kevin Whelan, 'Ireland, Scotland and Britain in the long eighteenth century', in Brotherstone, Clark and Whelan (eds), *These Fissured Isles*, pp. 58–60.

4 Stephen Conway, *The British Isles and the War of American Independence* (Oxford, 2002), pp. 134–5, 173–4; H. V. Bowen, *The Business of Empire: The East India Company and Imperial Britain, 1756–1833* (Cambridge, 2006).

5 Aled Jones and Bill Jones, 'The Welsh world and the British Empire, c.1851–1939: an exploration', in Carl Bridge and Kent Fedorowich (eds.), *The British World: Diaspora, Culture and Identity* (London, 2003), p. 57; John M. MacKenzie, 'Irish, Scottish, Welsh

and English worlds? A four-nation approach to the history of the British Empire', *History Compass*, 6 (2008), 1252–3.

6 Gwyn A. Williams, *The Welsh and their history* (London, 1982), pp. 174–85.

7 A point made forcibly in Andrew Thompson, 'Empire and the British state', p. 51; H. V. Bowen, *Elites, Enterprise and the Making of the British Overseas Empire, 1688–1775* (Basingstoke and London, 1996), p. 153.

8 David W. Howell, 'The economy of landed estates of Pembrokeshire, c.1680–1830', *WHR*, 3 (1966–67), 265–83.

9 Prys Morgan, *The Eighteenth-Century Renaissance* (Llandybie, 1981), pp. 13–14; R. J. W. Evans, 'Was there a Welsh Enlightenment?', in R. R. Davis and Geraint H. Jenkins (eds), *From Medieval to Modern Wales. Essays in Honour of Kenneth O. Morgan and Ralph A. Griffiths* (Cardiff, 2004), pp. 142–59.

10 C. A. Bayly, *Imperial Meridian: The British Empire and the World, 1780–1830* (London, 1989), pp. 81 and 101; James Horn, 'British diaspora: emigration from Britain, 1680–1815', in P. J. Marshall (ed.), *The Oxford History of the British Empire*, vol. 2: *The Eighteenth Century* (Oxford, 1998), pp. 30–9; E. D. Evans, *A History of Wales, 1660–1815* (Cardiff, 1976), pp. 251–62; Ned C. Landsman, 'The Middle Colonies: New Opportunities for Settlement, 1660–1700', in Nicholas Canny (ed.), *The Oxford History of the British Empire*, vol. 1: *The Origins of Empire* (Oxford, 1998), pp. 361–2.

11 Jenkins, *History of Modern Wales*, pp. 34–216; Angus Calder, *Revolutionary Empire: The Rise of the English Speaking Empires from the Fifteenth Century to the 1780s* (London, 1998), pp. 486, 526–7.

12 S. J. Connolly, 'Varieties of Britishness: Ireland, Scotland and Wales in the Hanoverian state', in Alexander Grant and Keith J. Stringer (eds), *Uniting the Kingdom: The Making of British History* (London, 1995), p. 199; Thompson, 'Empire and the British state', p. 51.

13 Evans, *A History of Wales*, pp. 261–2; Evans, 'Was there a Welsh Enlightenment?', 157–8.

14 Devine, *Scotland's Empire*, p. 260.

15 Jones and Jones, 'The Welsh world', p. 63.

16 'Anglo-Welsh' is taken to mean an individual of Welsh parentage born and brought up in England.

17 Emrys Jones, 'The Welsh in London in the seventeenth and eighteenth centuries', *WHR*, 10 (1981), 461–72, and Jones, 'The age of societies', in Emrys Jones (ed.), *The Welsh in London, 1500–2000* (Cardiff, 2001), pp. 54–87.

18 BL, IOR, H/78, p. 107; B/53, pp. 164 and 223; B/71, p. 347.

19 BL, IOR, B/41, p. 99.

20 Stuart Handley, 'Price, Robert (1655–1733)', in H. C. G. Matthew and Brian Harrison (eds), *Oxford Dictionary of National Biography* (Oxford, 2004), vol. 45, pp. 311–13; Robert Thomas Jenkins, 'Sir Richard Lloyd', *Welsh Biography Online* [accessed 11 January 2009].

21 BL IOR, B/51, p. 201; TNA, PROB 11/569, p. 402.

22 Eveline Cruikshanks, Stuart Handley and D. W. Hayton (eds), *The History of Parliament: The House of Commons, 1690–1715* (5 vols, Cambridge, 2002), vol. 5, pp. 203–9.

23 P. Lawson, *The East India Company: A History* (London, 1993), p. 72; Søren Mentz, *The English Gentleman Merchant at Work: Madras and the City of London, 1660–1740* (Copenhagen, 2005), pp. 229–39.

24 BL, IOR, B/43, pp. 697–8.

25 BL, IOR, B/49, pp. 794–5, 827.

26 J. G. Parker, 'The Directors of the East India Company, 1754–1790' (PhD dissertation, University of Edinburgh, 1977), vol. 1, pp. 146–9, 154–6, 225–8.

27 Geraint H. Jenkins, *The Foundations of Modern Wales, 1642–1780* (Oxford, 1993), p. 88; Jenkins, *History of Modern Wales*, p. 17; E. A. Wrigley and R. S. Schofield, *The Population of England, 1541–1871: A Reconstruction* (London, 1981), pp. 531–5; Geoffrey Holmes and Daniel Szechi, *The Age of Oligarchy: Pre-industrial Britain* (London, 1993), pp. 345–50.

28 In an effort to be sensitive to the Principality's internal economic, social and linguistic diversity, the country is divided into three regions. South Wales is taken to mean: Monmouth, Glamorgan, Carmarthen and Pembroke; East Wales: Flint, Denbigh, Montgomery, Radnor and Brecon; North and West Wales: Cardigan, Merioneth, Caernarvon, and Anglesey.

29 BL, IOR, J/1/16, pp. 313–19 and 408–10.

30 Philip Jenkins, 'The creation of an "ancient gentry": Glamorgan, 1740–1840', *WHR*, 12 (1984–85), 30, 41–43; Jenkins, *History of Modern Wales*, pp. 170–1.

31 *Ibid.*, pp. 69–70; Jones, *Modern Wales*, p. 103.

32 Gareth Elwyn Jones, *Modern Wales: A Concise History, c.1485–1979* (Cambridge, 1984), pp. 23–5; Philip Jenkins, *The Making of a Ruling Class: The Glamorgan Gentry, 1640–1790* (Cambridge, 1983), pp. 218–20; Jenkins, *History of Modern Wales*, pp. 3–5.

33 BL, IOR, J/1/3, pp. 198–200; J/1/4, pp. 357–60.

34 B. S. Cohen, 'Recruitment and training of British civil servants in India, 1600–1860', in Ralph Braibanti (ed.), *Asian Bureaucratic Systems Emergent from the British Imperial Tradition* (Durham, NC, 1966), pp. 87–140.

35 National Archive of Scotland, Edinburgh [NAS], Grant of Seafield Muniments, GD 248/227/1/1, Mrs Cumming of Penrose to Sir James Grant of Grant, from London 15 August 1775.

36 TNA, PROB 11/755, pp. 78–79.

37 Gerald James Bryant, 'The East India Company and its Army, 1600–1778' (PhD dissertation, University of London, 1975), p. 35; Gerald Bryant, 'Officers of the East India Company's army in the days of Clive and Hastings', *Journal of Imperial and Commonwealth History*, 6 (1978), 203–6.

38 For important exceptions see, P. J. Marshall, 'British immigration into India in the nineteenth century', *Itinerario*, 14 (1990), 28, and 'British society in India under the East India Company', *Modern Asian Studies*, 31 (1997), 89–108; Mentz, *The English Gentleman Merchant*, pp. 64–70.

39 H. V. Bowen, 'The East India Company and military recruitment in Britain, 1763–1771', *Bulletin of the Institute of Historical Research*, 59 (1986), 79–81; National Library of Scotland [NLS], Minto Papers, MS 11041, fols. 42–8.

40 BL, IOR, L/MIL/9/111-120: 'Early Cadet Papers, 1800–1810'.

41 Anthony Bruce, *The Purchase System in the British Army* (London, 1980), pp. 22–35.

42 P. J. Marshall, *East Indian Fortunes: The British in Bengal in the Eighteenth Century* (Oxford, 1976), pp. 16–17; P. J. Cain and A. G. Hopkins, *British Imperialism: Innovation and Expansion, 1688–1914* (Harlow, 1993), pp. 319–23; M. McLaren, *British India and British Scotland, 1780–1830: Career Building, and a Scottish School of Thought on Indian Governance* (Akron, 2001), pp. 11–33; Gerald Bryant, 'Scots in India in the eighteenth century', *Scottish Historical Review*, 64 (1985), 29.

43 For the remarkably divergent patterns of involvement by Scots and Irish within the ordinary rank and file of the Company's armies, see Bryant, 'Scots in India in the eighteenth century', 23; Thomas Bartlett, 'The Irish soldier in India, 1750-1947', in Michael Holmes and Denis Holmes (eds), *Ireland and India: Connections, Comparisons, Contrasts* (Dublin, 1997), pp. 14–16.

44 P. E. Razzell, 'Social origins of officers in the Indian and British home army: 1758–1962', *British Journal of Sociology*, 14 (1963), 249–50; Linda Colley, *Britons: Forging the Nation, 1707–1837* (New Haven and London, 1992), pp. 14, 128–9, 156.

45 Michael Hechter, *Internal Colonialism: The Celtic Fringe in British National Development, 1536–1966* (London, 1975), *passim*.

46 BL, IOR, B/87, pp. 354–55; J/1/16, pp. 91–4, 308–11.

47 Hodson, *List of the Officers of the Bengal Army*, vol. 4, pp. 36 and 39.

48 A. Mackillop, 'Europeans, Britons and Scots: Scottish sojourning networks and identities in Asia, c.1700–1815', in A. McCarthy (ed.), *A Global Clan: Scottish Migrant Networks and Identities since the Eighteenth Century* (London, 2006), pp. 19–47.

49 H. V. Bowen, 'Privilege and profit: The commanders of East Indiamen as private traders, entrepreneurs, and smugglers, 1760–1813', *International Journal of Maritime History*, 19: 2 (2007), 43–88; BL, IOR, B/89, p. 495.

50 C. H. Philips, *The East India Company, 1784–1834* (Manchester, 1961), pp. 80–4; Bowen, *Business of Empire*, pp. 89–90.
51 BL, IOR, L/MAR/C/651: 'List of Commanders with their respective rank in the Company Service, 1737–1832'.
52 Marshall, *East Indian Fortunes*, pp. 24–5; P. J. Marshall, 'Private British investment in eighteenth-century Bengal', in P. Tuck (ed.), *The East India Company*, vol. 4: *Trade, Finance and Power* (London, 1998), pp. 127–141.
53 Bowen, *Business of Empire*, p. 274.
54 Joseph Price, *Some Observations and Remarks on a Late Publication Entitled Travels in Europe, Asia and Africa* (London, 1783), pp. 30 and 71, and *The Saddle Put on the Right Horse: Or, An Enquiry into the Reason Why Certain Persons Have Been Denominated Nabobs, With Arrangement of those Gentlemen into Their Proper Classes or Real, Spurious, Reputed, or Mushroom Nabobs* (London, 1783), p. 107.
55 BL, IOR, O/5/27, 'General List of Europeans not in H.M.'s or the Honourable Company's Service for the Year 1812'; O/5/31, fols. 1–4, 'Register of Europeans & Inhabitants who are not in the service of the Honourable Company residing in the Black Town and its Environs, Ft. St George, 1 October 1786'.
56 The Company's practice in this regard challenges the classical formulation of the link between empire and Britishness. See Colley, *Britons*, *passim*.
57 Jones and Jones, 'The Welsh world', pp. 58–9.
58 See for example, BL, IOR, L/MIL/9/255, 'Cadet Appointments, 1775–1791'; *A List of the Hon. and United East India Company's Civil and Military Servants on the Bengal Establishment, 1785* (Calcutta, 1785).
59 BL, IOR, J/1/1–19, pp. 21–26, 'Writers' Petitions 1749–1813; L/MIL/9/107–127, 'Early Cadet Papers, 1789–1813'.
60 Hodson, *List of the Officers of the Bengal Army*, II, p. 68.
61 Farrington, *Biographical Index*, pp. 328–9, 480–1, 636–8.
62 Devine, *Scotland's Empire*, xxvi.
63 Jones and Jones, 'The Welsh world', p. 60.
64 *Ibid*, pp. 57, 67–71.
65 N. Glaisyer, 'Networking: trade and exchange in the eighteenth-century British Empire', *Historical Journal*, 47 (2004), 451–75; Z. Laidlaw, *Connecting Colonies: Metropole and Professions, 1815–1845* (Manchester, 2003), ch. 2; Douglas Hamilton, *Scotland, the Caribbean and the Atlantic World, 1750–1820* (Manchester, 2005); D. Dickson, J. Parmentier and J. Ohlmeyer (eds), *Irish and Scottish Mercantile Networks in Europe and Overseas in the Seventeenth and Eighteenth Centuries* (Ghent, 2007).
66 BL, IOR, L/MIL/11/110–113; L/MIL/10/122–123; O/5/26–27, 30–31.
67 BL, IOR, L/MIL/9/85, 89: 'Embarkation Lists, 1753–63, 1775–81'.
68 Price, *Some Observations*, p. 77; Price, *The Saddle put on the Right Horse*, pp. 88–9.
69 TNA, PROB 11/1145, p. 391; BL, IOR, LAG/34/29/185 [1782], pp. 101–2, p. 158;
70 TNA, PROB 11/489, p. 134.
71 BL, IOR, L/AG/34/29/5/5 [1784]; Bowen, *Business of Empire*, p. 274.
72 Hilton Brown, *Parrys of Madras: A Story of British Enterprise in India* (Madras, 1954), pp. 1–49.
73 Robert Thomas Jenkins, 'John Evans', The National Library of Wales, *Welsh Bibliography Online* [accessed 11 January 2009]; Evans, *A History of Wales*, pp. 261–2; TNA, PROB 11/425, pp. 158–9.
74 George McGilvray, *East India Patronage and the British State: The Scottish Elite and Politics in the Eighteenth Century* (London, 2008), *passim*; R. B. McDowell, *Ireland in the Age of Imperialism and revolution, 1760–1801* (Oxford, 1991), p. 139; NLS, Melville Papers, MS 1074, fol. 148.
75 Jenkins, 'The creation of an "ancient gentry"', 41–4; Jenkins, *Making of a Ruling Class*, pp. 203–4.
76 Catherine Hall, 'Introduction: thinking the postcolonial, thinking the empire', in Catherine Hall (ed.), *Cultures of Empire: Colonisers in Britain and the Empire in the Nineteenth and Twentieth Centuries* (Manchester, 2000), pp. 15–24; Kathleen

Wilson, 'Introduction: histories, empires, modernities', in Kathleen Wilson (ed.), *A New Imperial History: Culture, Identity, and Modernity in Britain and the Empire, 1660–1840* (Cambridge, 2004), pp. 1–3, 17.

77 Jenkins, *History of Modern Wales*, pp. 41–55; J. P. Jenkins, 'The demographic decline of the landed gentry in the eighteenth century: a South Wales study', *WHR*, 11 (1982), 33–42; M. J. Dowden, 'A disputed inheritance: the Tredegar estates in the eighteenth century', *WHR*, 16 (1992), 36–41.

78 T. M. Devine, 'Scottish elites and the Indian Empire, 1700–1815', in T. C. Smout (ed.), *Anglo-Scottish Relations from 1603–1900* (Oxford, 2005), pp. 213–29.

CHAPTER 7

Asiatic interactions: India, the East India Company and the Welsh economy, c.1750–1830

H. V. Bowen

In the previous essay Andrew Mackillop explained why only comparatively small numbers of Welsh men and women found their way to Asia during the long eighteenth century. In view of this, it is quite reasonable to assume that any interactions that occurred between Wales and Britain's growing empire in the east were somewhat limited. Indeed, logic would appear to dictate that the process of British territorial and commercial expansion in Asia which gathered pace after the East India Company's conquest of Bengal between 1756 and 1765 bore only very lightly upon Wales; and it is hardly surprising that historians have never been much inclined to look beyond the Atlantic world as they have sought to locate the development of the Welsh economy within wider terms of reference. As a result, little of substance is known about the extent to which the establishment of an empire in India affected patterns of economic activity in Wales, and even when scholars have identified 'East Indian' influences they have only noted them in passing. This has served to confirm a general impression that Wales lay at the very outer edges of the domestic world of the East India Company, barely touched by some of the expansion-driven economic processes that were at work in other parts of Britain.[1]

But a failure by Wales to supply large numbers of personnel to the East India Company should not be translated automatically into an inability of Welshmen to take advantage of the opportunities that were available to Britons in the ever-expanding sphere of British imperial and commercial activity in Asia. As has been well documented, men such as Sir William Jones, Sir Harford Jones and Sir William Nott were more than capable of making their mark as scholars, diplomats and soldiers, but others were just as successful in the spheres of trade, business and enterprise, even if they are rather less conspicuous in the historical literature. Some very substantial Welsh East Indian fortunes were made in Asia, and part of this wealth found its way back into the domestic economy, where it was put to work alongside other profits of empire that were generated directly or indirectly from activity in the east. To be sure, the sum total of this wealth was never remotely sufficient to transform the Welsh economy as a whole – and it would be quite wrong to suggest otherwise – but in parts of Wales funds generated directly and indirectly from the expansionist process in Asia did contribute to processes of capital formation which in turn influenced local economic development in a number of different ways. Indeed, if this wealth is considered alongside that emanating from commercial activity taking place in the Atlantic world, then it has to be acknowledged that the eighteenth-century Welsh economy was rather more significantly affected by imperial influences than has hitherto been recognised by historians. In other words, the tangled skeins of trade and empire ensured that parts of Wales were already being integrated into, and reshaped by, the wider imperial economy well before 1830, and East Indian connections played a part in this process, thereby ensuring that Welsh economic development was driven by external as well as internal factors.

Of course, any direct transfer of wealth from India to Wales was dependent in the first instance upon the ability of Welshmen to get out to the subcontinent in order to make money. The number who found their way to India was indeed small, but those who did get there arrived by design, not by accident, and the factors that determined their passages to the east were broadly similar to those that enabled passages to be made from other parts of Britain. Most of the Welsh who went to India were younger sons motivated by innate sense of adventure who were willing to take a risk in an unfamiliar and far-distant land; and most were driven by a desire to make a fortune that could set them up in comfort for the rest of their lives. But personal ambition alone was not enough to secure reward, because individuals seeking entry to the monopolistic East India Company needed influence to be exercised on their behalf, and in this context Andrew Mackillop has emphasised the importance of the networks of Welshmen that had long existed in London. In their essential characteristics, therefore, the aims and *modus operandi* of those from Wales were exactly the same as those of others from Britain, and it would be quite wrong to suggest that because comparatively few Welshmen served in Asia this was because they somehow acted in way that was fundamentally different from the English, Irish or Scots. There was no unique or strikingly different career path for Welshmen, and they took their place within the general processes that facilitated the movement of all Britons to Asia. It is only because they were heavily outnumbered and often cannot be easily identified in the historical record that the activities and patterns of behaviour of those from Wales have been obscured by the presence of those who can be more easily analysed by the historian.

It has long been recognised that the Scots and Irish were especially adept at building long-lasting networks of connections and contacts that enabled individuals to obtain posts in the East India Company and then receive the support necessary for them to establish themselves within the Company's trading and imperial world. Little systematic work has ever been undertaken on the English employees of the East India Company, but countless individual examples indicate they too routinely made good use of family, social, political and commercial contacts; and this often led to the creation of semi-permanent networks of connections that linked different provinces to London and then extended out from the metropolis into Asia. Of course, many British East Indian networks were not defined strictly along subnational lines, and there can be little doubt that Welshmen were able to take advantage of what, on the face of it, might appear to have been 'English' webs of connection and patronage. As a result, traditions of East Indian service were established in some Welsh families, and, for example, over several generations the interconnected Elliot–Grant–Voyle families of Pembrokeshire sent many men to serve in the Company's armed forces and medical service; while the Carne family of Nash, Glamorgan, had a similarly long-lasting link with the Company.[2] Nonetheless, in certain circumstances some in Wales were themselves able to establish their own networks in order to support and promote the interests of those who wished to participate in the fierce competition that existed for appointment and promotion in the Company. But it should also be stressed that the process of network-building created webs of connections with the Indian empire that served to channel return flows of wealth, information and people into particular localities, and this in large part explains the geographical distribution of East Indian economic, social and cultural influences that manifested themselves across different parts of Wales.

In the decades after 1750 the part of Wales in which East Indian influence was most evident was the large area that today forms the county of Powys, comprising the former shires of Brecknock, Montgomery and Radnor. Indeed the most important East Indian network connecting Wales to London and the Indian empire was centred upon Brecon, from where the influential Walter Wilkins used his connections within the Company to pave the way for local men hoping to find their way to India. Wilkins (1741–1828, MP for Radnor 1796–1828) had entered the Company's service as a writer in Bengal in 1758 before rising to become the first Governor of Chittagong province and a member of the Supreme Council of Bengal. Following his return home in 1772, he made good use of personal contacts within the Company's Court of Directors in London, and this enabled him to secure appointments for a number of young men drawn from across his local region. Wilkins thus developed his own East Indian network, and, as noted below, several former Company servants were later to be very prominent in and around the town of Brecon itself. But Wilkins also acted in association with members of the interconnected Clive and Herbert families who were endeavouring to establish a cross-border political power base, and he helped them create a larger web of East Indian connections that extended from Shropshire into mid-Wales as well as other English counties.[3] As a result, it was soon acknowledged that Wilkins was capable of exercising considerable influence on behalf of his associates and protégés.[4] Moreover, Wilkins's own personal longevity and assiduous renewal of contacts within the Company helped to ensure that he launched the Indian careers of more than one generation of local men. Thus, for example, he paved the way for Frederick Jones (1758–1834) of Pencerrig, Radnorshire, to enter the Bombay army in 1778, and then twenty years later did exactly the same for Jones's nephew, Humphrey.

The men who enjoyed the favour and patronage of Wilkins also benefited from practical support from other prominent figures closely connected with Brecknockshire and Radnorshire, as became evident when they stayed in London before embarking on the Company ships that would take them to Asia. In this respect, the businessman and Brecknockshire landowner Evan Thomas (1702–90) of Parliament Street, and the politician, wit and *bon viveur* Chase Price (1731–77, MP for Radnorshire 1768–77), were also key figures in the emerging mid-Wales East India network because they both entertained and generally looked after those from the region who were bound for India. Hence, in 1776 when Frederick Jones enjoyed a brief time in London before heading out to serve in the Company's army in India he stayed with his cousin Rice James, and found himself regularly in the company of both Thomas and Price.[5]

Nothing better illustrates the workings of this important Welsh East Indian network than the experience of David Price (1762–1835) who was born near Brecon, at Merthyr Cynog.[6] Price was eventually to acquire a very large fortune in India and on his retirement to Brecon he became a noted orientalist and translator of Persian manuscripts. But the early stages of his passage to India were very difficult indeed and only timely interventions from compatriots rescued him from impending personal disaster. This situation arose because, in an act of desperation, Price had originally entered the Company's army in late 1780 in order to escape from Britain after a series of misjudgements and financial difficulties had brought an abrupt and premature end to his career as an aspiring scholar at Cambridge. In a state of some distress he signed on with the Company's army as an ordinary soldier, only then to experience a horrific confinement on the ship *Queen* which was waiting to depart for India. Help was at hand, however, when Price was brought before a sympathetic Welshman who was chaplain to the Company's shipping at Gravesend. This unnamed individual told Price that he was his 'countryman' before informing him that he was indebted to Price's father for his education. As a result, the chaplain acted with Thomas Evans, who had recently been appointed as a surgeon in the Company's maritime service, to secure the release of Price from his 'present state of bondage and destitution'. The two saviours then moved swiftly to represent Price's case to the aforementioned Evan Thomas who, through his connection with Lord Weymouth, obtained for Price a cadetship in the Bombay army, a posting that was in the gift of William James, the Chairman of the East India Company.[7] This rescue operation was successful, and Price was transferred to Evans's ship, *Essex*, which was commanded by the 'superannuated Arthur Morris'. To his great astonishment and 'unspeakable relief', Price found himself 'admitted to mess with the midshipmen, of whom I was gratified to discover that no less than four were natives of the principality; the second officer Mr [Henry] Smedley, who had commanded the Grand Trimmer, a privateer of considerable force, being a North Wales man'.[8] The experiences of Price were certainly not typical for those from Wales who travelled to Asia but they do nevertheless underscore the point that the early East Indian careers of some could be advanced and supported by networks and connections established by Welshmen within the world of the East India Company.

Although domestic networks enabled some Welshmen to gain access to the East India Company, it is doubtful that any of these webs of connection and influence extended very far into Asia. The scattering of a small number of Welshmen across the ground in the east meant that it was simply not possible for individuals to maintain close contact with their compatriots in the way of the Scots and the Irish who were often clustered together in different branches of the Company's service in India and elsewhere. Instead, necessity determined that domestic Welsh East Indian networks folded into those established by others on the subcontinent, and this meant that most Welshmen endeavoured to advance themselves through associations and activities with men who came from elsewhere in Britain. Of course, it was possible for a well-established entrepreneur such as Thomas Parry (1768–1824), who was originally from near Welshpool, to base the long-term development of his firm upon the recruitment of family members from Wales,[9] but circumstances usually dictated that most Welshmen in late eighteenth-century India acted in isolation from one another, operating as individuals or in partnership with associates from other parts of Britain.

If some Welshmen were able to create East Indian networks, then so too a significant number of those who went to India were able to achieve their primary objective of making money. Needless to say, there were some who failed miserably and died in penury, but those Welshmen who made fortunes demonstrated an ability to make money in all branches of the East India Company's service, as well as in private trade. There was no one more successful than Thomas Parry, previously mentioned, who during the course of a long career combined official service with a very wide range of entrepreneurial activities conducted on his own account including shipping, marine insurance, agency work, 'country trading' around the Indian Ocean, manufacturing and procurement of raw materials. Parry first arrived in Madras in 1788 and by 1793 he had already created a 'snug fortune', although he then had to weather several commercial storms before he was able firmly to establish the large firm which as 'Parry's of Madras' still remains one of the best-known companies in India.

Not all were able to match the long-term success of Parry, but different branches of the Company's service provide striking examples of Welshmen making the most of their opportunities and combining skill, acumen and good fortune in order to accumulate considerable personal riches. As was the case with all Britons, there was no common pattern of wealth acquisition, and while some steadily accumulated wealth over a long period of time, others hit the jackpot when circumstances presented them with a windfall that could not have been anticipated. Into the latter category fell David Price, who lost a leg during the siege of Dharwar in 1791 and then became judge advocate and Persian translator of the Bombay army. It was Price's great good fortune to be present at the storming of Tipu Sultan's citadel at Seringapatam in 1799, after which he was appointed as the army's prize agent and charged with handling record amounts of booty. Being in the right place at the right time enabled Price to acquire the wealth that set him up in a considerable degree of comfort for the rest of his life.

Few were as fortunate as Price and most had to apply themselves to private enterprise, often combining foul means as well as fair as they pursued their own interests alongside those of the Company. This was the case, for example, with another army officer, George Herbert, who came from Park in Montgomeryshire and whose entry into the Company's military service was based upon a recommendation from Robert Clive.[10] In 1771 Herbert became a brigade paymaster in the Bengal army, a plum posting which presented him with the 'certain prospect of making a very large fortune with honor and honesty and without the dreadful ideas of having oppressed or injured anyone, ideas which must render riches the most terrible curses'. Herbert claimed to have had £30,000 passing through his hands every month, and, whether or not he did actually manage to behave with 'honor and honesty', he certainly deployed some of these funds in a range of commercial activities, which enabled him to acquire a fortune 'upwards of £80,000' by April 1778.

Walter Wilkins gained a substantial fortune while serving in the civil branch of the Company's Bengal administration between 1758 and 1772, and by the time he died in 1828 he was worth £250,000.[11] This meant that he was one of the richest men in Wales, and indeed he was one of the most significant wealth-holders in Britain as a whole. The surgeon Thomas Phillips (1760–1851), who had strong family connections with Radnorshire, enriched himself from the commercial activity he conducted while employed in the Company's medical service between 1782 and 1817.[12] In the diplomatic sphere, Harford Jones from Presteigne, minister-plenipotentiary to Persia between 1807 and 1811, built a fortune based upon the private trade he conducted while stationed as a commercial agent at Basra (1783–94) and Baghdad (1798–1806). At Basra, Jones traded in a notably wide range of commodities including carpets, tobacco and sugar, but he was especially interested in the buying and selling of manuscripts because they could be purchased so cheaply and thus 'yield a handsome profit', and he encouraged his friends to 'command me freely' if they desired a diamond ring.[13] During a troubled and increasingly desperate time at Baghdad, Jones claimed to have acted 'with scrupulous honesty' when trading in only a parcel of jewels and one large consignment of coffee, but nonetheless he was able to calculate that his fortune amounted to almost £19,000 by the end of 1805.[14] Finally, as Ken Jones has shown in great detail, John Lloyd from Llawrtyd in Breconshire was able steadily to accumulate a considerable fortune from a career in the Company's maritime service as he rose through the ranks until, after commanding the Indiaman *Manship* on two voyages to Madras and Bengal, he retired to Brecon in 1796.[15]

Of course, the climate, disease, alcohol, enemy action and general misfortune took a heavy toll on Britons in India, and several of the Welshmen who did make considerable amounts of money in India never returned to Wales. Most notably, Thomas Parry died suddenly from cholera when visiting Porto Novo in southern India in August 1824, although it is not evident that he ever intended to leave the subcontinent. One wealthy Welshman who certainly did wish to return to Britain as soon as possible was George Herbert. Unfortunately for him, however, he was to die in unexplained circumstances during his journey home. Together with Richard Griffith, a senior financial officer and opium contractor at Patna, Herbert resigned from the Company's service in early 1779,[16] and both men were ordered to carry Company packets to London via the 'overland route' through Suez. Griffith duly arrived in London in the autumn of 1779 in possession of a fortune of between £60,000 and £90,000, although he was later to run into financial difficulties, after a failed investment in the Grand Canal Company in Ireland. He ended his days living in comparative obscurity at Holyhead where he served as Post Office packet agent.[17] By contrast, the exact fate of George Herbert is unknown because, after setting out for Suez, he was not heard from again, and by 1782 John Herbert was being described as the 'sole executor to his late brother'.[18] A substantial portion of George Herbert's East Indian fortune had already been remitted to Britain – £6,150 in 1774/5 and £16,050 two years later – and as a consolation for the loss of George these considerable assets were retained in the Herbert family when John inherited them. Through marriage, John Herbert had already acquired landed property near Machynlleth, and in a greatly strengthened financial position he then went on to become a leading figure in Montgomeryshire, serving as a JP and Deputy Lieutenant of the county.

It is evident that nearly all of the Welshmen who possessed an East Indian fortune aimed to return to home in order to establish themselves in landed society, and there was no migration of former Company servants from Wales to London and the Home Counties as there was from Ireland, Scotland and provincial England. Most, it would seem, had ambitions that did not extend beyond exploiting the local opportunities for economic, social and political advancement that presented themselves in Wales itself, and they chose to live and invest in an environment that was familiar to them. As a result, it is possible to identify a good number of landed properties that were bought and developed by Welsh former servants of the Company. And, unsurprisingly in view of the patterns of networks and recruitment into the Company sketched out earlier, most of these estates were located in a swathe of territory that extended south-westwards from the English border with Montgomeryshire and Radnorshire, through Brecknockshire and across into Carmarthenshire and Pembrokeshire.

Upon his return from Persia in 1811 Sir Harford Jones, who assumed the additional name Brydges in 1826, settled in Radnorshire at Boultibrooke on an estate straddling the England–Wales border where he developed his newly acquired property and devoted himself to oriental studies and civic duties. Not far away, near Glasbury, was Walter Wilkins's home, Maesellwch Castle. In 1804 the re-built 'castle' was described as 'by no means a good one' by a writer who also took a dim view of Wilkins himself, noting that he was a 'very constant resident but with less popularity than generally awaits the resident gentry'.[19] To the south, close to Brecon, was the 893-acre Llanfranach estate of Wilkins's brother, Jeffreys (d. 1819), who had been a Company servant at Patna. Jeffreys Wilkins bought this land from the Anglo-Irish peer Viscount Ashbrook in July 1802, and he later built Maesderwen on it. Only a year earlier Captain John Lloyd had paid Ashbrook £13,460 for the neighbouring estate of Abercynrig, although he never actually took up residence in the house of the same name.[20] A short distance away in Brecon itself, David Price conducted his oriental studies at the well-appointed Watton House, from where he produced a stream a works, the most notable of which was *Chronological Retrospect; Or Memoirs of the Principal Events of Mahommedan History* . . . (3 vols, London, 1811–21). Operating at a rather less elevated level was Frederick Jones who similarly retired to Brecon. In addition to involvement in local politics and civic affairs, Jones wrote a brief account of the expeditions and sieges in which he had been involved while serving at Bombay between 1778 and 1787. His volume was first published in Brecon in 1794, when presumably it was intended for local circulation to his family and acquaintances, but, reaching out to a wider audience, Jones also arranged for copies of the book to be sold by a London bookseller.[21] Men such as Price and Jones had certainly accumulated substantial personal wealth in the service of the East India Company, but when they wrote about their experiences in India they were also adding to the local and national stocks of knowledge about Asia. In small ways, therefore, they were integrating Wales mentally and well as economically into the rapidly expanding British Empire.

Twenty miles or so to the west of Brecon was the home of Captain David Williams (d. 1819), from a local family, who served in the Bengal army between 1769 and 1786, during which time he commanded a battalion of Indian sepoys belonging to the Nawab of Awadh, a key ally of the Company. Williams, who was described by one of his correspondents as an 'old Indian delinquent',[22] used an East India fortune remitted in diamonds to purchase several parcels of land and property as he endeavoured to build up an estate around Henllys Fawr near Llandovery. Then on his return from India he became a figure of some considerable importance in local society, serving as a JP and colonel in the Carmarthenshire militia.[23] But Williams also had a highly controversial walk-on part in the most captivating national political drama played out during the late eighteenth century. This was because, in the course of lengthy impeachment proceedings conducted in Parliament against Governor-General Warren Hastings, it was alleged that in 1781 Williams, acting on orders passed down from the Nawab, had carried out the summary execution of a captured rebel leader, Mustafa Khan. As the thirteenth article of impeachment against Hastings put it, Williams had committed a 'cruel and atrocious murder'.[24] This put Williams at the centre of public attention in 1790 when Hastings's enemies used the allegation as a stick with which to beat the former Governor-General and his administrative regime. In the end, the much-vilified Williams only escaped from the limelight when a motion for an inquiry into the whole murky episode was dropped, although this was not before he was obliged to publish a robust and detailed defence of his actions which included a denial that he had been personally responsible for killing Mustafa Khan.[25] Even then, the allegations against him continued to resurface from time to time as the ultimately unsuccessful proceedings against Hastings dragged on until 1794.

Further to the south and south-west, former Company servants also sought to settle back into local society. Most notably, perhaps, the senior Company military officer Sir William Nott (1782–1845) retired to the place of his upbringing, Carmarthen, where shortly before his death he purchased the nearby Job's Well estate.[26] Near Llandeilo, the Aberglasney estate was bought for 10,000 guineas in 1803 by a retired Company surgeon Thomas Phillips (d. 1824) who had family connections in the locality.[27] During the late eighteenth century the Upton estate near Pembroke had been purchased by Captain John Tasker (d. 1800), who had 'acquired a competent fortune' in India and then 'retired to the place of his birth to enjoy it'.[28] From the Company's maritime service, John Jones (1751–1828) returned to his roots in Swansea, where in 1792 he purchased St Helen's House, using the profits he had accumulated from private trade conducted when he sailed to India and China as an officer and commander on board East Indiamen.[29]

Less well travelled than John Jones in a geographical sense was Jacob Richards (1774–1834) but he is noteworthy because of the striking trajectory of his upward social mobility. Richards does not quite provide an archetypal example of rags to fabulous riches but, unlike most of those discussed so far, he came from a humble background and used East India service to transform his own economic and social status. This served to establish him among the social elite of Tenby, the increasingly fashionable Pembrokeshire bathing resort which acted as a magnet for those such as the Voyle family who served in India, as well others who made money in the intra-Asian private 'country trade'.[30] Originally from Glamorgan, Richards was a labourer who was recruited into the East India Company's Bengal army in 1792 but within eleven years he had been promoted to sergeant major in the artillery. Little is known about how exactly Richards made his money but he appears to have been especially adept in financial matters. Indeed, when he returned to Britain in 1805 he was sufficiently wealthy to establish himself as a gentleman in Tenby where he purchased property and became actively involved in civic affairs, serving as mayor five times between 1812 and 1831. At the time of his death in 1834 Richards's estate was valued at £17,000, and his two surviving sons were in the early stages of their careers as officers in the Company's army.[31]

These were all men who returned to their roots after serving in the Company, but they were joined by others from across the border who also chose to channel all or part of their East India fortunes into Welsh land and property at a time when demographic changes were already causing widespread transfers across Wales to be made to incomers.[32] As such, East Indian wealth played a locally significant part in the restructuring of Welsh landed society. Robert Clive led the cross-border incursion as he endeavoured to add to his Walcot estate in Shropshire in an attempt to create a cross-border *bloc* of land and political influence. In 1768 and 1769 he bought the Monmouthshire estate of Piercefield (from Valentine Morris junior who held extensive land and investments in Antigua) and several other smaller parcels of land in the Usk and Trellech area for sums amounting to almost £50,000. A change of electoral strategy led to him selling his territory to the Duke of Beaufort for £57,500 in 1772, although by that time he had also purchased the Heightly and Rockley estates in Montgomeryshire, the county which had now become the primary object of his political attention.[33]

Others followed Clive's example, including the idiosyncratic John Zephaniah Holwell (1711–98) who had been temporary Governor of Bengal at the time of the 'Black Hole of Calcutta' episode of 1756. Holwell had a main residence in Middlesex but he was also a JP in Pembrokeshire and during the mid-1770s he invested heavily in the construction of the eccentric Castle Hall, Milford, which he then sold a decade later. Ralph Leeke made a similar short-term foray into Wales. On his return to Shropshire from India in 1786, he procured the Crugion estate and the manor of Nether Gordder in Montgomeryshire for £16,000, and then sold them for a profit of £22,000 in 1813.[34] In 1817 Francis Fowke, the Company's controversial Resident at Benares between 1775 and 1786 who had amassed a fortune of over £70,000 from trade in opium and diamonds, began the building of a large house on the site of a medieval castle at Boughrood in Radnorshire, where he died in 1819.[35] No doubt it was Fowke who encouraged his brother-in-law and former assistant at Benares, John Benn (1759–1825, later Sir John Benn Walsh), to invest part of his £80,000 fortune in Radnorshire. By 1821 Benn had acquired fifty-nine parcels of land, and this added greatly to the concentration of East Indian wealth in the county. Less wealthy English East Indians joined this often temporary movement into Welsh land and property, as was the case with William Crampton Green, a former major in the Bombay army who bought Kilvrough Manor near Swansea in 1806. Green lived at Kilvrough for only three years before he died, but the estate later passed into the hands of the Lyons family who themselves had very extensive East Indian connections.[36]

An especially enduring mark was left on the Welsh landscape by William Paxton (1744–1824).[37] Born in Edinburgh, Paxton served in the Royal Navy before entering the Company's ranks in 1774 when he was appointed Assay Master at Fort William in Bengal. Four years later he became the Master of the Calcutta Mint. At the same time, by acting in a private capacity Paxton used his entrepreneurial skills to set up one of the first commercial agency houses to be established in Calcutta, and this enabled him to offer a wide range of financial and shipping services to clients within the European community. The rapid growth of his business enabled Paxton to acquire a very large fortune, and when he returned to Britain in 1785 he established a branch of his company in London, which as Paxton, Cockerell, Trail & Co. became a bank as well as an East Indian agency house.

Paxton moved into Carmarthenshire when, seeking entry into Parliament and having been introduced to the area by his old Bengal associate Captain David Williams of Henllys Fawr, he spent £40,000 on the Middleton Hall estate, just outside Llanarthne. Paxton built a new mansion, laid out ornamental gardens and woodland, and created ponds that were serviced by an elaborate underground network of water pipes. His enthusiasm for improvement of the aquatic type led to him to introduce piped water to Carmarthen when he served as mayor in 1802, and he later paid for the building of an expensive public bath-house in Tenby. Paxton sought local approval for political purposes and his efforts to gain entry to Parliament led him to undertake other more direct forms of electoral expenditure. This meant that during the fierce battle for the Carmarthen county seat in 1802 he spent the astonishing sum of £15,690, which included payments for 11,070 breakfasts, 36,901 dinners, 684 suppers, 25,275 gallons of ale, 11,068 bottles of spirits, 8,879 bottles of porter, 460 bottles of sherry, and 509 bottles of cider. Paxton's largesse undoubtedly caused many hangovers, as well as a welcome short-term boost in trade for local brewers, hoteliers and tavern-keepers, but although the electors of Carmarthen were quite happy to gorge themselves on free food and drink many of them remained deeply suspicious of the fabulously wealthy incomer. As a result, despite his prodigious outlay, Paxton was unable to secure the votes necessary to defeat Sir John Hamlyn Williams in the poll. Yet, not easily deterred, Paxton was soon able to occupy the Carmarthen borough seat when John George Phillips vacated it in December 1803, and then during the election of 1806 he transferred his attentions back to the county seat, for which he was returned unopposed.

These intricate political manoeuvrings eventually enabled Paxton to derive some short-term satisfaction from entry to Parliament, but he failed to build up a strong local power base because many electors remained hostile towards the 'upstart nabob' and 'Scotch herring' who was 'heedless of the interests of our native land'.[38] As a result, he was unceremoniously unseated during the general election of 1807, and later attempts at a comeback ended in failure. But although Paxton enjoyed little success as a politician his spending did have a lasting impact on Carmarthenshire. At the time of his death, his fortune amounted to almost £300,000 and his 2,650-acre estate was dominated by 'Paxton's Tower', or 'Paxton's Folly' as it was known to the locals, a memorial erected in honour of Nelson who visited the area in 1802. The tower remains as a prominent landmark, and the National Botanic Garden of Wales is now located on the site of Paxton's former estate.

In many ways, the purchasing of land and the development of houses and estates in Wales by those returning from Asia conformed to a pattern of behaviour that has been identified by P. J. Marshall as having been common among holders of East Indian fortunes.[39] Many of those investing in Welsh property were thus recognisably 'nabobs', and were regarded by contemporaries as such, in the sense that they used their East Indian wealth to indulge in the comfort, leisure and luxury associated with a landed lifestyle. But it is noteworthy that at least of some of the East Indians in Wales also sought to channel part of their funds into economic activity and 'improvement' of the type undertaken by William Paxton around Carmarthenshire.

Such investment was especially evident in and around Brecon. Here, Walter Wilkins was a founding partner of the (old) Brecon Bank in 1778, and a partner in Wilkins, [John] Lloyd, Powell & Co.[40] Wilkins was joined as a partner in the Bank by his brother Jeffreys, probably from the outset, but certainly from 1792;[41] and both of them later invested in the Hay Tram Road. Captain John Lloyd undertook a yet more diverse range of investments. Following an attempt to develop the Dinas lead mine during 1794, he (together with Jeffreys Wilkins) became one of the four shareholders of the Brecknock Boat and Canal Company, which monopolised trade on the local canal and owned a colliery at Clydach; and he took up share capital and provided loan finance in order to help fund the initial construction of the Brecon to Abergavenny canal, and its subsequent onward extension to the Monmouthshire canal. In addition, Lloyd owned a fulling mill on the Honddu and (again with Jeffreys Wilkins) he became a founder investor in the local tramway known as the Watton 'railway'. In sum total, the interlocking investments of these three closely connected former East India Company servants were considerable, and there can be no doubting that they had a marked and enduring effect upon the financial, industrial and transport infrastructure developed in and around Brecon.

The transformative local effect of East Indian wealth manifested itself in a rather different way in Llandovery where the former East India Company surgeon, Thomas Phillips (not to be confused with his namesake of Aberglasney), chose to invest part of his very substantial fortune. In 1847, when he was in his eighties, Phillips was the main mover behind the establishment and building of the Collegiate Institute, which today exists as the public school known as Llandovery College. But Phillips did much more, having dedicated his retirement to philanthropic activity, and with almost obsessive zeal he channelled his East Indian fortune into Welsh education and learning. He endowed scholarships and a professorship at Saint David's College, Lampeter; funded scholarships for Welsh boys to study at Oxford; and, above all, he purchased vast quantities of books and artefacts, many of them 'Oriental' in nature, which were supplied not only to the colleges at Lampeter and Llandovery but also to towns throughout Wales and beyond.[42]

All of these purchases and improvements in Wales were funded by the investment of money made by individuals who, in one way or another, had participated directly in the process of commercial and imperial expansion in Asia: they went to the east, made money, and returned. The accumulation of riches in India catapulted Walter Wilkins and William Paxton into the ranks of the super-rich in Britain at a time when very few individuals in Wales held similar amounts of wealth. Other East Indians possessed lesser fortunes but were still marked out as men of unusual wealth and influence in the places where they settled. As such, contemporaries would have recognised that these high-profile local figures had derived very considerable financial benefit from the empire. Concealed from view, however, were individuals who had often never set foot outside Wales but indirectly derived profits from that the process of expansion. This was the case, for example, with those who invested in East India Company stock and were able to earn good rates of interest in the form of dividend payments which from 1793 onwards were secured on Indian land revenues and fixed at $10^1/_2$ per cent a year.

The total amount of East India stock owned by investors living in Wales was never large, and a list of stockholders compiled in March 1836 indicates that it stood at only £79,633 (1.3 per cent of the total) spread across thirty-nine accounts.[43] Nonetheless, this form of investment in empire attracted funds from across Wales, from well-established bankers such as the Morris family of Carmarthen through to small investors who had no obvious links with the Company, such as the spinster Jane Hughes of Aberdovey who owned £195 8s. stock, the Reverend Owen Gethin Williams of Rhiwlas, Anglesey (£77 2s. 5d.), and Elizabeth Williams, a widow of Croespyn, Anglesey (£115 19s. 1d.). These types of holdings are of interest because the existence of small East India investors across Wales reveals that by the mid-1830s the British investment market had become integrated to the point that individuals at some considerable distance from London were able to deploy capital in a leading gilt-edged fund such as India stock. And not all Welsh investors were 'passive' in the sense that they were content simply to collect annual dividends as a form of income. Some engaged in regular transactions, building up holdings of East India stock and then selling them at an opportune moment when a good price enabled them to make a profit. Hence by the early 1820s John Hunter of Llanidloes had built up a stock holding of over £5,000, which he then gradually sold off in small amounts;[44] while Edward Warren Jones of Llanina near Lampeter steadily accumulated stock throughout the 1820s so that by 1830 he owned £3,800.[45]

The other group of people who made money from expansion in Asia were industrial entrepreneurs and some of their East Indian commercial activities contributed very significantly to the deep and long-lasting changes that were occurring within the Welsh economy. Small consignments of 'Welch flannel' woollen textiles were routinely dispatched to India by the East India Company, but the most notable group of businessmen to benefit from trade with Asia were the copper smelters and manufacturers of the Neath and lower Swansea valleys whose enterprises and fortunes were profoundly influenced by the increasingly strong demand for their products that emanated from Indian markets. The significant late eighteenth-century growth of copper exports represented a great commercial success story for the East India Company at the very time it was under pressure to increase the overall volume and value of its trade, and this helped to ensure that Company orders exerted a powerful influence on a number of key firms. Indeed, it is possible to establish almost identical chronologies of growth, which indicates very strongly that the East India Company's expansion of its copper exports ran hand-in-hand with the early development of large-scale smelting in South Wales.

This mutually dependent relationship between the two processes was forged during the 1730s when the Company exported bulk cargoes of copper to Asia for the first time, and thereafter a sustained and increasingly diverse demand was felt in and around Swansea. With South Wales's copper also being channelled simultaneously into the slave-trade and the wider Atlantic economy, as outlined by Chris Evans in Chapter Two, it is evident that from the time the industry began to emerge as a large-scale concern it was to a very significant degree orientated towards markets in Britain's overseas empire. This process served very firmly to embed the region within the wider imperial economy during the second half of the eighteenth century, and it is quite erroneous to suggest that such integration only occurred during the nineteenth century as a consequence of the growth of the coal, iron, steel and tinplate industries. Of course, the distribution of those major industries across South Wales eventually ensured a much wider range of economic connections between the region and the empire, but copper led the breakout of heavy Welsh goods into worldwide markets and this very profoundly affected the outlooks, attitudes and mental horizons of those whose initiative, skills and resources shaped the process of development.

The East India Company had long exported small consignments of copper pots and utensils to Asia but in October 1729 it decided to test the market more extensively in India by exporting bulk cargoes of copper to Bengal for the first time. In undertaking this experiment the Company turned to 'Richard Lockwood & Co.', which was paid £3,150 for copper plates a few months later.[46] Encouraged by the results of the experiment, the directors of the Company returned to Lockwood with further orders – 100 tons of copper plates at £105 a ton in 1730/31, 80 tons in 1731/32, 60 tons in 1733/34, and 82 tons in 1734/35 – and copper became firmly established as one of the Company's staple export commodities.[47] Lockwood was evidently very well connected at East India House, not only through his long involvement in the Levant and African trade but also because he was a leading figure in the politics and finance of the City of London, and this enabled him to win these important supply contracts only a couple of years after he had diversified his commercial interests by becoming a partner in Robert Morris's copper-smelting works at Llangyfelach near Swansea. Established in 1727, Lockwood, Morris &

Co. developed its works on the site of the first copper-smelting enterprise in the Swansea valley which had been founded by Dr John Lane ten years earlier. To a large extent, therefore, Lockwood's success in winning the East India Company order was vital for the early growth of the fledgling firm, and remaining in favour with those at East India House meant that exports to Asia always formed an important branch of its operations, which were extended when a new works was opened at nearby Fforest in 1746. Indeed, a strong relationship with the East India Company endured until Lockwood, Morris & Co. ceased trading during the 1790s, and in most years substantial consignments of copper were dispatched to London for onward shipment to India. As a result, between 1750 and 1790 Lockwood, Morris & Co. supplied the East India Company with 4,449 tons of copper, and in return it was paid £488,438.[48]

Lockwood, Morris & Co. was the first copper-smelting company to exploit the opportunities arising from British commercial expansion in Asia, but others in the lower Swansea and Neath valleys were swift to follow, and some were also able to establish similar long-lasting relationships with the East India Company. Notably, firms in South Wales were well to the fore during the 1750s when the Company significantly increased its purchases of copper cake and brass and then began for the first time to procure evermore substantial quantities of 'manufactured' copper and the 'japanned' variety produced with a distinctive dark-sheen finish. This process of expansion and diversification helped to encourage the establishment of new works or the takeover of established enterprises in and around Swansea, and in most instances developments were led by incoming English entrepreneurs who brought capital and skills into the region from Bristol or London. In nearly all cases these firms had connections with the East India Company, and thus there was an increase in the number of commercial channels through which South Wales copper found its way to the East India Company. Most notable, perhaps, was the firm Joseph Percival & Co. which was re-formed as John Freeman & Co. in 1764, an organisational rearrangement which ensured that copper was supplied in significant quantities to the Company from the White Rock works throughout the second half of the century. In return, payments to the White Rock companies amounted to £670,367 between 1750 and 1800. From the Neath Abbey works the Mines Royal Company provided the Company with copper more or less continuously between 1755 and 1800, and it was paid £314,794. Other firms were less enduring but had important short-term relationships with the Company, as was notably the case with Chauncey Townsend & Co. (paid £135,434 between 1756 and 1764) and George Pengree & Co.

(paid £194,281 between 1765 and 1785), both of which smelted at the Middle Bank works. A further surge in exports during the late 1770s brought yet more firms from the region into the Company's orbit, notably Sir Herbert Mackworth and the Gnoll Copper Co. (1777–87) which operated the Melincryddan works near Neath; and Fenton (or Chacewater) & Co. (1776–85) which established the Rose works in 1780. By way of a supplement to this large-scale supply of copper to the East India Company, some of the smelters also found an outlet for their produce through sales of occasional bulk consignments to those who were engaged in licensed private trade with Asia.[49] And, no doubt, some copper smelted in Swansea would also have been shipped to the east by private traders who routinely engaged in a lively and often extensive illicit export trade that operated either directly or via ports in Europe.[50]

It has been estimated that by the 1780s between one-sixth and one-quarter of annual domestic copper output was being directed towards South Asia,[51] and the East India Company's records indicate that a very large proportion of this supply to the Indian market emanated from the smelting works located in and around Swansea. Indeed, for much of the time the existence of cartel-type arrangements among the smelting firms ensured that, in addition to fixing prices, the South Wales works were able to exert considerable control over the supply of copper to the Company. This was especially so between 1750 and 1770 before fierce competition within the association of smelters ensured that some concessions were made to firms from Cornwall and the north-west of England who were able to secure a wider distribution of orders. But a near-monopoly of supply of copper from South Wales to the Company was restored during the late 1780s through the formidable efforts of the 'copper king', Thomas Williams, whose organisational integration of the industry led to Anglesey replacing Cornwall as the main source of the ores used by the Swansea smelters.[52] Williams, whose Parys Mine Company procured the Upper Bank works in Swansea in 1782, ruthlessly undercut rival smelters to such an extent that he was able to secure the vast majority of the orders made by the Company at a time when it was obliged by statute to export 1,500 tons of copper a year. In return, the Company made very considerable payments to Williams, and £1,132,164 exchanged hands in the ten years after 1788. These payments fed the sustained growth of Williams's concerns, at least until the supplies of Anglesey ore became depleted at the beginning of the nineteenth century, but the spin-off effects were also felt across an extended commodity chain by a large supporting cast of individuals who participated in a host of different ways in the mining, smelting, manufacture, rolling, cutting and shipping of copper. Of course, these people did not become wealthy in the way of the industrial magnates but nonetheless, whether they realised it or not, their livelihoods were dependent to a considerable extent on the ebb and flow of East India Company commercial activity in Asia.

One must be careful not to exaggerate the localised effects of the growth of the copper industry on the port and town of Swansea, because the very nature of copper-smelting was such that output and the size of the workforce were both modest by comparison with the later emerging ferrous metal industries of the region.[53] Nonetheless, copper-smelting stimulated other industrial activity, notably coal mining, and the late eighteenth-century effects of interconnected expansion upon Swansea are reflected across a range of statistical indicators. Thus, to take just one example, the number of ships entering the harbour increased from 694 in 1768 to 2,590 in 1800, and the registered tonnage of these vessels rose from 30,361 to 154,264 during the same period.[54] And the spin-off effects were felt further afield in Wales, especially in Anglesey where Thomas Williams's large-scale extraction of copper ore from Parys Mountain stimulated activity across different sectors of the local economy and led to a marked growth in the number of ships dedicated to the carrying of bulk consignments of ore to Swansea.[55]

It is evident that the volume of demand from Asia exerted an important influence on a maturing heavy industry, but also of some significance to the developmental process was the *type* of copper required by the East India Company in order to meet the demand of purchasers in India. The Company repeatedly experimented with different varieties of copper in an attempt to identify what was best suited to Indian markets, and this meant that over the course of the half century after 1750 it extended it purchases beyond copper plates, cake and brass. In addition to standard battery copper, consignments of manufactured copper sent to India contained a wide range of bars, rods and ingots of differing shapes, sizes and finishes. In particular, the production of imitation 'japan' copper required the application of specialist techniques in order to create the dark-sheen finish often favoured in Indian markets, and after a successful trial conducted in 1754 the volume of this commodity exported by the Company increased substantially from annual average of 66 tons during the 1760s to 191 tons during the 1780s.[56] But under the heading of 'general merchandise' in Company commerce ledgers is to be found evidence that Welsh copper manufacturers were also producing a range of finished products for export to South Asia. These were not generic items that could have been dispatched to any market, but instead were commodities manufactured to very exact specifications in line with instructions formulated by the Company on the basis of information sent to London from India. Notable here was the output of the Mackworth and Gnoll Copper Company which during the 1780s supplied a range of finished goods, including copper bottoms for salt boilers, copper pitch kettles, copper linings for stationary cases, copper plates for mill bedstones, and copper nails, as well as copper for casting brass ordnance.[57] Sales of this type to the East India Company did not occur on any great scale but they do demonstrate the early capacity of some firms to adapt productive processes to the special demands of different global markets. Indeed the successful and rapid penetration of Indian markets by the copper-smelting firms of south-west Wales had a considerable long-term effect upon the maritime economy of Asia. As a detailed quantitative study demonstrates, from the 1760s the importation of copper into India from Britain eclipsed the long-established inward flow of that commodity from Japan, and this process of substitution supports the justifiable claim that 'it was British copper, not British cotton textiles, which acted as the harbinger of the Industrial Revolution to the world economy'.[58]

British commercial and imperial expansion in India thus had a direct and sustained influence upon the growth of copper-smelting, the industry which drove the early development of the south-west Wales economy, and in turn this had a considerable effect on the local environment and landscape. Such profound Asiatic influence was not so evident in the somewhat later growth of the ferrous metal industries, but key firms in the region were nonetheless keen to break into the Indian market during the late eighteenth century. Richard Crawshay, who owned the great Cyfarthfa ironworks at Merthyr, was deeply frustrated by his inability to secure any contracts to supply bulk consignments of bar iron to the Company until the very end of century. But, undeterred, he was able to fall back on supplying iron to private traders, and from the middle of the 1780s he was able to derive at least some benefit from the Company by occasionally selling it steel, iron shot and iron guns.[59] These sales to the Company enabled Crawshay to gain a foothold inside East India House, which meant that he was in a good position to take advantage when the Company's regular sole supplier of iron, John Wilson & Co., faltered and fell by the wayside between 1799 and 1804. As a result, he was able to step into the breach and provide the Company with a significant proportion of the mixed consignments of 'English' and Swedish bar iron it required during the first two decades of the nineteenth century. In total, the volume of iron directed by Crawshay towards Asia through the East India Company was not especially large, but his company maintained a position as a key supplier until, after the loss of its Indian trade monopoly, the East India Company began to wind down its commercial operations during the mid-1820s, and at times it was joined by other Welsh firms such as Homfrays & Fennell, the Dowlais Iron Company, and Guest, Lewis & Co.

This essay has identified a range of connections that existed between Wales and the early British empire in India. Wales was perhaps at the outer reaches of the domestic world of the East India Company, but it was nonetheless shaped in important ways by the interlinked processes of imperial and commercial expansion that were occurring in South Asia. By piecing together scattered evidence it has been possible to create a more detailed picture of the East Indian influences that were at work within Wales as that expansion gathered pace after 1750. In particular, this still-emerging picture suggests that at any given moment significant direct and indirect economic effects were being felt in Wales, especially across mid- and south-west Wales where the physical manifestations of inward flows of East Indian wealth were becoming more visible on the rural, urban and industrial landscapes. Certain houses, gardens, estates, financial institutions, transport infrastructure, urban improvements, industrial concerns and educational establishments all had their development shaped either wholly or to a considerable degree by investments made by individuals who had derived personal benefit from participation in the expansionist process. This attracted very little comment at the time because East Indian investment tended to be localised, and contemporaries would not have been able to identify connections between developments in Brecon, for example, and those of a very different nature that were occurring in the lower Swansea valley. But connections there undoubtedly were because what bound these developments together is that the individuals and firms that lay behind them all derived advantage from the opportunities offered by the East India Company, and as a consequence they reaped financial benefits in the form of salaries, dividends, perquisites, plunder and commercial profits. As stressed at the outset, this is not to argue that East Indian influences were in any way central to the economic development of Wales as a whole, and indeed many of them were not even locally transformative, but they did feed into the various dynamic processes that underpinned improvement and as such their importance should not be underestimated. Moreover, these external influences should not be seen as operating in isolation, and they need to be interwoven with others, such as those emanating from the Atlantic world, for only then can a full assessment be made of the multifarious economic interactions that occurred between Wales and the wider world during the long eighteenth century.

Notes

1 For the effects that expansion in Asia had upon Britain as a whole see H. V. Bowen, *The Business of Empire: The East India Company and Imperial Britain, 1756–1833* (Cambridge, 2006). The various East Indian influences that were at work in the domestic economy are examined in chs. 2, 4, and 9. I am grateful to Michael J. Franklin, Ken Jones and Louise Miskell for their very helpful comments on an earlier draft of this essay.

2 Steve van Dulken, 'The Voyle family of Pembrokeshire and India', *Journal of the Pembrokeshire Historical Society*, 6 (1994/95), 47–60; Philip Jenkins, *The Making of a Ruling Class: The Glamorgan Gentry, 1640–1790* (Cambridge, 1983), p. 150.

3 For the alliance between the Clive and Herbert families (which was later consolidated by marriage) and its effects upon Shropshire and Welsh politics, see Lewis Namier, *The Structure of Politics at the Accession of George III* (London, 2nd edn, 1965), pp. 235–98.

4 See, for example, Wiltshire and Swindon Record Office, Chippenham, 947/2145/2 (no foliation), George Herbert to John Herbert, from Calcutta, 1 April 1773.

5 NLW, MS 23794C, Journal of Captain Frederick Jones (1758–74), fol. 37.

6 This paragraph is based upon, and the quotations therein are derived from, NLW, MS 23575C, 'Major Price's [manuscript] autobiography', vol. 1, pp. 33–44. Henry Smedley later commanded the Company's ship *Raymond* on five voyages to Asia. Price's manuscript autobiography later formed the basis of *The memoirs of the early life and service of a field officer on the retained list of the Indian army . . .* (London, 1839).

7 James's origins are obscure, but it is likely that he was from Pembrokeshire and this might explain why he was able to provide Price with a much better position in the Company's army.

8 Smedley later went on to command the Company ship *Raymond* on five voyages to Asia. Company records do not indicate whether or not Morris was Welsh but, in view of the number of Welshmen on board *Essex*, it is very likely that he was.

9 For Parry's life and the long-term development of his firm, see G. H. Hodgson, *Thomas Parry. Free Merchant at Madras, 1768–1824* (Madras, 1938); N. S. Ramaswami and S. Muthiah, *Parrys 200: A Saga of Resilience* (New Delhi, 1988). Parry established the firm in 1788, and after 1809 he recruited his nephews David and Joseph Pugh who both served as partners.

10 The information on Herbert to be found in this paragraph and elsewhere in the essay is derived from a collection of his letters in Wiltshire and Swindon Record Office, Chippenham, 947/2145/2 (no foliation).

11 William D. Rubinstein, *Who Were the Rich? A Biographical Directory of British Wealth-holders. Volume one: 1809–1839* (London, 2009), pp. 278–9.

12 D. T. W. Price, 'Phillips, Thomas (1760–1851)', *Oxford Dictionary of National Biography* (Oxford, 2004) [www.oxforddnb.com/view/article/22175, accessed 2 July 2009].

13 For good examples of Jones's trading activities at Basra, see his unfoliated letter-book of 1791–92, NLW, MS 4904E. The quotations are from his letters to Samuel Manesty, 24 June 1791, and to Charles Watkins, 5 July 1791.

14 Jones's complicated diplomatic and commercial activities at Baghdad can be reconstructed from his letter-book covering the period 1804 to 1806, NLW, MS 4905E. The quotation and details of his fortune are taken from his letter to James Willis, 22 December 1805. Apart from diplomatic problems and differences of opinion, while at Baghdad Jones was troubled by poor health and allegations that he had misused the funds that the Company had allocated to him to establish the Residency. For a balanced assessment of Jones and his diplomatic activity see M. E. Yapp, *Strategies of British India. Britain, Iran, and Afghanistan, 1798–1850* (Oxford, 1980).

15 Ken Jones, 'John Lloyd (1748–1818): an adventurous Welshman, part I', *Brycheiniog*, 33 (2001), 59–92; 'John Lloyd (1748–1818): an adventurous Welshman, part II', *ibid.*, 34 (2002), 67–108; 'John Lloyd: personal life and private trade, part III', *ibid.*, 37 (2005),

45–80; 'John Lloyd part IV [*sic*]: Captain John Lloyd and Breconshire, 1796–1818', *ibid.*, 39 (2007), 61–111.

16 The Bengal Council to the directors, 1 February 1779, *Fort William – India House Correspondence*, vol. 8: *(Public Series): 1777–81*, ed. Hira Lal Gupta (New Delhi, 1981), p. 445.

17 Of Welsh descent, Richard Griffith was born in Dublin in June 1752. For a detailed study of his career and business activity see J. R. Owen, 'A nabob at Holyhead: Richard Griffith, Post Office packet agent, 1815–1820', *Maritime Wales*, 25 (2004), 27–55.

18 BL, IOR, B/97, p. 533 (2 January 1782).

19 Benjamin Heath Malkin, *The Scenery, Antiquities and Biography of South Wales From Materials Collected During Two Excursions in the Year 1803* (London, 1804), p. 272.

20 Jones, 'John Lloyd part IV', 88–90.

21 Frederick Jones, *A Brief Account of the Tullanganum Expedition from Bombay; and likewise of the Sieges of Bassien, Arnoll, Callian, and Cananore, on the Western Side of India: During the Course of the War, Commenced the 21st November 1778, Extracted from the Journal of an Officer, Who was Actually Employed on Those several services* (Brecknock and London, 1794). For edited extracts of Jones's diary which throw considerable light on his activities after his return to Wales see E. C. B. Oliver (ed.), 'The diary of Captain Frederick Jones (Part I: 1789–1799)', *Transactions of the Radnorshire Society*, 53 (1983), 28–56; '(Part II: 1800–1804)', *ibid.*, 54 (1984), 41–57; '(Part III: 1805–1811)', *ibid.*, 56 (1986), 52–71.

22 James Dunn to David Williams, November 1786, a loose letter in a small collection of Williams's papers to be found in NLW, Miscellaneous Records, 546.

23 For a letter-book of Williams covering the period 1782–86 which contains details of some of his remittances from India and investment instructions to his father and attorneys see *ibid.*

24 For this episode see Alfred Cobban and Robert A. Smith (eds), *The Correspondence of Edmund Burke*, vol. 6: *July 1789–December 1791* (Cambridge, 1967), pp. 99–100.

25 *Captain Williams's Narrative; In Which is Contained Particulars Relative to the Execution of Mustapha Cawn; . . . .* (London, 1790).

26 For an outline of Nott's career see R. H. Vetch, 'Nott, Sir William (1782–1845)', rev. James Lunt, *Oxford Dictionary of National Biography* (Oxford, 2004) [www.oxforddnb.com/view/article/20372, accessed 2 July 2009].

27 This Thomas Phillips is not to be confused with the Thomas Phillips, also a Company surgeon, noted below.

28 Richard Fenton, *A Historical Tour Through Pembrokeshire . . . to Which are Now Added the Notes Made for a Second Edition by Richard and John Fenton* (Brecknock, 1903), p. 137. I am indebted to Professor David Howell for drawing this reference to my attention.

29 For a detailed study of Jones see H. V. Bowen, 'Welsh commanders of East Indiamen: a case-study of John Jones (1751–1828)', *Maritime Wales*, 31 (2010), 21–36.

30 For the local activities of John Rees and others who traded in eastern seas see Douglas Fraser 'Tenby's legacy of the opium trade', *Pembrokeshire Life* (February 2007), 12–16 and 'All the tea in China', *ibid.* (December 2009), 10–14.

31 For two letter-books of Jacob Richards (covering the period 1807–34) see NLW, MSS 22870D and 22871D. I am greatly indebted to Mr Brian Price who brought these rich sources to my attention and then very generously supplied me with transcripts of the letter-books. The information on Richards and his career is derived from Mr Price's transcripts and supporting notes which are based upon extensive archival research. It seems abundantly clear that there was considerable East Indian activity and investment in and around Tenby and it is to be hoped that a clear and detailed picture can be built up through further research.

32 For the broad changes that occurred to patterns of landownership in Wales see Geraint H. Jenkins, *The Foundations of Modern Wales, 1642–1780* (Oxford, 1993), pp. 264–6.

33 P. D. G. Thomas, 'The Monmouthshire election of 1771', *Historical Research*, 72 (1999), 45–6, 56; Melvin Humphreys, *The Crisis of Community: Montgomeryshire, 1680–1815* (Cardiff, 1996), p. 123.
34 *Ibid.*, p. 123.
35 Eileen and Harry Green, *The Fowkes of Boughrood Castle. A Study in Social Mobility* (Tenby, 1973).
36 Margaret Walker, 'The Penrice and Lyons families of Kilvrough. Part 1. The Penrice family', *Gower*, 56 (2005), 37–46, and 'Part 2. The Lyons family', *ibid.*, 57 (2006), 34–48. I am indebted to Nigel Jenkins for drawing these articles to my attention.
37 The following two paragraphs are based in large part on W. G. J. Kuiters, 'William Paxton (1744–1824): The history of an East Indian fortune', *Bengal Past and Present*, 111 (1992), 1–19. See also Willem G. Kuiters, 'William Paxton, 1744–1824. Merchant and Banker in Bengal and London' (MA dissertation, University of Leiden, 1992). I am indebted to Dr Kuiters for supplying me with a copy of his dissertation.
38 Quotations in R. G. Thorne (ed.), *The History of Parliament. The House of Commons 1790–1820* (5 vols, London, 1986), vol. 4, p. 736.
39 P. J. Marshall, *East Indian Fortunes. The British in Bengal in the Eighteenth Century* (Oxford, 1976), pp. 214–56.
40 Margaret Dawes and C. N. Ward-Perkins, *Country Banks of England and Wales. Private provincial banks and bankers 1688–1953* (2 vols, Canterbury, 2000), vol. 1, 83.
41 *Ibid.*
42 D. T. W. Pryce, 'Thomas Phillips of Brunswick Square', in William Marx (ed.), *The Founders' Library, University of Wales, Lampeter. Bibliographical and Contextual Studies. Essays in memory of Robin Rider*, Trivium, vol. 29/30 (Lampeter, 1997), pp. 169–76; Gwyn Walters, 'Books from the "nabob": the benefactions of Thomas Phillips at Lampeter and Llandovery', *Transactions of the Honourable Society of Cymmrodorion*, new series, 5 (1999), 36–61.
43 BL, IOR, L/AG/14/5/248. For an overall profile of East Indian stockholders see Bowen, *Business of Empire*, ch. 4.
44 BL, IOR, L/AG/14/5/37, pp. 283, 285, 289, 290.
45 *Ibid.*, pp. 332–3, 335.
46 BL, IOR, L/AG/1/5/13, p. 85.
47 *Ibid.*, pp. 121, 127, 141, 176, 195, 301, 315, 351, 356, 366, 381, 382.
48 These figures and the information that follow have been extracted from *ibid.*, vols. 16–26.
49 See, for example, the private supply of copper by the Mines Royal and Mackworth & Co. to commanders of East Indiamen in 1781, BL, IOR, H/22, pp. 147–8, 156–8, 169–71.
50 For the content, scale, and organisation of this smuggling trade see H. V. Bowen, 'Privilege and profit: The commanders of East Indiamen as private traders, entrepreneurs, and smugglers, 1760–1813', *International Journal of Maritime History*, 19:2 (2007), 1–46.
51 J. R. Harris, *The Copper King: A Biography of Thomas Williams of Llanidan* (Liverpool, 1964), p. 11. During the 1790s exports to Asia accounted for 60% of total exports of 'brass and plated goods' and 35% of total wrought copper exports: *Report of the Committee [of the House of Commons] Appointed to Enquire Into the State of the Copper Mines and Copper Trade of This Kingdom (7 May 1799)*, appendix 33, pp. 166–9.
52 For a detailed study of Williams, see Harris, *The Copper King.*
53 For the place of copper-smelting in the wider economic development of Swansea, see Louise Miskell, *'Intelligent Town': An Urban History of Swansea, 1780–1855* (Cardiff, 2006), ch. 3.
54 *Number and Register of Tonnage of Steam and Sailing Vessels Entering Swansea Harbour Each Year, Ending December 31st, from 1768 to 1921* (no place of publication, 1921).

55 For the growth in the number of Anglesey ships that accompanied the late-eighteenth-century expansion of copper-mining operations on the island see Aled Eames, *Ships and Seamen of Anglesey, 1558–1918* (London, republished edition, 1981), pp. 184–92.
56 *An Account of the Annual Quantity of Cake, Manufactured, and Japan Copper, With the Quantity of Brass Shipped by the Honourable East India Company for the East Indies, and the Prices Purchased at Per Ton, From the Year 1731–2 to 1791–2* (no place of publication, 1793).
57 See, for example, BL, IOR, L/AG/1/5/20, pp. 272, 342; 22, p. 20; 23, p. 238.
58 Ryuto Shimada, *The Intra-Asian Trade in Japanese copper by the Dutch East India Company During the Eighteenth Century* (Leiden, 2006), ch. 5 (quotation on p. 79).
59 See, for example, BL, IOR, H/22, pp. 80–1, 107–9; L/AG/1/5/22, pp. 274, 336, 441.

AFTERWORD

Taken together, the essays in this volume point to Welsh relationships with the British overseas empire that were complex, multilayered and at times contradictory; and by bringing together a very wide range of evidence they significantly advance our understanding of the different ways in which Wales interacted with the wider world. The authors have measured participation in imperial activity, mapped overseas connections, marked out similarities and differences by comparing Wales with other parts of the British and Irish Isles, and assessed the impact of empire on Wales itself. But it has to be admitted that little has been written about what the Welsh actually *thought* about the empire and its indigenous peoples. And herein lies perhaps the greatest challenge ahead if the foundations laid out in this volume are to be built upon in future studies of Wales and the empire during the long eighteenth century.

Some of those contemporaries with enquiring minds who went abroad naturally wrote about what they saw and experienced, and their views and opinions occasionally found their way into print. Hence in 1786 David Samwell published a rather lurid pamphlet entitled *A Narrative of the Death of Captain James Cook . . . and Observations Respecting the Introduction of the Venereal Disease into the Sandwich Islands* (1786), while tucked away among Sir William Jones's voluminous works of oriental scholarship is to be found a detailed topographical study, 'Remarks on the Island of Hinzuan or Johanna', which was published in *Asiatic Researches* in 1799.[1] But many did not record their thoughts on the wider world in print or even in their personal letters and diaries, and, for example, the correspondence of the Welsh in India during this period is strikingly businesslike in tone and content, which is perhaps not surprising since most of them were concerned primarily with making money. And the overseas empire does not appear to have excited much comment among those who stayed at home. Indeed, although London-based Welsh radicals such as Richard Price and David Williams were prominent critics of the government during the War of American Independence, the colonial crisis of the 1770s and early 1780s failed to create in Wales the types of the local political tension and divisions that were experienced elsewhere in the British Isles.[2] Since, as noted earlier, Wales had few direct contacts with the empire this might simply be a case of 'out of sight, out of mind', but it does raise the possibility that a majority of the Welsh stay-at-homes had limited mental horizons and were not much interested in, or even aware, of the interactions with the empire that were taking place around them.[3] Whatever the case, it seems that the empire did not loom large in the everyday lives and consciousness of people in Wales, but this is an important matter that requires further investigation.

The second major challenge that lies ahead for historians is to assess what happened to Welsh relationships with the empire after 1830 as new influences and interactions began to have an effect on Wales and its people. By the 1830s not only was the empire changing, with the slave system being dismantled and the end coming into sight for the East India Company, but also Wales itself was maturing into an industrialised nation that was being shaped in deep and profound ways by the rapid export-led growth of the coal and iron industries. These processes eventually gave rise to the 'imperial South Wales' of the late nineteenth century invoked by Gwyn Alf Williams, but surprisingly little attention has been devoted to the establishment of the new and direct economic connections that were forged between Wales and the empire. Wales was quite suddenly, and indeed violently, integrated into the wider British imperial economy, and this undoubtedly had a considerable effect upon Welsh attitudes, outlooks, identities and self-confidence. At the same time, other types of relationships with the overseas empire were becoming established, and these drew new groups in Welsh society into direct contact with the processes of expansion. By the 1830s Nonconformist religious fervour was being channelled into more organised forms of missionary activity in South Asia and Africa, and this gave rise to two-way flows of knowledge and information between Wales and the wider world. And migration to Britain's white settler colonies not only broadened the geographical extent of the Welsh diaspora but also gave rise to the establishment of communities whose linguistic and cultural practices made them self-consciously and enduringly Welsh in their identities.

All of these interactions served to reconfigure linkages between Wales and the overseas empire, yet it cannot be assumed that any new or strengthening connections meant that those in Wales had necessarily become enthusiastic or indeed willing participants in British imperial enterprise. Industrial, religious and migratory imperatives were always the primary domestic drivers behind the establishment of links between Wales and the empire, and of course many Welsh connections with the wider world extended well beyond Britain's imperial boundaries. Thus while the empire provided opportunities for some in Wales, it by no means exerted the only 'pull' force on those who wished to broaden their horizons. And, again, there is a need to know much more about what Welsh people thought about the empire after

1830. For while the emergence of a Nonconformist and eventually Liberal Wales undoubtedly gave rise to powerful strains of anti-imperial sentiment in some circles, little is known about whether the general public mood towards the empire developed along similar lines or, alternatively, was supportive, ambivalent or perhaps just indifferent. As is the case for the long eighteenth century, there is a need for a full assessment to be made of Welsh attitudes towards the empire that is sensitive to the different contexts provided by region, class, gender and language.

It is evident, then, that much work remains to be done if Wales is to be fully integrated into the British imperial historiography and the empire is to be afforded a central role in the writing of Welsh history. Certainly as a next step it is important that research on the post-1830 period is consolidated and brought together in a sequel to this volume. If this can be achieved, it will be possible for the first time to place Welsh interactions with the empire in a proper long-term perspective. Scholars can then proceed with a much greater degree of confidence to identify any distinctive aspects of the Welsh relationship with the empire, and they can begin to make much better informed comparisons and contrasts between the imperial experiences of the Welsh and those of the English, Irish and Scots.

Notes

1 Jones had visited Johanna (today Anjouan/Nzwami) in the Comoro Islands when sailing to India in 1783. He produced a detailed study of the island, during the course of which he described one valley as being more agreeable than any he had ever seen, 'even in Switzerland or Meirionithshire'. It has been suggested that Jones's experiences as a barrister in Wales brought distinctive influences to bear upon his career as a judge of the Supreme Court at Calcutta during the 1780s. See Michael J. Franklin, 'Jones, Sir William (1746–1794)', *Oxford Dictionary of National Biography*, (Oxford, 2004) [www.oxforddnb.com/view/article/15105, accessed 14 January 2010]

2 P. D. G. Thomas, *Politics in Eighteenth-Century Wales* (Cardiff, 1998); Stephen Conway, *The British Isles and the War of American Independence* (Oxford, 200), pp. 134–5, 173–4.

3 It is notable, for example, that the empire barely features at all in the diary of William Thomas despite the fact that it was written at a time of recurrent imperial crisis and war. See R. T. W. Denning (ed.), *The Diary of William Thomas of Michaelston-super-Ely, near St Fagans Glamorgan, 1762–1795* (Cardiff, 1995).

INDEX

CPSIA information can be obtained at www.ICGtesting.com
Printed in the USA
BVOW08s2114130616

451906BV00003B/59/P

9 781784 993528